from Redwood Wish List

In Defense of Things

ARCHAEOLOGY IN SOCIETY SERIES

SERIES EDITORS
Ian Hodder, Stanford University
Robert W. Preucel, University of Pennsylvania

In recent decades, archaeology has expanded beyond a narrow focus on economics and environmental adaptation to address issues of ideology, power, and meaning. These trends, sometimes termed "postprocessual," deal with both the interpretation of the past and the complex and politically charged interrelationships of past and present. Today, archaeology is responding to and incorporating aspects of the debates on identity, meaning, and politics currently being explored in varying fields: social anthropology, sociology, geography, history, linguistics, and psychology. There is a growing realization that ancient studies and material culture can be aligned within the contemporary construction of identities under the rubrics of nationalism, ethnoscapes, and globalization. This international series will help connect the contemporary practice of archaeology with these trends in research and, in the process, demonstrate the relevance of archaeology to related fields and society in general.

Volumes in this series:

In Defense of Things, Bjørnar Olsen (2010)

Appropriated Pasts: Indigenous Peoples and the Colonial Culture of Archaeology, Ian J. McNiven and Lynette Russell (2005)

Archaeology of Performance: Theatre, Power, and Community, edited by Takeshi Inomata and Lawrence S. Coben (2005)

Collaboration in Archaeological Practice: Engaging Descendant Communities, edited by Chip Colwell-Chanthaphonh and T.J. Ferguson (2007)

Archaeology and the Postcolonial Critique, edited by Matthew Liebmann and Uzma Z. Rizvi (2008)

The Social Construction of Communities: Agency, Structure, and Identity in the Prehispanic Southwest, edited by Mark D. Varien and James M. Potter (2008)

Dwelling, Identity, and the Maya: Relational Archaeology at Chunchucmil, by Scott Hutson (2009)

In Defense of Things

Archaeology and the Ontology of Objects

Bjørnar Olsen

ALTAMIRA
PRESS

A division of
ROWMAN & LITTLEFIELD PUBLISHERS, INC.
Lanham • New York • Toronto • Plymouth, UK

Published by AltaMira Press
A division of Rowman & Littlefield Publishers, Inc.
A wholly owned subsidiary of The Rowman & Littlefield Publishing Group, Inc.
4501 Forbes Boulevard, Suite 200, Lanham, Maryland 20706
http://www.altamirapress.com

Estover Road, Plymouth PL6 7PY, United Kingdom

British Library Cataloguing in Publication Information Available

Library of Congress Cataloging-in-Publication Data

Olsen, Bjørnar.
  In defense of things: Archaeology and the ontology of objects / Bjørnar Olsen.
    p. cm. — (Archaeology in society series)
  Includes bibliographical references and index.
  ISBN 978-0-7591-1930-7 (cloth : alk. paper) — ISBN 978-0-7591-1932-1
(electronic)
  1. Archaeology—Philosophy. 2. Material culture. 3. Landscape.
  4. Phenomenology. 5. Actor-network theory. I. Title.
  CC72.O48 2010
  930.101—dc22   2010000867

♾ ™ The paper used in this publication meets the minimum requirements of
American National Standard for Information Sciences—Permanence of Paper
for Printed Library Materials, ANSI/NISO Z39.48-1992.

Printed in the United States of America

Contents

List of Illustrations

1

Introduction

But has my mise-en-scène thus mortified the quartz, drained it of any material vitality, its very shimmer dulled by being subjected to an archaeological epistemology where its role, within this too harmonious scene we call history, is never to be itself but always, always to represent something else?

—Bill Brown, *A Sense of Things*

In his book from 1987, *Material Culture and Mass Consumption*, Daniel Miller referred to material culture as "a surprisingly illusive component of modern culture," which "has consistently managed to evade the focus of academic gaze, and remains the least understood of all central phenomena of the modern age" (1987:217). Twelve years later, Michael Schiffer wrote that social scientists have "ignored what might be most distinctive and significant about our species . . . [that] human life consists of ceaseless and varied interaction among people and myriad kinds of things" (1999:2). And well into the new millennium, Bruno Latour has confirmed that little has changed:

Much like sex during the Victorian period, objects are nowhere to be said and everywhere to be felt. They exist, naturally, but they are never to be given a thought, a social thought. Like humble servants, they live on the margins of the social doing most of the work but never allowed to be represented as such. (2005:73)

Irrespective of the different perspectives and disciplinary entanglements of their authors, these quotes signify the growing concern with the neglect of things in the social sciences. Despite the grounding and inescapable materiality of the human condition, things seem to have been subjected to a kind of collective amnesia in social and cultural studies, leaving us with a paradoxically persistent image of societies operating without the mediation of objects. Needless to say, there are of course exceptions and brave attempts at repatriations that throughout the last century have included figures as varied and famous as Bergson, Heidegger, Benjamin, and Merleau-Ponty. However, despite the nuances and exceptions that any attempt at a gross generalization will encounter, it can still be argued forcefully that the material components of what we have come to think of as "social life" have been marginalized—even stigmatized—in the social sciences and philosophy during the twentieth century.

Why has this marginalization taken place? Why has the physical and "thingly" component of our past and present existence become forgotten or ignored in contemporary social science research to such an extent? How has this attitude affected those disciplinary fields still actually devoted to the study of things, most notably archaeology? These questions form some of the background to this book. With the possible exception of the last one, these questions are of course not novel to material culture studies (Miller 1987:3ff.; Dant 1999:9ff.; see Olsen 2007). My own motivation for readdressing them is partly based on a felt need to provide more convincing answers. More important, however, is the fact that these questions are closely related to the main inquiries which form the basis of this book: How do things and objects "mix" with human beings to form those configurations we call *society* and *history*? What role do things play in enabling and securing social life? Moreover, if things make a difference, which they obviously do, are these differences grounded in qualities that go beyond their relational significance? In other words—and challenging the semiotic and structuralist mantra—is things' difference, and thus capacity to act, grounded in qualities unique and essential to them?

These inquiries transgress disciplinary concerns while at the same time being strongly linked to archaeology. *Archaeology* has become a popular (if somewhat worn out) catchphrase among philosophers, psychologists, social scientists, and literary critics. However, few of those fascinated by its metaphorical payoff have bothered to think seriously about what an archaeological contribution to the topics they address might have actually looked like. In this sense, this book is also about reclaiming a concept. However, this should not be misconceived as either an attempt at repatriating or restricting it to a confined disciplinary field or an attempt to reaffirm a traditional concern with the distant past. Archaeology in my opinion is first and foremost a concern with things, and when the object now seems to reenter social and cultural discourses, archaeologists, as the most dedicated students of things, should naturally make their voices heard. Archaeology's long-held concern with things constitutes an intellectual skill that is clearly highly relevant to these debates. Moreover, due to our concern with things, I also find it appropriate that writing and reading theory from an archaeological point of view should make a difference. Our theorizing, although in part dedicated to common phenomena and the processing of similar philosophies, should be distinguishable—at least to some extent—from other theoretical discourses. This book is also written to contribute to this difference.

CREDO: NOT ALL THAT IS SOLID MELTS INTO AIR

During the last two decades we have witnessed a new interest in things, materiality, and landscape in a number of disciplines. However, for some reason, this interest has largely left void the intrinsic *material* significance of things and the qualities they possess beyond human cognition, representation, and embodiment. Although serious and pertinent criticism has been voiced against the textual and linguistic reductionism implied in many former interpretive archaeologies, a dominant trope is still that material culture and landscapes are sites of "inscription," metaphorical "stand-ins" that always represent something else and more importantly: the "social," the "cultural," the "political," and so forth—all implicitly conceived of as extramaterial entities. A subtext in most contemporary approaches is an implicit conception of culture as somehow "prior" to or detached from matter, with an assumption that cultures, "already different," approach the material world in unique ways, causing a variety of material expressions and meanings. Thus, despite much talk about somatic experiencing and bodily practices, things and landscapes seem to have little to offer to this experience beyond being plastic, open ended, and receptive.

Given its title, I reveal no big secret by admitting that this book has been provoked by a growing discomfort not only with the dominant antimaterial conception of culture and society within the human and social sciences, but also with the way archaeology and material culture studies, despite their self-proclaimed success (cf. Miller 1998a:3; Buchli 2002), have to such an extent moved away from the material qualities of things and subsumed themselves to hegemonic antimaterial and social-constructivist theories.[1] Thus, the following observation made by Schiffer in 1999 is still pertinent:

> beyond being marginalized material-culture studies often suffer from a more severe problem: they simply project conventional ontology and theories into new empirical domains, treating people-artifact interaction as secondary to

processes of culture. The manufacture and use of artifacts is regarded, for example, as just one more arena in which people negotiate culturally constituted meanings. (6)

This book is grounded in a realist attitude in the sense that I do believe the material world exists and that things constitute a fundamental and persistent foundation for our existence. Things, materials, and landscapes possess real qualities affecting and shaping both our perception of them and our cohabitation with them. A large portion of recent studies in archaeology, anthropology, geography, and cultural studies seems to have been guided by a "hermeneutics of suspicion" (Ricoeur 1970) in which "all that is solid melts into air,"[2] including things and the physicality of the world—which sometimes seem reduced to little more than discursive objects or "phenomena" of the subjects' cognitive experience. As noted by Judith Attfield, the material world has become dematerialized to the extent that we can no longer "believe our eyes" (2000:42). Denying or ignoring any integrity and autonomy to that which is beyond our perception, we are left with an "intentional world" held together almost solely by human cognition (cf. Ingold 2000:40–41).

Figure 1.1. "Societies or nation-states are not cognitive sketches resting in the minds of people; they are real entities solidly built and well tied together." Walltown Crags (Hadrian's Wall), Northumberland, UK (photo: Alfredo González-Ruibal).

SOCIETIES CONSTRUCTED OF WHAT?

Symptomatic of this anthropocentric attitude, if also somewhat semantically misleading, are the antiessentialist buzzwords of invention and construction. Tradition and cultures are *invented*, nations *imagined*, and knowledge *constructed*. Even far outside the relativist settlement, it has become commonplace to say that social reality is "constructed" (cf. Hacking 2001; Latour 2005:88ff. for a general discussion). Of course, tradition and cultures are invented and societies constructed, but this does not make them unreal or false. Societies or nation-states are not cognitive sketches resting in the minds of people; they are real entities solidly built and well tied together. As the etymological roots suggest, facts are made and the real is fabricated. Rather than "revealing" entities as constructed and made up, our attention should be devoted to analyzing how these entities (e.g., societies and cultures) are put together and the real building materials—the concrete and steel, rebar and pillars—involved in their construction. In other words, we should pay far more attention to the material components that constitute the very condition of possibility for those features we associate with social order, structural durability, and power (Latour 1999b, 2005).

It would be a grave overstatement to say that these building materials play any central role in the various conceptions of society applied in the social and human sciences. Marxism represents an exception, but even here, things, albeit important, are largely reduced to a confined structural feature and the means of production within the total social formation. Societies and cultures are otherwise rather consistently treated as collectives of humans held together by social relations and social forces—in short, by *people without things*. In a textbook aimed at university students, anthropologists Thomas Eriksen and Torunn Sørheim define *society* as "a system of roles, obligations, and relations between humans sufficiently extensive enough to facilitate that most of its inhabitants get most of their needs satisfied" (Eriksen and Sørheim 2006:40, my translation). We further learn that culture consists of the "thoughts, knowledge, and skills that humans have acquired as members of society. . . . Culture can thus be considered as a kind of *mental matrix for action*, the sum of all the experiences, knowledge, and values that we carry with us and that ground our actions" (41, my translation, emphasis in original).

Even in an apparently thing-specific subject such as gift exchange, the objects providing the logic to its naming are often trivialized or regarded as being more or less irrelevant. Here, too, a common assumption is that the gift's role is epiphenomenal to the primary social relations between persons. Thus in his study of ancient Norse gift exchange, Aron Gurevich arrives at the conclusion that "what mattered was not the transferred object itself, but the persons who owned the object and the fact that they had chosen to transfer it" (Gurevitch 1992:179). This typifies a common attitude within social studies by which persons or subjects constitute categories that can easily and naturally be bracketed off from things and, in this unequipped state, become sufficient to explain the phenomena in question. However, as argued by Þóra Pétursdóttir in her discussion of gift exchange as narrated in the Icelandic sagas,

> The object was not just an incidental substitute, a "stand-in," which represented "social" relations and transactions, but was in itself of central importance in the establishment and maintenance of the relationship—without it the relation was unthinkable. . . . A friendship, or any other relation, was therefore not formed between two parts in a vacuum but through collective interactions between entities of things and people. The objects were not abstracted, incidental things but constantly engaged, concrete manifestations, and thus fundamental parts of these associations. (2007:61)

In order to understand how society works—and thus is made possible—we have to become more liberal and inclusive and to acknowledge that far more constitutive entities than humans (and their thoughts, knowledge, and skills) are woven into its fabric. In other words, we have to take into account that societies consist of myriads of real and co-working entities composed of both humans and nonhumans. In this respect, some of the founding sociologists such as Emile Durkheim provided glimpses of insights that seem much more sensitive and humble toward the material world than the perspectives of later fellow sociologists and philosophers (cf. Joerges 1988:224).[3] In *The Suicide* (published in 1897), Durkheim wrote that

> it is not true that society is made up only of individuals; it also includes material things, which play an essential role in common life. The social fact is sometimes so far materialized as to become an element of the external world . . . in houses and buildings of all sorts which, once constructed, become autonomous realities, independent of individuals. It is the same with avenues of communication and transportation, with instruments and machines used in industry and private life. . . . Social life, which is thus crystallized, as it were, and fixed on material supports, is by just so much externalized, and acts upon us from without. (1951:313–14)

To Durkheim, for this moment at least, artifacts were also *social facts*. Unfortunately, however, neither he nor the vast majority of his successors paid much attention to this fact in their research. Actually, as noted by Joerges, "the closer one moves to the sacred inner circles of theory-building and systematic empirical generalisations, the more devoid of things social science becomes" (1988:223).

THE SOLITUDE OF THE BODY

There are signs of change, of course, and the timely advent of the body in social and cultural studies during the past twenty to thirty years has been particularly promising (e.g., Butler 1993; Meskell 1996; Williams and Bendelow 1998; Tilley 1999; Hamilakis, Pluciennik, and Tarlow 2002; Sweeney and Hodder 2002; Joyce 2005; Waskul and Vannini 2006). The material potential of this somatic turn, as especially reflected in various readings inspired by Maurice Merleau-Ponty, seems obvious: as human beings we are somatically inserted in the world, and prior to the Cartesian "I think" it is necessary to acknowledge a practical lived component expressed in routinized practices and actions, in bodily habits (Merleau-Ponty 1962:137ff.; Macann 1993:175–76; cf. foreword to Meskell and Joyce by Turner, 2003; Joyce 2005).

From this corpus of phenomenological thinking we have learned that knowledge is not something just sitting in our heads. It is also acquired through and stored in our bodies. Once a certain habitual skill has been learned, we only need a short time to familiarize ourselves with a new city, a new car, or another archaeological museum. The time is too short to develop completely new sets of conditioned reflexes—our familiarity with organized spaces and with materiality and things, in short our material habitual competence, permits us to project a potential for movement and actions that can rapidly be modified to accommodate specific differences (such as coming to a new house or city; Merleau-Ponty 1962:145–47; Macann 1993:176). As the famous American phenomenologist John Travolta stated after returning to America from three years of fieldwork in Amsterdam: "It's the same as here, but different" (Travolta teaching his gangster buddy about cultural differences in *Pulp Fiction*, quoted after Löfgren 1997:106).

This somatic turn, also as inspired by (and reflected in) the works of de Certau, Foucault, and others, clearly paved the way for less logocentric approaches in social studies. It also contained the potential for challenging the taken-for-granted primacy of language as the means for coming to grips with the world, although sometimes rather the opposite was proposed (cf. the discussion of Butler's work in chapter 3). However, despite its indisputable material potential, there is usually something crucial missing in most of these accounts of the competent body found in disciplines such as philosophy, literary studies, sociology, and anthropology: the *things* that the body relates to and blends in with—in short, the material components of the world it is *being in*. One often gets the impression that in these disciplines, the human body is the only flesh of the world, and that this lived-in body roams the ground rather unconstrained by other types of beings.

Consider the concept of *habit memory*, a very important concept that we owe to Henri Bergson (see chapter 6). It refers to how memories are stored in the body as dispositions and habits. In contrast to so-called cognitive or recollective remembrance, habitual memories are lived and acted rather than represented (cf. Merleau-Ponty 1962; Casey 1984; Bergson 2004). Biking is often used to exemplify this type of memory, here nicely formulated by Elaine Scarry: "What is remembered in the body is well remembered. When a fifteen-year-old girl climbs off her bike and climbs back at twenty-five, it may seem only the ten-year interval that her body has forgotten, so effortless is the return to mastery" (Scarry 1985:109). Something rather essential, however, is missing in this story: *the bike*. The other half is entombed in the celebration of the clever body, and we are once more left with the sound of one hand clapping. But try to bike without a bike; try to think of your day-to-day practices without things. Think how the routines, movements, and social arrangements of our daily lives are increasingly prescribed, defined, and disciplined, as well as helped or encouraged, by assemblages of material agents. All we need to do is to think about moving around a house, a university campus, or a city to realize how they ground programs of action that schedule and monitor our day-to-day activities (Boast 1997:188). In all of our daily conduct, objects are involved as (more or less) taken-for-granted and inherent aspects of our doings. They do not just provide frames, scenes, or background for our actions (cf. Miller 1985), but are intrinsically and indispensably involved in enabling those very actions. Thus, the time seems overdue to credit them some social recognition. This is not to say, of course, that things are the only vital component of social order and constitute the site where all our attention from now on should be focused. As remarked by Latour, "there might exist many metaphysical shades between full causality and sheer inexistence" (2005:72).

For obvious reasons, one would expect the picture to be very different in the growing number of archaeological studies of the body (cf. Meskell 1996; Hamilakis, Pluciennik, and Tarlow 2002; Joyce 2005). Here, however, the body seems taken even more literally. Guided by the long-held concern with signaling and identity formation (status, gender, ethnicity, personhood, etc.), the material cultural focus has been primarily related directly to bodily display and inscriptions (ornaments, dress, tattooing) and iconic manifestations such as figurines, masks, anthropomorphic rock art, and so on. Despite the claim that "under the influence of phenomenological approaches" the focus has shifted to analyses of "the production and experience of lived bodies" (Joyce 2005:152; cf. Hamilakis, Pluciennik, and Tarlow 2002), the pivotal role of the human being is rarely challenged. Rather than exploring the possibilities opened by focusing on somatic experiencing and, consequently, on being as a materially entangled being, many archaeologies of the body may actually be seen as reinforcing the anthropocentric bias. (See, however, Meskell and Joyce 2003; Meskell 2004). This adopted bias accentuates my initial claim that archaeological theorizing should make a difference by always and consistently remembering things.

REMEMBERING THINGS

A main part of the agenda of this book is thus to suggest a more egalitarian attitude in the way we perceive society and culture, a more "symmetrical" way of attending to past and present lifeworlds. This is founded on the premise that *things*, all those enormously varied physical entities we by effective historical conventions refer to as "material culture," are beings in the world alongside other beings such as humans, plants, and animals. All these beings are kindred, sharing certain material properties, "flesh," and membership in a dwelt-in world (cf. Merleau-Ponty 1968). They all share the capacity for making a *difference* to the world and to other beings (Harman 2002:167). *Symmetry*, if we stick to that concept (see Latour 2005:77), does not imply that they are equal—hence reducing everything to sameness. Entities are of course different, in fact they exhibit—between and among themselves—extremely varied forms of beings that actually constitute the very basis of collective action (see chapters 7 and 8). However, this difference should not be conceptualized in compliance with the ruling ontological regime of dualities and negativities; it is a *nonoppositional* or *relative* difference that facilitates collaboration, delegation, and exchange (cf. Pickering 1994; Latour 1999b:180–82).

However far back we go into "talkative history and silent prehistory" (Serres 1987:209), humans have extended their social relations to nonhumans with whom they have swapped properties and formed collectives (Serres 1987:209; Latour 1999b:198). According to Michel Serres, this capacity of advanced material bonding becomes constitutive of what it is to be socially human; it is the main difference between our society and a society of animals:

> Our relationships, social bonds, would be airy as clouds were there only contracts between subjects. In fact, the object, specific to the Hominidae, stabilizes our relationships, it slows down the time of our revolutions. For an unstable band of baboons, social changes are flaring up every minute. . . . The object, for us, makes our history slow. (1995a:87)

If there is one historical trajectory running all the way down from Olduvai Gorge to Postmodernia, it must be one of increased mixing: that more and more tasks are *delegated* to nonhuman actors, and more and more actions are mediated by things. Only by increasingly mobilizing things

Figure 1.2. "If there is one historical trajectory running all the way down from Olduvai Gorge to Postmodernia, it must be one of increased mixing: that more and more tasks are delegated to nonhuman actors, and more and more actions are mediated by things." Bay Bridge and San Francisco (photo: Wernher Krutein/photovault.com).

could humans come to experience "episodes" of history such as the advent of farming, urbanization, state formations, industrialization, and postindustrialization. The features we associate with historical change and the attributes we ascribe to development and progress were all made possible by humans increasingly becoming more entangled and "assemblaged" with nonhumans (cf. Renfrew 2004).

The important thing-lesson entailed in this story is that these other entities do not just sit in silence waiting to be embodied with socially constituted meanings. Landscapes and things possess their own unique qualities and competences that they bring to our cohabitation with them. Throughout history, the properties of soil and water, bone and stone, bronze and iron, have been swapped with those of humans. Thus, the claim of such an egalitarian or symmetrical archaeology becomes very different from that of Karl Marx (and Gordon Childe): man did not make himself!

OUTING THE OBSTACLES

Remembering things may seem to be an obvious task in order to conduct adequate studies of society and culture. Only a brief reflection on our current existence, irrespective of being lived through the bodies of a shopkeeper, a philosopher, a reindeer herder, a novelist, or a cybermedia artist, will reveal to us how inextricably it is enmeshed with things and with objects always-already combined and included in all our everyday doings. Just try the (impossible) experiment of imagining an existence without things, without matter. The more we realize how past and present human existence is mixed with materials, the more extraordinary and paradoxical becomes the blacklisting of them from the social sciences.

However, and for various reasons, relearning to ascribe action, power— or, to use that old mantra, *agency*—to entities other than the human subject has proved a very difficult task. One major obstacle is that it implies opposing what Graham Harman (2002:4) has termed "the long dictatorship of human being" held in philosophy, social theory, and the social and human sciences at large. This is a persistent and vital regime, well defended by the effective history of Western thought and successfully infiltrating the most remote corners of the academic landscape. This epistemological and ontological legacy has entombed most of our thing experiences and made us inattentive to the being of things (cf. Benso 2000). According to this legacy, things do not act (outside mechanical causality) and have no meanings, goals, or any other qualifying properties that may facilitate their enlistment into the social. These are qualities reserved for the rational and intentional subject—in short, for humans only.

Attempts to do away with this regime have largely been dismissed, obstructed, or prevented. To ascribe more than usefulness and aesthetics to things has largely been seen as mystifying and fetishistic, a dangerous primitivism prescribed for the other, the premodern. Thus, an important aspect of our social and academic education has been not to confuse social relations with object relations or to ascribe what is thought of as human properties to objects. As noted by Miller, the dominant imperative has been "that primary concern should lie with direct social relations and 'real people'" (Miller 1987:11). So we have one set of relations that are taken for granted as real, authentic, and honest (humans among themselves) and another set that a priori are false. Transgressing the border between the "us" and the "it" easily leads to dismissal and moral contempt.

This border and these sanctions are, of course, related to the wider moral-political legacy of modernity (see chapter 5). Numerous philosophers and social theorists saw the emergence of the mass-produced, mass-distributed, and mass-consumed object from the late nineteenth century onward as a sign of an illusory and deceptive world. The new consumer capitalism, filling the world with goods, replicas, machines, and inhuman technology, became the incarnation of our inauthentic, estranged, and alienated modern being (Heidegger 1993; Young 2002). It also gave rise to a powerful and persistent definition of *freedom* and *emancipation* as that which *escapes the material* (Latour 1993:137–38, 2002). Things were increasingly seen as a threat against authentic human and social values, as tellingly manifested in the Marxist (and social-theorist) vocabulary of "objectification," "reification," and "instrumental reason." "Materialism" too soon became a self-explanatory term of abuse, embodying all negative features of modern living. In other words, things ended up playing the villain's role as humanism's "other," also giving their relegation from disciplines studying genuine social and cultural practices an effective moral justification (Olsen 2003, 2007). No wonder then that during the twentieth century to study "just things" became a source of embarrassment (cf. chapters 2 and 5).

THING THEORY AND BRICOLAGE

Outing these philosophical obstacles should not be confused with dismissing the legacy of modern thinking or interpreted as a plea for a nostalgic return to premodern conditions (Domańska and Olsen 2008). There are of course many ontological and epistemological shades within what we probably too conveniently tend to compartmentalize as the modern episteme or "modern thinking" (cf. Thomas 2004). Although entailing a somewhat ambiguous conception of things, Martin Heidegger's work, for example, signals that there were attempts, successful or not, that tried to oppose the dominant anthropocentric regime. The works of philosophers and social theorists such as Bergson, Walter Benjamin, and Merleau-Ponty are all of great relevance to the study of things, as are those of a number of late-twentieth-century scholars including Michel Foucault, Serres, and Latour. In this work, I shall draw on many of these brave attempts. Even philosophies deeply embedded in the Cartesian legacy raise issues important to the topic of this book and to the questions posed at the outset.

Trying to deal with these questions has required some risky expeditions into the vast terrain of philosophical thinking and social theory, ranging from poststructuralism to actor-network theory (ANT). The aim of these excursions has not been to prepare the ground for any tour de force overview or to provide any deep insights into all fields and deep valleys of this misty landscape. In compliance with my initial plea for an archaeological difference, the goals of my theoretical hiking are far more limited: What aspects of these philosophies and theories are of relevance to our understanding of things? Do they help us to come to grips with how things relate to us, and can they help in explaining the sad fate of things in our talkative discourses? How do these philosophers and theorists themselves approach the material world, things, objects, and artifacts? In other words, what differences would an archaeological reading of them bring forth?

Needless to say, even these more modest goals cannot be accomplished in any exhaustive way, and some people will no doubt be searching in vain for their theoretical loved ones. The actual body of theory approached in this book is a reflection of a hard-to-untie knot of personal theoretical dedications and commitments, the relevance and convenience of former readings, and the likes and dislikes that much research is based on (although rarely expressed). However, in my defense, the theories actually dealt with have—with a few exceptions—all been important to what has become known as "material culture studies" over the past twenty to thirty years. I reapproach some of these theories to see if more can be said about them—have we sensed the proper thing-lesson of, for example, phenomenology?

Without denying the sympathies that undoubtedly shine through, I have tried not to commit myself too much to any distinctive approach. Rather, I have attempted to let myself be guided by a *bricoleur* attitude, searching around for usable bits and pieces that may be reassembled with other appropriate spare parts. Even if one approach as a whole may be of limited interest to my topic, some nuts and bolts may still be very useful—if by that term we mean that they inform, enlighten, nuance, or challenge the way we conceive things. This eclectic attitude is, of course, a vulnerable and risky approach. Risky in the sense that it confronts the idea of compatibility—which in and of itself is not a bad idea, though it is often grounded in an all-or-nothing model of commensurability. In this model, programs and philosophies are labeled, united, and held together by founding totemic scholars. Thus, phenomenology stands to ANT as "Heidegger" to "Latour," and never shall they meet. Moreover, it confronts the customized politeness of authorial obedience (phenomenology cannot be fused with ANT—just look how many times Heidegger is ridiculed by Latour; symmetry has no credibility as a concept due to Latour's mocking of it, etc.).

Another version of this politeness is the respect of authorial maturing. As many authors change their perspectives and become retrospectively chronologized into early and late beings (e.g., Heidegger, Foucault, Barthes), we are somehow expected to flow with the author, conducting what Harman has termed "developmentalist readings" (2002:7), and to have more trust in the late rather than the early. However, as Harman notes in relation to his somewhat controversial reading of Heidegger:

> I regard it as irrelevant the question of whether Heidegger *meant* to grant the prominence to tool-being that it receives in this book. . . . A philosophy is

not a private introspective diary to which the philosopher has unique access. Better to think of it as a thought experiment, a process of smashing frag- ments of reality together to see what emerges. . . . You and I have the right to pursue the implications of tool-being in ways that Heidegger might not have suspected, and even in ways that he might have condemned. (2002:5–6)

Proposing theoretical bricolage requires that we allow for some "intra- paradigmatic" autonomy: that elements carry an importance by them- selves that may be activated and even increased when dislocated from their original setting. In other words, it requires that we refrain from thinking of theoretical fragments as adhesive either/or representations, which when sympathetically touched upon inevitably lead to the enroll- ment in, and thus commitment to, an entire positioned corpus of thinking. The only consistency test that such an eclectic approach can be put to is whether it "works" and performs consistently in relation to my research objectives. In other words, it enables a better understanding of things: of their ontology, of their oblivion in academia, and of their contribution to society and history.

However, some qualifications are still called for. Defending open- minded and risky theorizing is not a plea for the ignorance of strong intellectual traditions and the hard work that has made them successful. Avoiding swearing allegiance to this or that theoretical regime is not to say that we should be unconcerned with their content and their integrity or that any use or representation of them is acceptable. Thus, defending eclecticism does not mean defending more versions of "anything goes." There is obviously a lot that does not go, that cannot be mixed or should not be presented under well-established intellectual brand names (cf. chapter 2). Even if theoretical insights may be combined and used fruit- fully in ways different from those intended by the original authors, this does not render them open to any uses or deprive them of their critical potential. Theories also have objectives that object to uses that are too liberal.

My own "soft" eclecticism has emerged as an attempt to pursue the ways in which productive reasoning discovered in one body of work can be enlightened, improved, or strengthened by joining it with similar proposals observed in other bodies, while also trying to take into consideration the possible tensions and contradictions that exist between other parts of these bodies. Despite the internal controversies and contradictions that may arise, such an eclectic approach seems far more fitted to dealing with the complex mass we call "things." Things themselves have repeatedly proved to be too complex, different, and unruly to be captured by any single philosophy or social theory (cf. Latour 1999b: 176).

WRITING THINGS, THEORIZING THINGS

Theorizing on and writing about things in their inconspicuous ready-to-hand mode, as well as trying to depict their tacit, thingly affordances and importance, is obviously a task inflicted with its own contradictions and problems. How can the reticent be expressed and still be considered tacit? In what way can people's practical and everyday engagement with things be properly dealt with in academic discourses prone to abstract categories and theorizing? Are we doomed to the linguistic absolutism and pessimism by which Ludwig Wittgenstein ends his *Tractatus* ("Whereof one cannot speak, thereof one must be silent")?

In a recent paper, Tim Ingold expresses some of these concerns in relation to what he diagnoses as a susceptibility to abstraction in material culture studies that threatens to alienate the thing theorists from the things actually studied (2007a). Depressed by a conference he attended, Ingold reflects about what this "academic perversion" is all about:

> As anthropologists, I thought to myself, might we not learn more about the material composition of the inhabited world by engaging quite directly with the stuff we want to understand: by sawing logs, building a wall, knapping a stone or rowing a boat? Could not such engagement—working practically *with* materials—offer a more powerful procedure of discovery than an approach bent on the abstract analysis *of* things already made? (2007a:2–3, emphasis in original)

One may easily sympathize with Ingold's frustration, which fortunately did not take him in the suggested direction—he actually continues by quite conventional academic means in discussing concepts developed by psychologist James Gibson. While much may be learned from the suggested practical engagements, it seems based on a problematic conception of both things and academics. The latter are "thinkers" dislocated (and thus alienated) from the real (read: rural) world in which authentic practices and proper things have their *Heimat* (cf. Miller 2007:25–26). Although common Norwegian experiences, which include rowing, sawing and chopping logs, skiing, snow shuffling, fishing, hunting, tenting, gardening, house building, house cleaning, cooking, baking, and child nursing may be less widely shared (at least from what I can observe in my current Californian writing diaspora), Ingold seems to misrepresent or underestimate our own modern habitual knowledge and involvement with things. People from all over the globe and in all contexts intimately engage with things. Our ready-to-hand involvement with things and materials has probably never been greater and more diverse. Each academic conducting an "abstract analysis *of* things already made" possesses an enormous reservoir of tacit knowledge related to driving, biking, walking, food preparation, IKEA furniture assembling, computer work, dressing, writing, drinking, eating, teaching, book handling, shopping, and so forth. All these experiences are material encounters involving constraints, objecting objects and processes of "tuning in" (cf. Ingold 2000:352–54). Academics also hunt, fish, garden, sail, climb, and build, and even those who do not still have their life much more grounded in a tacit mode of "knowing how" than an intellectual "knowing what."

Thus, even if the idea of going back to a more direct encounter with authentic raw materials may be useful for certain purposes (such as understanding log building or flint knapping), it is not the lack of material engagements or competences that explains the problems of abstraction that Ingold addresses in his paper. The question is rather to ask why our habitual knowledge about "the material composition of the inhabited world" has been excluded to such an extent from our discourses. As already hinted at, and as will be argued in more detail later (see chapter 5), I conceive this void as an outcome of a very effective history of thing oblivion and displacement in Western thinking rather than a lack of material experience and engagement. In other words, the problem is not that we lack practical knowledge. Quite the contrary, we have probably never been more experienced in dealing with things and technology; never has human life been more of a "meshwork," to use Ingold's own term (2007a, 2008). However, due to a dominant intellectual legacy, the material component of this mess has mostly been treated with suspicion and rarely allowed more than a provisional and derivative existence.

In building alterative approaches, it is also doubtful whether the strategy of exiling certain concepts (such as materiality, material culture, and artifacts) is very helpful (Ingold 2007a). Using language necessarily involves transformations and abstractions—the word *ax* is by necessity different from the concrete object. Academic exchange is primarily conceptual, and although concepts may be ranked according to their relative proximity to experience, they are nonetheless concepts. As concepts they participate in another order, a linguistic discourse in which their rhetorical, aesthetical, and allegorical values are also of importance. Favoring materials over materiality, as Ingold (2007a, 2007b, 2008) prefers, may be useful in addressing certain issues and making an argument convincing, such as the one that dealing with things and authentic raw materials in a concrete manner is better and nobler than abstracted concerns with materiality.

However, attempts to ban, eliminate, and expel concepts from our vocabulary are rarely effective and their voids are soon filled with equally abstracted and generalized concepts. In the very same paper in which Ingold has a go at the concept of *materiality* (which actually appears frequently in his own writings), closely related age-old abstractions such as the *mental*, the *material*, and *matter* proliferate, as do concepts that similarly carry taken-for-granted disciplinary and cultural assumptions about the order and division of the world. (And what about new abstractions such as *meshwork, network, agency, mediators, ANT,* etc.?) This is not to say that conceptual critique is redundant, as such exegeses may indeed be useful and thought provoking—as exemplified by Heidegger's meticulous language toil. However, it is questionable whether the attempted campaign of conceptual policing helps very much in developing fruitful approaches to things and materials. Rather than certifying proper concepts, we should concentrate on sensible usages.

Moreover, despite the long-held tyranny of written texts and spoken language, I am convinced that things can also be cared for in written texts. I do not subscribe to the "abyss" doctrine grounding many social constructivist approaches, arguing that things (and the "world") are separated from language by some untraversable abyss, making any statement just a linguistic construction. Siding with authors as varied as Benjamin and Latour, I believe things also contain their own articulations that can be translated to language as well as being mediated by other means of expression (cf. Benjamin 1996:70; Latour 1999a:144).

WHAT THIS IS NOT A BOOK ABOUT

Writing a book about thing theory easily leads to expectations of something that can be immediately used to inform archaeological inquiries about the past and even of being provided with instructions for proper usage. In this book, however, theories are not played out in a "case study," the compartmentalized applied field that constitutes such a dominant trope in most archaeological and anthropological books of this kind. Those who search for a methodology or an interpretive strategy will therefore most likely be disappointed. A concern with things, however, is found consistently throughout the entire book. Thus, before heading on, it may be appropriate to end this first chapter by saying a few words about what *not* to expect from this book and why.

A primary concern is with the ontology of things: what things are, how their difference affects our life, how their being challenges our conceptions of time and history, and why things, despite their importance, have been dismissed and ignored to such an extent in social science studies. Needless to say, in my opinion these are all issues that are important both to archaeology and to the emerging number of scholars and artists concerned with things. Even for the methodologically devoted archaeologist there should be something to be achieved; the concern with things as data or sources should not be kept separate from a concern with the nature of their being. However, ontological issues are not easily played out in a case study because, for a start, it is hard to envisage any exhaustive "case" in which things' being can be put on trial. What seems more useful and achievable is a stepwise argumentative approach that links theory and things. Given the aims and scope of the book, I have thus tried to produce a text that constantly engages with things in their varied manifestations. These things include archaeological entities but also ordinary things embedded in our present everyday life. Since we all have such intimacy and familiarity with things, and in this sense are *all* fellow archaeologists, everyday objects and doings become an important heuristic device for making the arguments familiar and sensible.

This "distributed" integration of things also serves another mission. Despite its "theoretical" orientation, this book challenges the primacy of theory and the separation of things from theory that often, if not necessarily, grounds the urge for "application." I do not think things "speak" to us because of theory or that things only become meaningful through theoretically informed readings. Things are already meaningful and essential to the world and—despite my minor objections—Ingold (2007a, 2008) is clearly right that there is a lot to learn from our direct involvement with them. Thus, what is needed is not necessarily recourse to more cases or new things, but means by which to activate the implicit thing knowledge we already possess, as well as means to become more sensitive to the inherent qualities of things themselves.

Some readers may object that I have omitted central contributions or debates within archaeology and material culture studies, such as the research on cognition and material culture (e.g., Renfrew 2001, 2004). This is mostly a deliberate choice based on a care for my own topic, interests, and research questions. Rather than attempting the impossible task of being all-inclusive, I have—and despite the unavoidable excess of compulsory references—chosen to engage in more detail only with those works and authors I consider directly relevant and important for my arguments. There is, of course, always the risk of not being aware of works that would have informed one's discussions. In this respect I am mostly worried for contributions made outside the dominant languages and publishers, a concern I am sure most of my British, French, and U.S. colleagues also sincerely share. (See, however, Olsen 1991.) Still, as their enormous production witnesses, this burden of concern does not prevent them from writing. In other words, to write is also to be selective and to include what one knows and, for various reasons, considers relevant.

Finally, this is not a book about things unusual, conspicuous monuments, elaborately decorated artifacts, enigmatic figurines, or astounding ritual deposits. It is even less about the ephemeral, the void, the momentary, the transitory, and all other borderline phenomena that seem to have such attraction in many theoretically oriented works in archaeology and (material) culture studies more generally. Leafing through the titles and keyword listings of books, papers, and conference sessions from the last decade, it is rather astonishing to note how rarely we encounter ordinary things as matters of concern: streets, tube stations, logs, chairs, sewer pipes, bridges, cargo ships, meadows, fishing grounds, hearths, wells, and cooking stones—in other words, stable materials, things in their reliable everydayness. This is not at all to say that spectacular things, grand monuments, and strange and momentary phenomena are without interest, but taking into account their relative frequency and importance in past and present life-worlds, they seem a little overemphasized and probably a little overrated. Why do the growing cadres of thing-students forget or avoid those things we normally mix with, rely on, or excavate? Although probably less exciting and appealing to those constantly preoc- cupied with the search for something *behind* the material, a "return to things" can never be accomplished without also bringing in these missing masses. Besides, the thingness of the thing is probably easier to grasp in the less conspicuous, ordinary, and thus far more common objects.

2

Brothers in Arms?

Archaeology and Material Culture Studies

The whole productive idea of using artefacts to reconstruct the whole of
an extinct society saw artifacts as leftovers, not as essential to the very
existence of social life.

—Mark Leone, "Beginning for a Postmodern Archaeology"

The outset of this book was devoted to the fact that things have been
ignored in twentieth-century social science research. Today, this of
course is little more than a commonplace reminder. Throughout my research, I have encountered this claim in quite an astonishing number of
works, which has provided me with an impressive list of fellow mourn-
ers. Archaeologists are prominent, but quite a few sociologists, anthropologists, and philosophers have also voiced this bias. Michel Serres, for
example, has noted the paradoxical situation that despite the fact that
things are seen as being diagnostic of humanity ("Humanity begins with
things; animals do not have things"), they play no role in the study of this
humanity. Thus, "in the current state of affairs the so-called human or social sciences seem at best to apply only to animals" (Serres 1995b:165–66,
199–200).

With such a critical awareness of things' exile from the human and
social sciences being exposed, actions taken to repatriate the object would
of course be expected, and this is precisely what the buzz tells us. Thus,
a popular claim lately is to say that things have recaptured much of their
lost territory. As voiced by historian Frank Trentmann, "Things are back.
After the turn to discourse and signs in the late 20th century, there is a
new fascination with the material stuff of life" (Trentmann 2009:283).

While the 1970s and 1980s became known for the linguistic or textual turn, we have for some time now envisaged a "turn to things" in the sociocultural fields (cf. Andersson 2001; Bakker and Bridge 2006; Benso 2000; Brown 2003; Domańska 2006; Fahlander and Østigård 2004; Hahn 2004; Miller 1998a, 2005a; Nilsson 2003; Preda 1999).

In this chapter, I shall review some of these attempts at "(re)turning to things." One obvious field of its manifestation is the growth of what is often labeled as "material culture studies" in its various forms, such as consumption studies. However, an even more pertinent field to explore is the development within archaeology, the discipline of things par excellence. Despite being little but a "material culture study," which for several decades has also included analyses of contemporary societies (Rathje 1984, 1991, 1996; Schiffer 1991, 1999, 2003), it is for some reason rarely placed at the forefront when the new material culture family (including ancestors and fiancés) are presented (Miller 2002:240; cf. Appadurai 1986b; Miller 1987; Buchli 2002; Trentmann 2009). Its consistent devotion notwithstanding, archaeology's relation to things still remains somewhat ambiguous, as this chapter will try to outline. While it obviously does not have to turn—or return—to things to confirm its identity, archaeology has been seriously affected by the shifting intellectual conceptions of things and materiality both in academia and society at large.

This chapter is not at all intended as any exhaustive review of material culture studies or the shifting role of things in archaeology and other disciplines. For this purpose, the reader should look elsewhere (cf. Buchli 2002, 2004; Fahlander and Østigård 2004; Hahn 2004; Hodder and Hutson 2003; Julien and Rosselin 2005; Knappet 2005; Lucas 2001; Meskell 2004, 2005; Miller 1987, 2005a; Pearce 1997; Preucel 2006). Rather, it is an attempt at diagnosing some trends and tendencies in this research. Although theories, their use, and their application are commented on, they are themselves not scrutinized in much detail. The purpose of this, and the following chapter, is to prepare the scene for my more detailed plea in defense of things in the chapters to follow.

ARCHAEOLOGY: THE DISCIPLINE OF THINGS

Saying that material culture has been ignored in the social and human sciences is utterly unfair to one discipline that has stubbornly continued to engage with things: archaeology. As already noted, archaeology is the foremost discipline of things, and there was a time way back when archaeologists loved objects—one may even recall a certain obsession. In fact, it was a passion shared by several disciplines such as anthropology, ethnology, and a wide field of what we, at least retrospectively, may call cultural studies (cf. Fenton 1974:19–21; Klausen 1981; Stocking 1982; Strathern 1990:38–39).

However, it is an equally well-known fact that most of our former allies soon abandoned the world of things in favor of more social and human concern, leaving archaeologists, ethnologists, and museum curators rather alone in their concern for the object. When anthropology turned social (or cultural), things were no longer assigned any role in mediating the relationship between the anthropologists and the culture that was studied. From now on, societies and the cultural contexts were to be accessed "directly" through the new disciplinary imperative of dialogue and participant observation (Miller 1987:111; cf. Kuper 1978). Increasingly concerned with the motivation of the native's otherness, the "social framework" needed immediate and full dedication:

> It led to the position that one should really be studying the framework itself (the social context=society). The artefacts were merely illustration. For if one sets up social context as the frame of reference in relation to which meanings are to be elucidated, then explicating that frame of reference obviates or renders the illustrations superfluous: they become reflections of meanings produced elsewhere. (Strathern 1990:38)

Complying with the justificatory habit associated with most ruptures and revolutions, the well-proved tactic of self-definition through negation also became generously applied by the newly converted anthropologists. Thus, after becoming social (or cultural), they more than willingly testified to things "objectifying" function, feasible only, we were told, within outdated evolutionary and diffusionist conceptions of culture—or within "conjectural" history. Throughout the first three quarters of the twentieth century, anthropologists repeatedly launched cautionary tales to reaffirm their vision of culture as social or cognitive. In his 1961 attempt to define culture, Fredrik Barth thus still found it necessary to make a cautionary tale: "It often seems that . . . *even artifacts* are treated analytically as if they were cultural elements. It ought to be clear that patterns of behavior described as 'customs' or artifacts in a museum are not cultural elements. . . . Culture consists of ideas" (Barth 1961:39, my translation and emphasis). In this context, where the social (and soon the political and ethical) increasingly became flagged as a categorical imperative within the social and human sciences, to study "just things" became a task in need of justification. It became a source of embarrassment, a reactionary heritage of mindless antiquarianism surviving in dusty museum spaces—leaving, in short, little honor to the discipline of things.

And gradually a change could also be discerned in the archaeological rhetoric: the material was only a *means* to reach something else, something more important—cultures and societies: the lives of past peoples, the

Indian *behind* the artifact. The social scientists remained rather unimpressed, however, and even after the discipline had turned "new," Edmund Leach continued to lecture us that "in the last analysis, archaeology must be concerned with people rather than with things" (1973:768). Others recalled an almost negative learning curve, claiming that throughout the twentieth century[1] archaeology had become "*increasingly* obsessed with objects as such, and treating them as having independent behaviour in a manner that separated them from any social context and which amounted to a genuine fetishism of the artefact" (Miller 1987:110–11, cf. 143; my emphasis).

Tribal songs notwithstanding, it is a fact that archaeologists during the last century became increasingly concerned by their dubious reputation as students of things. A small but growing number of theoretically minded archaeologists started to question the rationale for the disciplinary habit of collecting and classifying things. This concern was already discernable in the writings of Vere Gordon Childe and Aarne Michael Tallgren back in the 1930s (Childe 1933; Tallgren 1937) and is more fully fleshed out by later "dissenters" such as Walter Taylor (1948) and the postwar pessimists (cf. Gjessing 1951; Hawkes 1954; see even Piggott 1965). At the very heart of their concern was the pivotal issue of not confusing culture with things: "Culture is unobservable, is non-material. . . . Even behavior, though observable, is non-material. . . . Therefore, the term material culture is a misnomer and the dichotomy between material and non-material relates only to observable results of cultural behavior, not to culture itself" (Taylor 1948:102). Culture was a nontangible realm, which things related to only in an epiphenomenal way—as was society. The fallacy of the archaeological project was that we had to rely on dead things providing poor and accidental access to (once) living cultures.

The outcry a decade later that "archaeology is anthropology or it is nothing" (Willey and Phillips 1958:2) grasped this new disciplinary zeitgeist of yearning for a world behind the artifacts. However, it also signaled a new optimism that cleared the way for a new, anthropological archaeology that shrugged off the negative image of the archaeologists as being hopelessly victimized by their accidental and fragmentary material record (Binford 1962). Given that the right procedures and epistemology were applied, things would speak loudly and convincingly about the cultural dynamics that they originated from.

FUNCTIONAL ARTIFACTS OR TEXTUAL FRAGMENTS: ACCESSING "THE BEHIND"

Throughout the ensuing decades of processual and postprocessual archaeology, *how* and *what* to grasp beyond the artifact became the crucial issue of debate. In this debate, at least as it unfolded up until the 1990s, one may discern two main identities ascribed to material culture, simultaneously designating two respective "spheres of behind" that things may provide access to. On the one hand, we had the processualists or "new" archaeologists who were concerned with explaining things' functional, technological, and adaptive importance, while on the other hand we had the postprocessualists struggling to interpret their social and cultural meaning (their role as signs, metaphors, symbols, etc.; cf. Binford 1962, 1972, 1983; Gibbon 1989; Hodder 1982b, 1986; Johnson 1999; Preucel 1991; Shanks and Tilley 1987; Thomas 2000).

Although their differences were considered to be very essential—as the vague memories from the science war remind us—what was shared in most processual and postprocessual approaches was a longing for realms beyond the material itself. *Material culture* became an ambiguous term for reaching a culture that itself was not material (although it must be admitted that the processualists provided us with a less airy conception). Things were studied primarily as a means to reveal something else, something more important—the societies and cultures, women and men, *behind* the artifact. The material was a *source* material, treated not for its *thingness* or sociality, "but rather as a mediating window onto ancient life" (Meskell 2004:14). The archaeological record, past things in the present, was conceived of as an incomplete *representation* of the past, as traces of an *absent presence*—not as part of the past society (or the past) itself. As pertinently remarked upon by Mark Leone, "things, or artifacts, were indicative of and not essential to culture. . . . The whole productive idea of using artifacts to reconstruct the whole of an extinct society saw artifacts as leftovers, not as essential to the very existence of social life" (2007:206).

The following quotation may be seen as representative (if not exhaustive) of the general archaeological attitude toward material culture:

> The main aim in archaeology is to write culture history. Our primary data for this reconstruction are the artifacts, or the material remains of past human activity. This material is the product of people's ideas (culture). To understand the relationship between the material remains and the cultural processes which produced their distribution, is the critical problem in archaeology. (Håland 1977:1)

Thus, things are primarily studied for methodological and epistemological reasons: to reveal the extramaterial cultural processes that produced them (e.g., behavior, action, mind). Or as concisely summarized by Clive Gamble: "Getting at people is the core activity in archaeology" (2001:73).

Some familiar memories: in the 1960s and 1970s, material culture turned adaptive and functional. Variation in material culture reflected differences in ecological adaptation and social status. In the early 1980s, we learned about material culture as active and communicative, as symbols in action. Later on, pots, megaliths, and rock carvings were written into the limitless text of poststructuralism and (late) hermeneutics. Literary analogies abounded: *reading the past* (Hodder 1986), *reading material culture* (Tilley 1990a), *material culture as text* (Tilley 1991; see Preucel 2006:138–42). Concepts such as biography (Kopytoff 1986) and narrative (Joyce 2002) added to the obvious impression that "things ain't what they used to be" (Miller 1983). In fact, they were hardly things at all anymore (cf. Ingold 2007a). One way of seeing this development is that the conception of things became further and further removed from their own intrinsic material qualities—in other words, that conceiving of things qua things became far less attractive than conceiving of them as text, symbol, and narrative.

Thus, contrary to the often voiced accusation of being "too concerned with things" (*pace* Leach), we may rather claim that archaeology throughout most of its processual and postprocessual career suffered from being *undermaterialized*. Despite the claim of an "active" material culture, actions continued to originate primarily from the human sphere. The materiality of past societies, tellingly conceived of as *traces* or *remnants*, becomes epiphenomena of historical and social processes that are not in themselves material (cf. Soja 2000:7; Strathern 1990:37–38). As pertinently observed by Daniel Miller, archaeologists are by and large considered to be profound or good at their work "to the extent to which they are able to transcend the merely manifest in the objects which they uncover and see through these fragments to the reality of the social and cultural lives of which they are mere remnants" (Miller 2005b:212). The division between a material and a social world seems to be taken for granted (cf. Richards 2008:206), and accessing the dematerialized latter should be the primary goal of our inquiries. No wonder then that the material qualities of things have increasingly been covered up by the piles of epistemologies invented to make them as transparent and compliant as possible, in which their role is never to be themselves "but always, always to represent something else" (Brown 2003:82).

PHENOMENOLOGIES OF LANDSCAPE

During the 1990s, however, we witnessed a gradual move away from this somewhat one-sided focus on the symbolic/communicative and representational aspects of material culture. In particular, this shift was reflected in studies of landscapes and monuments in compartments of British archaeology. (For alternative approaches, see Shanks 1995, 1998; Boast 1997; Pearson and Shanks 2001; Meskell 1996, 2004; Meskell and

Joyce 2003.) Based partly on phenomenology and partly on a wide range of social theory running from Pierre Bourdieu to Michel Foucault, several archaeological studies from the mid-1990s onward seem to be founded more on people's doings and their lived engagement with the world (e.g., Barret 1994; Bradley 1998, 2003; Edmonds 1999; Meskell and Joyce 2003; Thomas 1996; Tilley 1994, 1999, 2004).

While the social theory mobilized can be seen as part of the postprocessual legacy, *phenomenology* represented a new theoretical engagement that became an importance source of inspiration for many archaeologists (cf. Gosden 1994; Feldt and Basso 1996; Thomas 1996, 2000, 2004, 2006; Karlsson 1998; Ingold 2000; Meskell and Joyce 2003; Meskell 2004; Fuglestvedt 2005). This was a rather predictable move. After all, phenomenology was launched as a way of "relearning to look at the world" (Merleau-Ponty 1962:xx), a return "to the things themselves"[2] and to practical "lived experience" unobscured by abstract philosophical concepts and theories (even if the experience of actually reading Edmund Husserl and Martin Heidegger may appear as a continuous falsification of that statement).

The phenomenological inspiration was particularly strong in studies of landscapes and monuments. Attention turned toward how materials and landscape, through active interaction with humans, served to shape experiences, memories, and lives. This was clearly an important and promising move, although there was a tendency for it to be overshadowed by the constant urge to include individual experiences and the human dimension of landscape. The effective history of postprocessual thinking and the wider sociopolitical concern with individualism, human agency, and intentionality (cf. Olsen 2006) probably made it difficult to take on the potential radical consequences of a philosophical project claiming to challenge the subjectivist and humanistic regime of modern Western thinking (see chapter 4). The filtered or domesticated version of phenomenology that made its way into archaeology and landscape studies may be seen as a negotiation of these conflicting objectives and interests.

Immensely influential was Christopher Tilley's *A Phenomenology of Landscape* (1994), later described as "a path-breaking and highly praiseworthy attempt to introduce phenomenology to archaeology" (Hodder and Hutson 2003:119; cf. Smith 2003:64). In this work, Tilley attempted to break away from disengaged approaches to landscape and monuments by putting the active experiencing and embodied subject in place. It was an approach, to use Julian Thomas's words (1996:20), which took into account the fact that the body is not just something we live *in*, but a means by which we experience the world, something we live *through*. However, Tilley's book hardly posed any challenge to the humanist and anthropocentric legacy that postprocessual archaeology was so firmly embedded in. Rather, it tried to accommodate (or add) phenomenology to this legacy (cf. Meskell 2004:10). Actually, its title notwithstanding, phenomenology constitutes only one among a formidable lineup of theoretical candidates—itself presented in less than three pages (Tilley 1994:11–14).

Despite Tilley's attempt to transfer a sharing of experience from mind to body, the experiencing power remains firmly anchored within the human individual: the centrality of the human body becomes a taken-for-granted universal (cf. Tilley 1994:16, 74). Tilley's initial definition of phenomenology as "the understanding and description of things such as they are experienced by a subject" (1994:12; see also Tilley 2004:1) confirms some of this subjectivism and clearly conflicts with the phenomenological maxim "to the things themselves" (although it must be pleaded in Tilley's defense that even to the phenomenologists it proved hard to live up to Husserl's slogan). In an attempt to elaborate his early conception of phenomenology, Tilley provides the following descriptions:

> [Phenomenology] is about the relationship between Being and Being-in-the-world. Being-in-the-world resides in a process of objectification in which people objectify the world in order to set them apart from it. This results in the creation of a gap, a distance in space. To be human is both to create this distance between the self and that which is beyond and to attempt to bridge this distance through a variety of means—through perception (seeing, hearing, touching), bodily actions and movements, and intentionality, emotion and awareness residing in systems of belief and decision-making, remembrance and evaluation. (1994:12)

This may function well as a summary of a theory of objectification (and "embodiment"; cf. Miller 1987), but it is hard to find justification for most of this in the works of Heidegger and Maurice Merleau-Ponty that are claimed to be the pivotal sources. The objectifying "gap," the intentional striving to overcome it, and a Being separated from Being-in-the-world, just to mention some very problematic notions, are hardly conceptions in compliance with the twentieth-century phenomenological project as laid out by these philosophers. (See chapter 4 for a more thorough discussion of phenomenology.)

Superficially, Tilley's phenomenology may seem to be just another example of the theoretical bricolage defended at the outset of this book. However, it is an intellectual problem when the phenomenology, which is emblematically adhered to, is difficult to identify in the works of those scholars it is said to originate from. Thus the problem is not so much what is done, if one wants to adopt a humanist and idealist perspective, but rather how a different and potentially challenging perspective is abducted in order to do so. This is not to make phenomenology itself immune to criticism. As will be shown later (chapters 4 and 5), there are numerous problematic conceptions involved in this philosophy. This also includes a lurking anthropocentric tendency that probably has fueled some of the humanist readings. (Cf. the discussion of "desevering" in chapter 4.)

Tilley's book is in many ways an admirable one, but it is firmly located in the effective historical legacy of postprocessual thinking. Thus, the struggle for a "humanized space" (as opposed to "spatial science") may well have been fought without bringing in phenomenology as an emblematic concept. It is somehow ironic that despite later works that suggested more subtle and worked-through approaches (including Tilley's subsequent works), it was this first "phenomenology" that proliferated in material culture studies and archaeological textbooks in the years to come (e.g., Ashmore and Knapp 1999; Jameson and Shaw 1999; Johnson 1999; Edmonds 1999; Evans 2003; Scarre 2002; Hodder and Hutson 2003; Hamilton et al. 2006; see however Meskell and Joyce 2003 and Meskell 2004 for a somewhat different approach). Thus, when Ruth Van Dyke and Susan Alcock (2003) summarize the strength of the phenomenological approach in archaeology (i.e., that it "allows us to think about the ways in which landscapes and built forms were experienced, perceived and represented by ancient subjects" [7]), it is clearly Tilley's initial definition that informs their view. Another irony of this was that it made phenomenology undeservedly vulnerable to much recent ill-grounded critique (cf. Johnson 2006; Bintliff 2007).

The conception of *landscape* that came out of this phenomenology depicted a subjective and supple sphere held together and made meaningful by people's thoughtful engagement with it. The landscapes one encountered were always open, multivocal, and ever changing—in other words, always relative to the situated actors' conception of them. As noted back in 1993 by Barbara Bender, "Landscapes are created by people—through their experience and engagement with the world around them" (1). In a more recent paper, we learn that a phenomenological approach "allows us to consider how *we* move around, how *we* attach meaning to places, entwining *them* with memories, histories and stories, creating a sense of belonging. . . . We have seen that landscapes are experimental and porous, nested and open ended" (Bender 2002:136–37, emphasis added). According to Gabriel Cooney, we "perceive, understand, and *create* the landscape around us through the filter of our social and cultural background and milieu" (1999:46, emphasis added). Wendy Ashmore and A. Bernard Knapp confirm that "today . . . the most prominent notions of landscape emphasize its socio-symbolic dimensions: landscape is an entity that exists by virtue of its being perceived, experienced, and contextualised by people" (1999:1). And summarizing Bender and Tilley's conception, Ashmore tells us that for these two scholars, "landscapes are primarily social constructs" (2004:260).

Two key terms, or tropes, seem to dominate the actual attempt of capturing this situated experience. One is *visuality*—the description and imaging of the way sights and visual fields change with the location of the viewer (Hamilton et al. 2006:33). The other is "adjectivity," wrapping up the landscape in adjective-filled narratives that pertain to the phenomenological sensibility of the archaeologist present (cf. Tilley 2004:27–28; Willams 2007:12; Bender, Hamilton, and Tilley 2007:335–36). I am not saying that all those advocating these conceptions of landscape saw themselves as doing phenomenology. However, the concept was conspicuously present in these discourses, and the difficulty of distinguishing those who explicitly advocated phenomenology from those who confessed to "social constructivist" and idealist perspectives, with some notable exceptions, is probably rather telling. For example, the interpretations Tilley offers in his 2004 book on landscape phenomenology are hardly distinguishable from those emerging from other theories popular among postprocessual archaeologists. Menhirs and rock art still are about structural oppositions, symbolizing principles of social order, identity, spirits, and ancestors. Discussing the Brittany menhirs, for example, we learn that the individuality of these primarily naturally shaped stones "would act to sustain a sense of social identity for the people who erected them and subsequently

Figure 2.1.   Landscapes—what difference do they make to the way we live, think, and act? Integrated living, southern Iceland (photo: Bjørnar Olsen).

lived with them. People would recognize themselves, where they were, and who they were through the material qualities and identity of the individual menhirs" (Tilley 2004:37).

Phenomenological or not, what is missing in most of these stories is what landscapes and places have to offer us. How do *they* affect our being-in-the-world? In the celebration of landscapes and matters as plastic and always constructed ("as something open-ended, polysemic, untidy, contestational and almost infinitely variable" [Bender 2002:137]), there seems to be little concern for the properties and competences possessed by the landscape itself. Mountains and plains, rivers and lakes, forests and fields, oceans and fjords—what *difference* do they make to the way we live, think, and act? Are they all just open ended, receptive, and polysemic, or do they have a say—also beyond suggesting metaphorical and ritual associations (see Bradley 2000; Tilley 1999, 2004)?

One may speculate as to whether the old ecofunctionalist school perhaps came closer to Heideggerian phenomenology than many of the self-proclaimed archaeologies of phenomenology. The ecological approach saw humans as an integrated part of a systemic whole; it emphasized how living in a particular landscape, in certain places, brought forth a certain way of living—a way of living made possible by responding to the forms and capacities "slumbering" in the environment. The new "phenomenological" (and symbolic) human, however, seems less receptive; it took on the role of ruler-creator, inventing ever-changing cognitive landscapes. Maybe this creativity was related to "practice," as frequently told. However, apart from the ever-present ritual toil, the people who are supposed to have been creating these landscapes seem strangely alienated from the everydayness of herding sheep, clearing fields, carrying water, building fences, cooking, cutting wood, and so forth.

The experiential primacy assigned to the visual field adds to this bias. Despite the acknowledgment that perception is also a somatic engagement, we are too often presented with actor-spectators who walk around contemplating and gazing at landscapes and monuments from different angles (cf. Tilley 1994:74–75). Though I cannot elaborate the relationship in any depth here, the emphasis on vision and view angles (cf. Tilley, Hamilton, and Bender 2000; Cummings and Whittle 2003; Bender, Hamilton, and Tilley 2007) connects this archaeology in more than one sense to the Cartesian perspectivalist tradition in landscape painting (cf. Jay 1998). Despite attempts to attach this as the stigma to the objectivist gaze (associated with maps, plans, and aerial photography; Willams 2007:288), perspectivalism is actually a very conspicuous trope in many phenomenologies of landscape. (For criticism, see Thomas 1993; Hamilakis 2001, 2002; Frieman and Gillings 2007). It may not be accidental that this complies well with Western metaphysics, in which the spoken resemblance between the "I" and the "eye" has always conveyed more than a phonetic association (Andersson 2001:79; Jay 1998). Bender pertinently notes the controlling power of this gaze as one that "skims the surface; surveys the land from an ego-centered viewpoint . . . the Western gaze is about control" (Bender 1999:31; see also Tilley 2004:14–16). However, little of this insight seems to be turned back on the "contemplative gaze" so often found in landscape archaeology (cf. Bender, Hamilton, and Tilley 2007).

RETURNING TO THINGS: CONSUMPTION STUDIES

As already noted, a (re)turn to things has been announced as a current trend more widely in the social and human sciences (cf. Andersson 2001; Bakker and Bridge 2006; Brown 2003; Domańska 2006; Foster 1996; Miller 1998a, 2005a; Preda 1999; Trentmann 2009). The growing field of modern material culture studies and the more general concern with design, "visual culture," landscapes, and the body constitute some of the components in what may be seen as a rehabilitation of things in contemporary studies of society. The chronology and key sites for this rehab are, of course, a matter of debate. One serious contestant would be the studies of modern household refuse pioneered by processual archaeologists, which in many ways was the first systematic attempt at challenging the subjective, linguistic accounts grounding much social research (cf. Rathje and McCarthy 1977; Rathje 1984, 1991, 1996; see Schiffer 1991, 1999).

Far more recognized, however, is what has become known as *consumption studies*, probably the most influential brand of modern material culture studies (cf. Douglas and Isherwood 1979; Appadurai 1986b; Miller 1987, 1998a, 1998b, 2001, 2005a; Baudrillard 1998; Dant 1999; Attfield 2000; Buchli 2002; Mullins 2004). A main concern has been how artifacts, primarily consumer goods, are actively used in social and individual self-creation, in which they become directly constitutive of our understanding of ourselves and others, "a means by which we give form to, and come to an understanding of, ourselves, others, or abstractions such as the nation or the modern" (Miller 1994:397). Objects are turned into signs and consumed *as* signs; their importance is their sign-value (Baudrillard 1998). According to Miller, one of the leading advocates of this approach, people appropriate objects from the manipulative forces of production and commerce and turn them into potentially inalienable and creative cultural products vital to their own identity formation:

> The key [criterion] for judging the utility of contemporary objects is the degree to which they may or may not be appropriated from the forces which created them, which are mainly, of necessity, alienating. This appropriation

consists of the transmutation of goods, through consumption activities, into potentially inalienable culture. (Miller 1987:215; cf. Miller 1998a:19, 2002:238–39)

This and related approaches to modern material culture within anthropology, cultural studies, sociology, and other disciplines have produced a wealth of studies of such things as graffiti, kitsch, surfboards, rugs, greeting cards, and home decoration (cf. the volumes of *Journal of Material Culture* published since 1996 for an illustrative segment). This has increasingly been the case since the late 1990s, when consumption studies became more and more narrowed toward shopping, the exchange of goods, the *desire* for objects, their aesthetization, and the media image of them (cf. Miller 1998b), rather than their uses and the ways material objects are *lived with* (Dant 1999:37; cf. Attfield 2000:136ff.; Brown 2003:4; Meskell 2004:33–38). As noted by Glassie (1999:77–84), within anthropology and modern material culture studies, things are increasingly read as

Figure 2.2.   "And it seems possible to say very little in these studies about the dull, ordinary, and inconspicuous materiality that people constantly engage with. . . . How do we 'sublate' a coal mine or a derelict town in the Russian North?" Apartment house, Lovozero, Kola Peninsula, Russia (photo: Bjørnar Olsen).

goods—as commodities and possessions (cf. Douglas and Isherwood 1979; Appadurai 1986a; Baudrillard 1998; Miller 1998b, 2001).

And it seems possible to say very little in these studies about the dull, ordinary, and inconspicuous materiality that people constantly engage with: walls, streets, fences, parking spaces, fishing grounds, and gas stations. How do we consume a highway, a university campus, or a subway system? How do we "sublate" a coal mine or a derelict town in the Russian North? To a considerable degree, consumption studies seem to have become the study of the "domesticated" and staged materiality of the private individual, the outfits and belongings of what Walter Benjamin denoted as "Das Etui Mensch" (cf. Benjamin 2002:38). They rarely extend beyond the domestic doorstep to include what Frank Trentmann calls the "brutal materiality of iron, steel, or bullets" (2009:287). The critical comments are still few, but in a brave—and early one—the Swedish ethnologist Orvar Löfgren questioned the overwhelming focus on the particular, the symbolic, and the visual in this field:

> In these studies of teenagers, home-makers and shoppers you sometimes feel that you are drifting through a symbolic forest or watching an exhibition of signs and messages . . . And in this focus on the symbolic there is also a total dominance of sight as *the* medium through which we experience the world. Like flaneurs and tourists—we *are* not in the world, we are only looking or gazing at it. (1997:102–3)

For Löfgren, it is a paradox that the return to material culture studies did not to a greater extent bring back the *material*. At the same time that more and more of our lives are caught up with materials, studies of material culture have become increasingly focused on the mental and representational: material culture as metaphor, symbol, icon, message, and text—in short, as always something other than itself (Löfgren 1997:103). This also makes many of these studies strangely vulnerable to the criticisms that Georg Simmel raised more than a century ago against what he saw as modernity's tendency to fragmentize, aestheticize, and symbolize the material world. In Simmel's diagnosis this was an attitude that "place[s] us at a distance from the substance of things; they speak to us 'as from afar'; reality is touched not with direct confidence but with fingertips that are immediately withdrawn" (1978/1906:474; see chapter 5).

ARCHAEOLOGIES OF EMBODIMENT

There is a line of argument running deep through consumption studies and social archaeologies of different types: that social relations are objectified or embodied in practices, artifacts, monuments, or landscapes. Taken as it is widely used, *embodiment* has come to mean the act by which people establish some kind of "quasi-social" relationship with objects in order to live out in a "real" material form their abstract social relationships (Dant 1999:2). Through processes of embodiment, the vague and ambiguous become concrete and the raw and physical are made meaningful. Embodiment becomes a process of materialization whereby selfhood, gender, cosmological entities, and so on are imbued in matter. This has proven to be a very flexible means indeed. Thus, Neolithic monuments are conceived as "a visible embodiment of ideas about the world" (Bradley 1993:72), and urban monuments become "the emblematic embodiment of power and memory" (Boyer 1994:321), while blouses and stockings are to transvestites "the material embodiment of the cultural values they would appropriate" (Suthrell 2004:136).

Despite the immense literature on embodiment in archaeology[3] and other disciplines, it is rarely debated what embodiment—as an act, a doing—actually implies in ontological terms (cf. Olsen 2007). In Lynn Meskell and Rosemary Joyce's otherwise excellent study of the embodied lives of ancient Mayas and Egyptians, the word *embodiment* is for obvious reasons very generously used, but it is hard to find any precise definition of the concept or a direct discussion of its ontological grounding. However, through such statements as "[embodiment is] a critical site of both social and personal *investment*" (2003:10, my emphasis) and "[the] social and individual work of embodiment . . . is *responsible* for the existence of a large part of the material culture, art and objects of 'high culture' that archaeologists have recovered" (10, my emphasis), it seems to imply a unidirectional process involving a human-social cause and a material effect. In her seminal book on object biographies, Meskell confirms this impression when commenting on recent attempts to grant agency to objects:

> Yet we should acknowledge that humans create their object world, no matter how many different trajectories are possible or how subject-like objects come. Materiality represents a presence of power in realizing the world, crafting thing from non-thing, subject from non-subject. This affecting presence is shaped through enactment with the physical world, projecting and imprinting ourselves into the world. . . . Such originary crafting acknowledges that there are no a priori objects; they require human interventions to bring objects into existence. (2004:3)

En passant, it should be noted that a possible thing agency does not rest in objects becoming human/subject-like but rather in their capacities of making a difference through the unique and complementary qualities they have to offer our shared world (see chapter 8).

The immense popularity of the concept of embodiment (only rivaled by *agency* in social archaeologies) and the confidence with which it is used seem grounded in a notion of embodiment as something given a priori, as something "revealed" about human-thing relationships rather than involving a particular ontology or way of thinking about this relationship (see Rowlands 2005). One condition that seems to ground it is the idea that without human intervention, that is, as beings beyond or outside our cognition, things and the world are intrinsically meaningless (cf. Holtorf 2008:266). Things only become meaningful by being inscribed with our sociality and intentions, simultaneously preparing the ground for interpretation as a rewinding of this very process of imbuement.

Introducing what is often referred to as a major breakthrough in the social study of things, *The Social Life of Things* (Appadurai 1986b), the editor sets the tone by telling us that "our own approach to things is *conditioned necessarily* by the view that things have no meanings apart from those that human transactions, attributions, and motivations endow them with" (Appadurai 1986a:5, emphasis added). The fact that Arjun Appadurai refers to his statement as a "formal truth" (1986a:5) reveals how "ontologized" this aspect of the rationalist and Enlightenment legacy has become. By casting matter as inert and meaningless, all qualities and ideas about it have to be located in the thinking subject (cf. Matthews 2002; Thomas 2004). What is removed in these archaeologies of embodiment is things' difference; their own voices are silenced, making their fate "always to live out the social life of men" (Pinney 2005:259). Our embodied traces are, to borrow Benjamin's phrase, clinging to things as private labels. Thus when we encounter home decoration, cloths, megaliths, and landscapes, what we are confronted with are really nothing but material mirror images of ourselves and our social relations (Latour 1999b:197). Even in Tilley's discussion of boat depiction in the Bronze Age rock art of southern Sweden we learn that, "in depicting boats, people were thus making fundamental statements about themselves to themselves and about the principles of social and political and cosmological order" (2004:201)

Rather than seeing human-thing entanglements as a "thrown" condition (in Heidegger's sense), *embodiment* as widely used seems to presuppose a rift, by implicitly suggesting the possible existence of a prior phase of separation ("nonembodiment") setting humans (and sociality) apart from matter—suggesting, in other words, that things, bodies, and nature are not originally part of the social, but may eventually be included and endowed with history and meaning by some human and social generosity. As such, the notion of embodiment reverberates with a common, albeit implicit, conception of humans (subjects, individuals, actors, etc.) in the social sciences as at the outset pure, noncomposite entities; in their "original constituency," they come unmixed and unequipped. From this blank state they *enter into* relationships with things and each other.

Personhood, selves, or collective identities never emerge *from* mixtures (Thomas 2000:148–52; see chapters 7 and 8).

CONCLUSION: RETURNING TO THINGS?

The recent debates on the meaning of material culture in archaeology and anthropology have largely been framed within the pretext of the social or cultural a priori. Cultural differences, social categories, and ethnic divisions exist as the given but nonobjectified backdrop that explains the circulation and consumption of things as well as their symbolic actions. Things may express ideas, embody social categories, and negotiate boundaries. However, the "social" and "cultural" is always the underlying *langue* to which all such expressions must be returned for confirmation. The key figure in this social and cultural primacy has traditionally been the human agent, the subject or the individual. This subject seems at the very outset devoid of things—a noncyborg whose nonobjectified condition is regarded as crucial to explaining his subsequent involvement with matter—and thus the never-ending transcendental imperative of searching for the Indian *behind* the artifact.

The various approaches within the new material culture studies have of course stimulated new thinking about things. Consumption studies deserve great credit for remembering things as a viable and necessary element in the study of contemporary societies. Through the work of Miller and others, things are increasingly acknowledged as a legitimate social subject matter. However, despite increasingly becoming matters of concern, things are still conceived mainly as alternative *sources* or intakes to those forces, institutions, and relations that they are believed to be epiphenomena of (Leone 2007:206). Despite the range of subject matter covered by the new material culture studies (such as consumption, exchange, style, and symbolism), and irrespective of mirroring, denying, or negotiating the templates that they are supposed to embody, the social derivative nature of things is rarely questioned. As pertinently observed by Richard Sennett, "'Material culture' too often, at least in the social sciences, slights cloth, circuit boards, or baked fish as objects worthy of regard in themselves, instead treating the shaping of such physical things as mirrors of social norms, economic interests, religious convictions— the thing in itself is discounted" (2008:7). Meaning is something being mapped onto things and landscapes, which themselves seem surprisingly drained of all significance to facilitate their so-called cultural construction (Ingold 2000:154). Little emphasis is placed on things qua things, and the possibility that they themselves might be indispensable constituents of the social fabric that is studied. In this sense, material culture studies have clearly succeeded in coming to terms with the old accusations of fetishism and objectification, making Leach's old advice to the archaeologist of becoming "concerned with people rather than with things" (1973:768) rather superfluous.

There are, however, alternative tendencies reflected in a growing number of studies in archaeology, anthropology, and other disciplines. Inspired by "thing-friendly" theoretical positions and work done in other fields such as science studies, these works try to shrug off some of the effective historical burden that has reared us to accept self-sufficient and tautological perspectives of social societies and cultural cultures mapping themselves onto things (e.g., Boivin 2004; Boivin et al. 2007; Dant 2005; Dolwick 2008; Edensor 2005; González-Ruibal 2006, 2008; Hicks 2005; Ingold 2000, 2007a, 2008; Jones 2007; Knappett 2005; Knappett and Malafouris 2008; Shanks 2007, 2010; Thomas 2007; Webmoor 2007; Webmoor and Witmore 2008, Witmore 2006, 2007). In these and other contributions, much more attention is paid to what things actually have to offer us and how they act as indispensable mediators in constructing those entities often thought of as self-sufficiently cultural and social. These approaches have started to explore how the varied intrinsic qualities of things make an immense difference to us. In other words, the materials of past (and present) societies are not seen as an epiphenomenal outcome of historical and social processes or as just an epistemological component through which these processes can be grasped, but actually as constituent parts—even explanatory parts—of these very processes. This also includes the study of the disciplinary past, which is not just a reflection of great minds, discourses, and sociopolitics, but also a history of engagement with instruments, sites, and academic architectures that facilitate those disciplinary practices and traditions we now take for granted (Olsen and Svestad 1994).

This book sides with that body of work in terms of the general scope and aims. We may disagree considerably in terms of theoretical orientation and even about how to conceive of things and the role they play. Still, what I find these studies amounting to—and I hope this work will pay its share—is a care for things' properties and differences. As anyone who has tried to walk a city, sail a boat, or assemble an IKEA bookshelf has experienced, things are not just submissive and plastic beings ready to embody our mental templates or the imperatives of our social wish images. That they may have also served that role is not an excuse to pay loyalty to the current regime.

3

Material Culture as Text

Scenes from a Troubled Engagement

A text is made of multiple writings, drawn from many cultures and entering into mutual relations of dialogue, parody and contestation, but there is one place where this multiplicity is focused and that place is the reader, not as hitherto was said, the author . . . a text unity lies not in its origin but in its destination.

—Roland Barthes, *The Death of the Author*

Throughout the last three decades of the twentieth century, the term *poststructuralism* came to be associated with a large number of topics and approaches within philosophy, literary criticism, and feminist studies. Poststructuralism also made its impact in studies of material culture. In some respects, this influence may be conceived of as rather limited and ambiguous, probably most conspicuously captured in the maxim "material culture as text," which constituted an important trope, especially in the so-called postprocessual archaeology during the late 1980s and early 1990s (Tilley 1990a; Preucel 2006:135–42, 255–58). Although the explicit use of poststructuralist theory was quite limited and selective, it contributed to setting a new agenda for thinking about things and landscapes, one that is still effective. Moreover, the poststructuralist campaign against everything firm and fixed led to a widespread suspicious attitude in cultural studies that directly and indirectly also came to mold the conception and interpretation of material culture.

Before exploring this connection in more detail, a few comments need to be attached to the concept of poststructuralism, which has proved to be an ambiguous one, and which has often been conflated with the even more elusive concept of postmodernism. Although these two "posts" are closely related, some identifying distinctions can nonetheless be noted. Writ large, postmodernism has been conceived of as an epistemic rupture that has shaken the foundational pillars on which modern life was built, announcing a new condition tellingly signified by the numerous "ends" it became associated with (of grand narratives, the nation-state, universal reason, authenticity, history, etc.). Probably more conspicuously (and less overstatedly), however, postmodernism has surfaced as a new aesthetic or "style" characterized by a playful allusiveness that stresses irony, genre mixing, eclecticism, and ambiguity (Connor 1997; Jameson 1984; Lyotard 1984). Although clearly related to the wider orbit of postmodernism (like fish to water, to paraphrase Michel Foucault), poststructuralism is distinctive in being confined mainly to academic discourses and more firmly located within a defined body of knowledge.

Poststructuralism can be associated with popular themes and topics in material culture studies from the late 1980s and onward, such as object biographies and narratives, and clearly contributed generously to the influential social-constructivist conception of landscape that entered many archaeological texts (although often under the guise of phenomenology). These topics and conceptions may all be linked to the poststructuralist mantra of "textualism," a term originally coined to characterize new modes of reading and analyzing texts, which directly and indirectly became the most important poststructuralist commodity in archaeology and material culture studies. In this chapter, I shall present and discuss features of this textual approach. In the first part, I explore some of its theoretical grounding and how it "worked" when exported to nontextual domains such as things and materialities at large. Next, I take a look at the debate on writing things, that is, how things are transformed into written discourse and, more generally, the relationship this establishes between things and texts. These initial and largely sympathetic exposures lay the groundwork for the concluding discussion of the severe problems associated with poststructuralism and the textual approach to things.

STRUCTURALISM AND POSTSTRUCTURALISM: CHRONOLOGIES AND CONFUSIONS

As an intellectual project, poststructuralism became heavily marked by its close (although oppositional) relations with the structuralist program, and the "post" added by a new generation of intellectuals should not be understood in any antithetical or purely negative way. Poststructuralism shares several basic conceptions with its "relational other": first, a nonessential conception of how meaning is constituted—that it is a product of the difference between entities rather than some inherent quality of the entities themselves; second, the conception that language (or texts) constitute a "model world" for any system of signification; and, third, a distaste for a dominant aspect of Cartesian ontology, identifying being (and self) with consciousness.

The poststructuralist revolt, however, was aiming at a much more far-reaching critique of Western metaphysics, a metaphysics that was still supposed to infiltrate structuralism. As foreshadowed by the antiessentialist philosophy of Friedrich Nietzsche and Martin Heidegger, modern thought was claimed to be dominated by a "metaphysics of presence" in which truth, knowledge, and being were argued and secured by reference to some foundational essence—a transcendent, originary center located outside discourse and practice (Derrida 1977, 1978). This metaphysic was argued to still be effective in the structuralist conception of language, giving priority to a fixed underlying structure or grammar (*langue*) of which the actual utterances (*parole*) were nothing but a precoded outcome. It conditioned even the very Saussurian concept of the sign (also as reflected in the signifier-signified split), in which the sign itself was always reduced to something secondary, a representation *of* or *for* something invariable and more "real" located outside discourse and difference (cf. Derrida 1977:43–44, 1978: 18–24).

The emergence of structuralism and poststructuralism are set far apart chronologically. Structuralism originates in the early-twentieth-century work of linguist Ferdinand de Saussure and was later modified and formalized by a number of scholars throughout the first half of the century, notably Roman Jakobson, Louis Hjelmslev, and Vladimir Propp. Somewhat ironically, at the point when structuralism began to gain academic fame outside its normal site of linguistics, thanks largely to the work of Claude Lévi-Strauss, it had simultaneously begun to come under attack on its own home ground. During the 1960s, a group of French philosophers and literary theorists such as Jacques Derrida, Foucault, Julia Kristeva, and Roland Barthes launched the critique to which the label "poststructuralism" was later added (cf. Sturrock 1979; Tilley 1990a; Preucel 2006).

It would be a grave exaggeration to claim that this revolt produced much of a stir within the disciplines devoted to the study of material culture. This is understandable, to be sure, given that a decade would pass before structuralism itself would begin to make its way into this field (although see Leroi-Gourhan 1964, 1965; Deetz 1967). When this actually happened, most notably in American ethnology and historical archaeology (Glassie 1975; Deetz 1977; Leone 1977; Beaudry 1978) and British "postprocessual" archaeology (Hodder 1982a, 1982b; Shanks and Tilley 1982), it was soon to be overtaken by scholars freshly familiar with the poststructuralist critique. This compression is most evident in early post-processual archaeology (cf. Hodder 1985, 1986), in which both structuralist and poststructuralist theories and approaches were advocated rather simultaneously from the mid-1980s onward, sometimes even by the very same authors (cf. Shanks and Tilley 1987; Olsen 1987; Tilley 1991).

Thus, while structuralism and its "post" are separated by close to six decades of research, their impact on material culture studies occurred late and almost simultaneously. It is hardly surprising that this partly overlapping chronology caused some confusion. What became known as the "textual analogy," the idea that material culture could be conceived of and "read" as text (cf. Patrik 1985; Hodder 1986; Moore 1986; Tilley 1990a, 1991; Buchli 1995) proved to be especially vulnerable. While the concept of text clearly was attached to the poststructuralist repertoire, involving a new, reader-centered epistemology, in material culture studies it was often confused with the structuralist conception of language and the idea of texts as structured and linear systems (cf. Patrik 1985; Hodder 1986; Parker Pearson 1995; Preucel and Bauer 2001). This confusion of a textual (poststructuralist) analogy with a linguistic (structuralist) one may well have provoked the feeling that the analogy was "fraught with danger":

> I can see that an artistic cycle, such as the glyphs on a Maya stele, or the paintings in an Egyptian tomb, may be read as a text. I can even concede that a building, the work of a single architect or designer, may be seen is this light . . . as the product of a single human mind, the analogue of the "writer" of the text. Even here, the analogue is not a strong one, for it is a feature of written text that they are in essence linear: the words need to be in the right order. One of the distinguishing features of the visual arts is that the lineal order need not matter. . . . When we turn to an archaeological site consisting of a palimpsest of structures and rubbish pits, constructed and deposited at different periods, the analogy breaks down altogether. (Renfrew 1989:35–36)

Even if this argument is relevant on the condition that texts are linear and material culture is not, it remains somewhat enigmatic that those who advocated it seem little concerned with its implications for the opposite move: in other words, how this proclaimed palimpsest of structures and fragments can be consistently and unproblematically transformed into linear scientific texts (cf. Parker Pearson 1995:370; Olsen 1997:119–20). However, to understand why Colin Renfrew's criticism is misplaced as an attack on the poststructuralist textual approach—which it was intended as—we need to consider this approach in more detail.

A ROUGH GUIDE TO POSTSTRUCTURALISM

Even if mostly a summarizing term of convenience, *textualism* can be regarded as a key nominative for the early poststructuralist movement. Despite the fact that it also carried serious ontological implications, it is most commonly associated with a new epistemology of reading that radically challenged existing interpretive premises. The transition to this new epistemology was marked by two important sacrifices: that of the author and that of structure.

In traditional literary criticism, as well as in the traditional hermeneutic conception of understanding, the author and the world of the author were regarded as the main entrance to a qualified interpretation of the text. Interpretation largely rested on the ability to grasp the author's intentions, to reveal the author and the author's world "beneath" the text: once the author is found, the text is explained (Barthes 1977:147). As noted by Barthes, "we try to establish *what the author meant*, and not at all *what the reader understands*" (1986:30, emphasis in original).

Poststructuralism did away with the traditional notions of authors as producers and readers as consumers of text. Interpretation or reading was a creative and productive task that involved a redistribution of power and responsibility from the author to the reader. This process of democratization, however, conditioned that the orthodox idea of the author as the father and owner of the work was dismantled. Thus, a new epistemology of reading—and the birth of the reader—could happen only at the cost of "the death of the author" (Barthes 1977:142–49).

Put in less absolute terms, this approach suggests that even the most self-conscious author can only circumscribe some aspects of meaning. Those who read the text—often in different historical and cultural settings—bring to it other voices and other texts and create meanings far beyond the author's intention. It is inconceivable that a play by Shakespeare, for example, should have a current meaning identical to the one it had at the moment of production or should conform to the author's intentions. We translate into the text the effective history of sociocultural development, expose it to new conditions and new regimes of meaning and truth, and transform it into a present product. Thus, the reader becomes an actor as well as a producer of meaning (cf. Olsen 1990:181).

The decentering of the author, however, was not in itself an attack on the structuralist approach; on the contrary, such a decentering may be argued to be well in concordance with the structuralist antisubjective agenda. The departure and "post" are evident in another operation involved in this new epistemology of reading. In a famous introductory remark to his book *S/Z* (1975), Barthes launches a veritable attack on the structuralist procedure, which, in his words, consisted in seeing

> all the world's stories within a single structure: we shall, they thought, extract from each tale its model, then out of these models we shall make a great narrative structure, which we shall reapply (for verification) to any one narrative: a task as exhaustive as it is ultimately undesirable, because the text thereby loses its difference. (3)

Thus, the new epistemology of reading conditioned more than the assassination of the author. The main act of the structuralist constitution, proclaiming that the text is just a manifestation of an underlying structure or grammar, also had to be sacrificed. The script of this act was sameness, not *difference*. The latter concept—or *différance*[1]—became a major mantra in poststructuralism, especially in Derrida's embrace of it. To put it in very simple terms, in his version, difference denies the possibility that a single element—a sign—can be present in and of itself, referring only to itself. It always refers to some "other" outside itself, which is not present, and which is itself constituted through this difference. Thus, every element is constituted on the basis of the trace it carries of other members of the signifying system, a "differential network, a fabric of traces referring endlessly to something other than itself, to other differential traces" (Derrida 1979:84; cf. Derrida 1973:138–40, 1987:26; see Yates 1990:114ff. for a more detailed discussion).

Difference is closely related to another key concept that emerged out of the early poststructuralist work, that of "intertext" as introduced by Kristeva. According to her, *intertextuality* refers to the transportation (or transposition) of textual material within the matrix of all texts, including nonwritten ones; the "transposition of one (or several) sign-system(s) into another" (1986:111). A text, a signifying practice, is never single or complete but always plural and scattered (Kristeva 1986:111). It should thus be conceived of as the site of intersection of other texts, a "multidimensional space in which a variety of writings, none of them original, blend and clash" (Barthes 1977:146; cf. Derrida 1987:33). Thus, every text is a work of translation, making the closure of any text impossible. As nicely summarized by Barthes,

> a text is made of multiple writings, drawn from many cultures and entering into mutual relations of dialogue, parody and contestation, but there is one place where this multiplicity is focused and that place is the reader, not as hitherto was said, the author. The reader is the space on which all the quotations that make up a writing are inscribed without any of them being lost; a text unity lies not in its origin but in its destination. (1977:148)

It remains somewhat enigmatic, however, why the author could not also be credited with such a role. If not assigned any role in creating the text's difference and intertextuality, every notion of experimental and poetic "writerly" writings also becomes futile.

This new epistemology of reading, or *deconstructive* reading, was aimed at shaking up the text's unity and individuality to reveal its polyvalence as a tissue of quotation from innumerable other texts (including the non-written texts of the world). This transgression was more than an interpretative turn: it clearly involved an ontological rupture, since any strict division between the world and the text was denied. Or rather, it was a denial of the possibility of living outside the infinite (inter)text. This inevitably brings us to probably the most debated and ridiculed dictums of poststructuralism, Derrida's "there is nothing outside the text."[2]

Contrary to the many vulgar and simplistic interpretations of Derrida's claim, it does not assert that there is no world or being outside texts or narratives. Rather, it opposes the idea of a strict divide between the world (or reality) on one side and the textual representation of it on the other. It proposes an ontology of the "limitless text," in which the meaning-constitutive quality of the text—the play of difference—is as relevant (and inevitable) to speech, thought, and the "world itself" as it is to writing. There is no meaning or significance outside the play of difference. Both in texts and in our lived experiences meanings are created within this web of innumerable relations of differentiation, where signs refer to signs and "where nothing is anywhere simply present or absent. There are only, everywhere, differences and traces of traces" (Derrida 1987:26). With special reference to the relationship between language and materiality, Judith Butler has captured this argument in the following doctrinal way:

> On the one hand, the process of signification is always material; signs work *by appearing* (visibly, aurally), and appearing through material means, although what appears only signifies by virtue of those non-phenomenal relations, i.e., relations of differentiation, that tacitly structure and propel signification itself . . . what allows for a signifier to signify will never be its materiality alone; that materiality will be at once an instrumentality and deployment of a set of larger linguistic relations. (1993:68)

Thus, following Derrida, to write is not a parasitic act or a dangerous and incidental supplement to a primordial unitary world. In fact, "there have never been anything but supplements" (Derrida 1978:159). Writing, interpretation, or science may be conceived of as replacing one signifying chain with another. In this sense, the world has always-already been written; difference as the meaning-constitutive quality has always existed—hence the futility of craving for an origin and presence outside this play of difference, in other words, an authentic invariable world where things have meaning without referring to other things and other systems of signification (Derrida 1977:158–59, 1987:28–29; Norris 1982:32–41).

MATERIAL CULTURE AS TEXT

The brief sketch outlined above distills the state of poststructuralist legacy as it started to influence material culture studies during the 1980s. Clearly, there were other intellectual linkages and strands, and Foucault's studies of power and disciplinary practices in particular, given their concern with the materiality of discourse, might have been expected to become more influential than they actually were. One of his important contributions to social theory was to show how systems of ideas and the exercise of regulatory power can never become effective without a material disciplinary and normalizing technology that ontologizes and fixes the desired categories and norms (i.e., by making them "visible" within a hierarchical and efficiently spatial organization; Foucault 1973, 1979; Tilley 1990b; Olsen and Svestad 1994; Svestad 1995).

This explicitly very material approach, however, received far less enthusiasm among students of things than the textual approach did. Even if it is beyond the scope of this chapter to elaborate on this in detail, I am inclined to believe that the more pleasing appeal of the latter was grounded in it being (mis)conceived as more "subjective" and "humanistic." The general public and intellectual attraction for the symbolic, the aestheticized, and the plastic, mixed with the late-twentieth-century obsession with the active individual, clearly made the "free" reader-centered interpretative approach more attractive than Foucault's somewhat dismal analysis of alienating disciplinary technologies (cf. Olsen 2003:88–94). Similar to the fate of phenomenology outlined in the previous chapter, it was thus a very selective and watered-down tap of poststructuralism that made its way to material culture studies.

To all this it must be added that, as with phenomenology, very few material culture studies can be claimed to be grounded explicitly in poststructuralist theory. (For exceptions, see Yates 1993.) Very often the approaches were blending a number of positions but with some references to aspects of poststructuralism, stressing multivocality, openness to interpretation, small stories/narratives, biographies, and so on (cf. Hodder 1989, 1999; Shanks 1992, 1999; Holtorf 1998; Bouquet 1991; Edmonds 1999). Thus, any compartmentalizing of them as "poststructuralist" must be seen as a retrospective choice of convenience rather than as a suggestion that there actually existed (or exists) a poststructuralist camp in archaeology or material culture studies, which clearly is not the case. It is more appropriate to talk about different degrees of influence.

Probably the most conspicuous poststructuralist influence within this field is well captured in the notion of "material culture as text." The claim voiced by this slogan was that material culture could be seen as analogous to text, or, rather, it could be read as text. Despite certain conceptual confusions (as noted above), the textual analogy proper was based on the disjunction between textual meaning and authorial intention. As a written text becomes separated from its author, things also become detached from their context of production and enter into dialogue with other texts through the dynamic act of interpretation. Related interpretive ideas had been presented in other theoretical camps such as among late hermeneuticans (Gadamer 1975; Ricouer 1981) and reception theorists (cf. Iser 1974, 1978), and the sources of inspiration for the textual analogy were somewhat mixed (cf. Johnsen and Olsen 1992).

Traditionally, material culture has been approached as carrying a final signified, to be disclosed through the act of interpretation. What does this awl mean? What is the significance of this design? Why is this pot decorated this way? The intentional act of producing/using endows the object with a grounding layer of meaning that can be exposed with the aid of proper methodological procedures. Central among these was the contextual approach of bounding things within their appropriate context (and/or to put oneself in the place of—or close to—the producers/ users). As argued elsewhere (Johnsen and Olsen 1992), this approach, both as conducted within different schools of archaeology (Müller 1884; Hodder 1986) and in anthropology (participant observation; cf. Strathern 1990:37–40), is basically a legacy of the early (romantic) hermeneutic conception of understanding. Actually, to some scholars, this procedure was so imperative to interpretation that it legitimatized the claim that "an object out of context is not readable" (Hodder 1986:141). Unsurprisingly, this origin-centered contextualism became an easy target for the poststructuralist counterclaims: How can we limit or close off a text or a context? How can it be bounded and shut off from readers and other texts? What is "outside" context? Timothy Yates, for example, argued that this traditional hermeneutics was totalizing and deterministic, a restrictive approach that limited the signifying potential of material culture. It was, he claimed, an attempt to endow things with a final signified outside the play of difference (1990:270–72).

A poststructuralist approach was supposed to work rather differently: it emphasizes *how* things mean and what thoughts they stimulate; it investigates and affirms the plurality of meanings obtained by things being reread by new people in new contexts. Such readings are claimed to be more a matter of translation and negotiation than of recovering. Consider the biography of a Neolithic megalith: this monument has continuously meant (or been read) since it was created some six thousand years ago. In the course of its career it has encountered Bronze Age warriors, Iron Age farmers, medieval priests, and eighteenth-century antiquarians, who have all established new intertextual connections and interpretations. Today the megalith still means something to tourists, farmers, archaeologists, artists, television producers, and advertising agents. Due to its veritable duration, this material text has opened itself up to infinite readings by continuously confronting new readers in altered historical situations. Rather than being endowed with a pre-given signified to be disclosed (burial, ancestral house, monument of power, etc.), its effective history of interpretation proves it to be a receptive and open site to signification. This openness to signification allows the megalith to establish ties to any historical moment and culture. If so, this material text can be claimed to be more radically plural, carnivalesque, and out of authorial control than any written text. In this sense, its origin was lost by its own creation. Only the material signifier remains more or less constant; the signified are repeatedly created and lost through the historical act of rereading (Olsen 1990:197–200; Holtorf 1998).

Figure 3.1. "Consider the biography of a Neolithic megalith." Megalith tomb of Dombate, Galicia, Spain (photo: Alfredo González-Ruibal).

Another example, if not poststructuralist by intention, may exemplify this perspective further. In his rich book entitled *Material Culture* (1999), Henry Glassie also discusses processes of material creation, communication, and consumption in relation to handicrafts and local communities in northern Turkey. Among other things, he is especially concerned with how certain artifacts, the carpets produced by the weaver Aysel, assemble history and contexts through their specific biographies. Although "inalienable" in their domestic origin, carrying memories, aesthetics, and tradition, Glassie depicts how the carpets made by Aysel, through processes of economic exchange, escape the circle of the village, leaving her, never to be seen again (45–58). The close and infiltrated (but not univocal) meanings attached to their cultural *Heimat* are replaced or extended as the carpets embark on a new life. Hence, the beautiful biography:

> A German couple buy a carpet in the Covered Bazaar in Istanbul. It becomes a souvenir of their trip to Turkey, a reminder of sun on the beach, and it becomes one element in the décor of their home, a part of the assembly that signals their taste. Their son saves it as a family heirloom. To him it means childhood. Germany replaces Turkey. The weaver's memories of village life give way to memories of an aging psychiatrist in Munich for whom the carpet recalls a quiet moment when he lay upon it and marshalled his bright tin troops on a rainy afternoon. Then his son, finding the carpet worn, wads it into a bed for a dog, and his son, finding it tattered in his father's estate, throws it out. It becomes a rag in a landfill, awaiting its archaeologists. (Glassie 1999:58)

To decide what meaning is the right or proper one, what context of interpretation is appropriate for interpretation, or even when the carpet is "out of context" seems futile (cf. McGuckin 1997). Even if the carpet stayed in Aysel's village, it would still be translated and intersected with other texts.

The folklorist or anthropologist studying such carpets as a manifestation of local material culture would bring to the analysis knowledge of other motifs; he or she would compare them with design patterns from other parts of the world, his or her former readings and studies would intersect, networks of theoretical and methodological resources would be activated, and so forth. Then, when this scholar's studies of the carpets finally became processed into finished products (paper, books, or Web pages), they would take on new and accumulated trajectories, enmeshing the carpets into new networks of readings. Even if the interpreter never traveled to the remote village, the carpets would still be intertextual products, patchworks that interwove materials, memories, kinship, inspirations, religious beliefs, and so on. Old carpets would be reread as the transformation of society, and knowledge and the global/local interface would supply the readers with new links, making possible the transposition of other signifying material. Thus, the imperative of an invariable context, or an authentic object that escapes difference, seems impossible to maintain. At this point there is clearly a connection between poststructuralism and the actor-network theory discussed later in this book (cf. Law 1999; see chapter 7).

MATERIALIZED TEXTS

Poststructuralism brought a new dimension to the epistemology of interpretation, emphasizing the processes by which meaning is produced rather than passively recovered. Interpretation was claimed to be a never-ending task, a creative act of production, not the disclosure of some fossilized strata of meaning. Within material cultural studies, the criticism it brought forward of narrow contextual hermeneutics was clearly an important and liberating turn. However, the somewhat biased enthusiasm for selected aspects of poststructuralist theory, especially those stressing multivocality and the plurality of meanings, seems to have encouraged a somewhat gamelike—even numerical—attitude toward interpretation: How many ways can a thing come to mean? How many layers of meaning can be accumulated? Furthermore, and despite the emphasis on the relational foundation of meaning (as activated by the "free play of the signifier"), the important sources of meaning always seem located *outside* the signifier (the object, the text) in question: in the reader, in other readings, or in other texts, who/which donate to it these new dimensions of meaning. And finally, even if the textual analogy was powerful and productive, few asked about the difference in the way things and texts mean. Do we experience a city, a house, or a landscape in the same manner as we *read* a textual or spoken statement? What is the difference between the somatic and nondiscursive experience of the former and the conscious intellectual engagement with the latter? Can the textual analogy be broadened to embrace the somatic experiences of matter?

Despite the obvious difficulties (and contradictions) involved, if material culture is to be compared to—and analyzed as—text in a more sophisticated and "material" manner, we need to complicate and extend the conception of *text*—maybe to such a degree that the text is as much an analogy of the material as vice versa. Trying to accomplish this within the theoretical orbit of poststructuralism alone is probably an impossible task. One productive step, however, may be to consider the (material) text as "writerly" rather than "readerly." Barthes coined this distinction to separate those texts that pretend (even if futilely) to have only representative functions, leaving the reader with no choice but passive consumption, from those texts that resist such simplistic mimesis and offer some kind of active coauthorship (1977:155–64). While the readerly text strives to erase itself in order to become as transparent and innocent as possible, the writerly text insists on being something more than a medium for communicating a preconceived meaning. Neither is it a mere blank slate for inscription or an arena for the free play of our imagination; in other words, it is not the case that we can read anything we like into—or out of—it, as is often portrayed in critiques that claim this to be a fallacy of poststructuralist interpretation (cf. Hall 1996:218). Rather, it implies a necessary redistribution of power and "agency"—not to the author, but to the text itself.

In striving toward symmetry, the writerly text neither admits any smooth passage between signifier or signified, nor provides an empty site where we may embody our own subjective and culturally dependent meanings. Contrary to any normal conception of texts, it has no beginning or linearity; it is a reversible structure offering numerous entrances, of which none can be claimed to be the primary. When the text's materiality,

Figure 3.2. "This 'conversation' is not intellectual rhetoric; it can be activated only by a 'physiognometic' dialogue that restores to things their own materiality, allowing them to speak to us in their own language." Leftover machinery in the abandoned mining town of Pyramiden, Svalbard, Norway (photo: Bjørnar Olsen).

nontransparency, and difference are acknowledged, it loses its status as a passive medium and becomes a site of contestation and negotiation, something to be worked upon, considered, and struggled with. To read such text is more than a purely intellectual enterprise: it entails somatic experience, a kind of wrestling in which the outcome is not given. It provides a sensation that is not one of a pleasing experience, a "comforting stimulation for weakened nerves," to use Georg Simmel's phrase (1978/1906:474), but one that unsettles and distorts (Barthes 1976:14).

Thus, if there is a "pleasure of the text" in Barthes's subtle conception of the term, it consists in materializing it, "to abolish the false opposition of practical and contemplative life. The pleasure of the text is just that: a claim lodged against the separation of the text" (Barthes 1976:58–59). Reading a text does not take the reader to something or somewhere else, a world beyond the text (be it the author's or the reader's). Rather, such texts may be seen as operating in an undifferentiated space that unhinges such oppositions, an intermediate role that, in some aspects at least, comes close to Kristeva's notion of the *chora*—the in-between (Kristeva 1986:93ff.; cf. Grosz 2002).

This involvement with a text that resists domination and transparency can be conceived of as based on a reversed analogy: on text as thing. Barthes's notion of writerly text involves negotiation, a plea for symmetry, something that resembles the reciprocity involved in Walter Benjamin's mimetic (and auratic) relationship to things. This is a relationship that cares for things' difference, and this otherness (or impenetrability) is precisely what makes them "speak" to us. This "conversation" is not intellectual rhetoric; it can be activated only by a "physiognometic" dialogue that restores to things their own materiality, allowing them to speak to us in their own language (Benjamin 2003:338).

WRITING THINGS

Poststructuralist textualism worked both ways; thus, it also triggered a debate and a series of reflections on the ways in which material culture was *written* and the formation processes involved as we move from things to text (cf. Tilley 1989; Baker and Thomas 1990; Olsen 1990; Hodder et al. 1995, Joyce 1994, 2002; Preucel 2006). To engage in an academic study of material culture is, by necessity, to also engage in textual activity. Things receive much of their identity as anthropological or archaeological objects by being realized as texts (field reports, catalogues, journal articles, and books), even if often supported by visualizing devices such as drawings, photographs, and exhibitions. Every description and analysis, ranging from the labeling of artifacts (Bouquet 1991) to social and historical synthesis (White 1973, 1978), involves textualization and the use of (oral/ written) language. Even the photographed and exhibited item often gets much of its identity from the metatext (the caption) that accompanies it (Olsen 1990:192).

Writing academic texts is by convention to write *about* the subject matter. Much as with the supposed processes of embodiment and materialization discussed in the previous chapter, the transformation is smooth and readerly; it is always supposed to move hierarchically and irreversibly from signified to signifier, from content to form, and from idea to text. This aspired-to ideal seems to be that of an erased or transparent signifier that allows the content "to present itself as what it is, referring to nothing other than its presence" (Derrida 1978:22). The common conception of academic language has been that it is merely a neutral device, a transparent instrument subjugated to a derivative hierarchy consisting of "on one side and *first of all*, the contents of the scientific message which are everything, and on the other and *afterwards*, the verbal form entrusted with expressing these contents, which is nothing" (Barthes 1986:4, emphasis in original).

One of the most profound poststructuralist contributions was to challenge this transitive conception of language and writing in which the text is believed unconditionally to mirror the world, constituting its simulacrum. As discourse, for example, anthropological and archaeological texts participate in the same structure as the epic, the novel, and the drama. Thus, to write is to make ourselves subject to narrative formation processes, to literary techniques and conventions (rhetoric, allegories, plots), blurring the strict border between scientific text and fictional literature (cf. Derrida 1977, 1978).

The concern with science and research as textual practices, as writing, also had an impact on the theoretical debate in archaeology and anthropology. This was also inspired by the metahistorical works of Hayden White (1973, 1978) and caused a new awareness of how literary form intervenes in the textual construction of the object. This was most noticeable in anthropology, in which the recognition of the constitutive character of ethnographical writing led to a debate on the representation and construction of the "other" (Clifford and Marcus 1986; Clifford 1988; Geertz 1988; Hastrup 1992; Hastrup and Hervik 1994; see Baker and Thomas 1990; Solli 1996; Edmonds 1999). Poetry (or "poetic" writing) and other experiments with literary forms were proposed as alternative and more adequate representations of the complexities and hybridities encountered in the field (cf. Prattis 1985; Fischer 1986; Giles 2001). According to George Marcus and Michael Fischer, the objective of experimental writing was to produce a more authentic representation of cultural differences (1986:42–43).

The sudden focus on autobiography, style, and aesthetics probably made an amount of narcissism unavoidable. Both archaeology and anthropology produced works where the concern for content sometimes obviously became secondary to what James Clifford once referred to as "our fetishizing of form" (Clifford 1986:21; for examples, cf. Campbell and Hansson 2000; Bender, Hamilton, and Tilley 2007). The new imperative of creating polyphonic texts also caused some questionable (although memorable) solutions. The devices applied to infusing dialogue and multivocality into the text often boiled down to adding a section with dialogue or conversation in an otherwise quite conventional narrative (often featuring the author and one or more opponents as participants, a solution probably inspired by Foucault's dialogic conclusion in *The Archaeology of Knowledge* (Foucault 1970:199–211; cf. Tilley 1991; Hodder et al. 1995; Hodder and Preucel 1996; Hodder 1999; Karlsson 1998; see Joyce 2002; Bender, Hamilton, and Tilley 2007). Even if encountering such a dialogue in scientific texts may have provoked some reflections, it may be read as another way of controlling reader's responses (producing both questions and answers), and thus actually reinstalling the author as the center of discourse. It is as if the author takes on the reader's and critic's roles, producing texts that are already fragmented and ready-made deconstructed (Shaw and Stewart 1994:22–23).

MIMESIS REGAINED?

The new emphasis on dialogue and plurality was clearly intended as a liberating turn. In ethnography, it was partly a project of empowering the "other" as more than an "informant," or, in Clifford's more modest words, an attempt "to loosen at least somewhat the monological control of the executive writer/anthropologist and to open for discussion ethnography's hierarchy and negotiation of discourses in power-charged, unequal situations" (1997:23).

Things are maybe less likely to be cared about as complex, historical agents or to be seen as in need of emancipation. However, their treatment in scientific discourses is somehow analogous to Western blindness toward the other (cf. Olsen 2003, 2004, 2007). This even includes a certain ambiguity (cf. Young 1995), being at the same time objects of ignorance (or contempt) and of desire. As noted by several commentators (e.g., Simmel, Benjamin), the modern attitude to things embroils this ambiguity: a fear of things in their thingly otherness and, simultaneously, a redemptive longing for the warmth of the atomized and humanized artifact (Simmel 1978/1906:404, 478; Andersson 2001:47–51; see chapter 5). Things' otherness and distinctiveness unsettle and distort us and urge means for domestication and subordination. By introducing the imperative regime of meaning, language and writings have clearly functioned as such means and largely managed to counter the objects' disquieting material obstinacy. One outcome of this labeling and narrativization is, of course, a world less and less sensitive to the way things articulate themselves, entombing the "material community of things in their communication" (Benjamin 1996:73). Intellectually, we encounter things as (pre)labeled, as enveloped by layers of linguistic meaning—what Benjamin termed "overnaming," the outcome of which is the silencing of things themselves (1996:73).

Accompanying things on display, a printed image, or a figure, the texts—even an innocent catalog label or figure caption ("Spear-thrower from Mas d'Azil"; "The sorcerer of Trois-Frères"; "The beautiful Bronze Age warrior: chiefly Urnfield equipment from northern Italy"[3])—load the object with a preconceived signified, a culture and moral that clearly reduce its possible signification (Olsen 1990:195). As noted by Barthes, "the text directs the reader through the signifieds of the image, causing him to avoid some and receive others; by means of an often subtle dispatching, it remote-controls him towards a meaning chosen in advance" (1977:40).

Against this background of sameness and uniformism, it is understandable that the introduction of new ways of writing things, which are more ambiguous and multilayered (such as double texts, experiments with hypertext and hypermedia, poetics, irony, etc.), was conceived of (and motivated) as acts of liberation. Such presentations clearly appear to be a more appropriate means of securing, realizing, or *making manifest* (cf. Shanks 1999) things' material diversity and polyphonic character. One (if not *the*) raison d'etre behind all this seems to be that whereas the former, realist writings misrepresented the world as simplistic and straightforward, poststructuralist (and postmodern) writings and presentations let the presumed complexity and hybridity shine through (cf. Marcus and Fischer 1986:31, 42–43). This point of motivation is well expressed by White in relation to historiography:

> Since the second half of the nineteenth century, history has become increasingly the refuge of all those "sane" men who excel at finding the simple in the complex, the familiar in the strange. . . . The historian serves no one well by constructing a specious continuity between the present world and that which preceded it. On the contrary, we require a history that will educate us to discontinuity, more than ever before; for discontinuity, disruption and chaos are our lot. (1978:50)

It is somewhat ironic that the plea for a more complex and diverse representation can actually be read as advocacy of a new *mimesis*. Although normally claimed to be the great fallacy of realism (which was accused

of conflating literary form with epistemological stance), experimental
writings and presentations may actually be a new way of creating what
Johannes Fabian has termed "representations that are (or pretend to be)
isomorphic with that which is being represented" (1990:765). Even if the
aspiration of creating better (or more realistic) representations should not
be the cause of any embarrassment, it clearly seems odd in relation to a
theoretical legacy that precisely questions such mimicry and, as it seems,
any representationist stance altogether.

THE TYRANNY OF THE TEXT

There is also another, in my opinion far more serious, issue at stake here,
similarly submerged in the ongoing debate about things and texts. This
concerns how the textual approach campaigned for by poststructuralists
(and others) has reinforced the hegemony of the text, allowing (in a very
literal sense) no space outside it. Finally fully conquered, the materiality
of things ended up as little more than an arbitrary quality in a dematerialized discourse (Beek 1991:359). In the wake of an idealist intellectual
tradition that has continuously devaluated, stigmatized, and demonized
the material (always bypassed, always made transcendental), to conceive
of any material experience that is outside of language becomes the subject
of suspicion.

   One example of how poststructuralism came to campaign for a textual
(and linguistic) colonialism against things is provided by Butler, whose
work has been hailed by a number of archaeologists and anthropologists
as providing a new framework for understanding materiality (despite
rarely addressing nonhuman matters; e.g., Thomas 1996, 2000, 2004; Gosden 1999; Meskell and Joyce 2003; Joyce 2005; Fowler 2001; Hodder and
Hutson 2003; Buchli 2002). Discussing the differentiation between sex and
gender, Butler (1993) convincingly argues how the latter term (by being
conceived of as socially and culturally constructed) came to reinforce the
naturalness and "given" quality of the former. Sex constitutes the invariable material bedrock on which gender is molded. Thus, by being conceived of as matter, the biological (sexual) body escapes cultural construction. According to Butler, however, this escape is precisely a product of
the metaphysics of presupposing a material first instance, an originary a
priori; in other words, it is based on a deceptive conception of materiality
as existing prior to, or outside of, language. Unmasked, this ontologized
matter (as opposed to the culturally constructed) is revealed as nothing
but a linguistic construct itself, something always discursively articulated. Thus, there is no materiality existing outside of language: "We may
seek to return to matter as prior to discourse to ground our claims about

sexual difference only to discover that matter is fully sedimented with discourses on sex and sexuality that prefigure and constrain the uses to which that term can be put" (Butler 1993:28).

Following Butler, materiality is nothing given, be it a site or a substance, but a "process of materialization that stabilizes over time to produce the effect of boundary, fixity, and surface we call matter" (Butler 1993:9). This interesting thought, however, is based on an inverted hierarchy of opposition in which materialization is seen solely as a process in service of (or an effect of) power. Thus, sex is a forcible materialization of a "regulatory ideal" (heterosexuality); to materialize the body's sex is "to materialize sexual difference in the service of the consolidation of the heterosexual imperative" (Butler 1993:2). Materialization and its byproduct matter end up as epiphenomena of something more primary (power, the heterosexual regulatory ideal, etc.). And, well in concordance with the effective history of modern Western thought, materiality continues to be viewed with suspicion and contempt, entailing the old vision of freedom and emancipation as that which escapes the material (cf. Latour 1993:137–38). Hence the conspiracy theory claiming that "'materiality' appears only when its status as contingently constituted through discourse is erased, concealed or covered over. Materiality is the dissimulated effect of power" (Butler 1993:35).

Despite Butler's promising introductory citation from Donna Haraway's cyborg manifesto ("Why should our bodies end at the skin, or include at best other beings encapsulated by skin?" [Haraway 1991:178]), her discussion and conception of materiality appear entirely anthropocentric, leaving little room for other "carnal beings" not covered with skin. Taking those nonhuman beings seriously should not be conflated with any imperative or desire of subjugating oneself to materiality as a "transcendental center" or "final signified" to which all discourse may be anchored. Such either/or logic is of course utterly misplaced. Rather, it is a claim to do away with such hierarchies or centers and to thus acknowledge the otherness of things and of materiality as providing a distinct sphere of experience—sometimes closely related to language, other times very remote from it.

The impact of Butler's textualism reminds us that despite the emerging somatic (and visual) frames of experience in material culture studies (cf. chapter 2), there is still a very persistent conception of the absolutism of language and text. Actually, how deeply this assumption is rooted can be exemplified by a few fragments from two archaeological books written well into the "posttextual" era. Countering the critique that recently has been directed toward the textual analogy, Robert Preucel finds it sufficient to simply posit a supposed a priori statement: "These critiques are largely misguided since it can be argued that textualisation is the central constitutive practice within social orders" (2006:141, see p. 256). In another fairly recent book, *Archaeology and Modernity*, Julian Thomas claims with equal conviction that "any notion of a pre-discursive materiality is incomprehensible, since we cannot articulate the pre-discursive other than in discursive concepts" (Thomas 2004:143; for related opinions, cf. Bender, Hamilton, and Tilley 2007:26). In an earlier paper, he is even more explicit, claiming that "language is the means by which the material world is revealed to us. We can recognize things because we have the concepts at our disposal to comprehend them" (Thomas 2000:154). As Gosewijn van Beek points out in his pertinent comment to the prophets of linguistic absolutism:

> Certainly, there is no escape from language when analysing and talking about material culture, especially as language is the preferred medium of scientific exchange. But this does not mean that the material aspect we necessarily talk about *in* language has no locus in other media of experience. The "hegemony of linguistic approaches to the object world" surely is a reification of the dominant form of scientific discourse which then is constructed as the substance of things we talk about. (1991:359)

Things of course are not experienced solely as linguistic signs or signifiers, despite their capability of being transposed and represented in other media. We may talk and write about New York as a concept or an idea, as a mental wish image, or as something social, symbolic, or purely textual. Still the concept of "New York" relates to, and emerges from, a complex material infrastructure of land, rivers, streets, bridges, buildings, parking lots, art, public transport, people, cars, and so on. As argued by Ian Hacking, with a different point of reference (the material infrastructure surrounding the idea of "women refugees"), you may want to call these structures "social" because their meanings are what matter to us, "but they are material, and in their sheer materiality make substantial differences to people" (2001:10).

The hegemony of the text may be seen as related to a general asymmetry in academia, and especially in the humanities, in which material life (technology, manual labor, dirt) has always been an object of contempt and thus utterly marginalized. This regime of subordination may actually be related to a central aspect of Derrida's deconstructionist theory: the hierarchies of opposites (Derrida 1977). In Western culture, pairs of opposites such as body/soul, matter/mind, form/content, and nature/culture play a fundamental role in ordering discourses. As Derrida points out, this is a hierarchy of value (even of violence) in which one side is always given priority over the other (here, the left side), which is conceived of as marginal, derivative, a supplement. His favorite example (even if a questionable one) is the way speech is prioritized over writing—the latter being conceived of as redundant, a "dangerous supplement" to speech (and thus to thought). However, another opposition of subordination is less talked about, that of writing (and speech) over things (cf. Benjamin 1996:72–73). This hierarchy of value in which matter is subordinate to text and language is well in accordance with the logocentric tradition outlined by Derrida—a tradition that has always privileged the human side (thought, speech, writing) and rendered matter passive, meaningless, or negative (cf. Olsen 2003; Thomas 2004:chap. 9). Thus, as noted by Graham Harman, it is time to break loose from the textual and linguistic ghetto that we have been constructing for ourselves "and return to the drama of things themselves" (2002:17).

CONCLUSION: WHAT DID WE LEARN?

Some of the initial criticism directed at the textual analogy in material culture studies was based on the traditional assumption of written texts as linear (and irreversible) structures and thus their incompatibility with the material world, with its chaotic palimpsest of things. Even if this criticism clearly was based on a misunderstanding of the poststructuralist conception of text, which was precisely palimpsestial in nature, one may still question why students of material culture needed the textual detour to discover their own subject matter's far more fragmented, reversible, and polysemic nature. This is not to say that the textual turn was just an ideologically enforced curve made in vain. By questioning the obviousness of the traditional hermeneutic approach to interpretation, poststructuralist textualism provoked reflection on how we interpret things, on what entities are involved in the meaning/creative process and on their mutual relationship. The poststructuralist discourse on these issues constituted a vital source of theoretical inspiration.

A major fallacy, however, was to conflate the textual and the material as ontological entities. Many of us inspired by poststructuralism all too easily came to ignore the *differences* between things and text—to ignore that material culture *is* in the world in a fundamentally different constitutive way from texts and language. Actually, only a minor part of the material world is "read" or interpreted in the way we deal with linguistic means of communication. Our dealings with most things take place in a mode of "inconspicuous familiarity"; we live our lives as "thrown" into the entanglement with ready-to-hand things. This entanglement fundamentally orients our everyday life in a predominantly nondiscursive manner (Heidegger 1962:85–105; see chapter 4). Thus, to conceive of our

Figure 3.3. "Many of us inspired by poststructuralism all too easily came to ignore the *differences* between things and text." Stranded vessel, Hópsnes, Iceland (photo: Bjørnar Olsen).

dealing with material culture as primarily an intellectual encounter, as signs or texts to be consciously read, is to deprive things of their difference and their ability to "talk back" in their own material way.

If our living with things is a predominantly somatic experience, a dialogue between material entities, then we also have to envisage a poetics that, although not untranslatable, is clearly of a very different kind (cf. Benjamin 1996:69–70). If things were invested with the ability to use ordinary language, they would talk to us in ways very banal, but also very imperative and effective: walk here, sit there, eat there, use that entrance, stop, move, turn, bow, lie down, gather, depart, and so forth. Our habitual practices, memory, and what is spoken of as social and cultural form, cannot be conceived of as separate from this "physiognometic" rhetoric. At the same time, our dialogue with the material world is a sophisticated discourse about closeness, familiarity, bodily belonging, and remembering, and it is extremely rich and polysemic, involving all our senses. Walking through a forest involves encountering the "numberless vibration" (*pace* Bergson) of the material world. We hear and smell the trees as much as we see them; we are touched by their branches, moistened by the dewfall. Sounds, smells, and touches admit proximity with the world; more than seeing, they mediate the corporeality and symmetry of our being in the world (Heidegger 1971:25–26; cf. Welsch 1997:158; Ingold 2000:249ff.).

This cacophony of sensations involved in our material living is well expressed in the writings of authors such as Proust, James, Benjamin, and Borges, making manifest a nearness to things, a kind of topographical mode of experience (cf. Andersson 2001; Brown 2003). Benjamin also explored the possibilities offered by images and photographic collages in order to emancipate historical representation from the constraints of linear narrativity (2003). Today, the new media reality has equipped us with far more tools to help this move beyond conventional forms of documentation and inscription. In addition, a growing number of archaeologists and artists are exploring the hybrid spaces between their respective fields, in order to express (or make manifest) the "ineffable" experience of place and materiality (see Coles and Dion 1999; Tilley, Hamilton, and Bender 2000; Pearson and Shanks 2001; Renfrew 2003; Renfrew, Gosden, and DeMarrais 2004; Witmore 2004; González-Ruibal 2008).

Exploring such hybridized spaces where scholarship and art cohabit creates a possible interface where things and bodily practices can be articulated outside the realms of wordy languages. Experimental and nonliterary ways of making manifest our engagement with material culture are very important and to be encouraged (see Andreassen, Bjerck, and Olsen 2010). This is not to claim, however, that the study of material culture should become some type of art or handicraft in which the only legitimate utterances are those performed, exhibited, or made manifest in stone or wood. Although words and things are different, this is not to say that they are separated by a yawning abyss (making any statement a linguistic construction). If we conceive of things as being possible to articulate, even to contain their own articulation, they may also be transformed (and translated) into discursive knowledge, even if this may take us through many links and to crossing many small gaps (Latour 1999b:67–79, 141–44). As argued by Benjamin, to move from the language of things to human language is a translation "from one language into another through a continuum of transformations. Translation passes through continua of transformation, not abstract areas of identity and similarity" (1996:70). Avoiding the absolutism of the "whereof one cannot speak, thereof one must be silent" (Wittgenstein) or any other linguistic (and material) idealism, the crucial point is rather to become sensitive to

the way things *articulate themselves*—and to our own somatic competence
of listening to, and responding to, their call.

To what extent poststructuralism can help develop such sensitivity is
doubtful. A major obstacle to the development of a sensitive and symmetrical approach to things is found in the limitations imposed by the
current territorial circumscription of knowledge and expressions (see
chapter 5). Modeled on its essentialist ontology, the legacy of the modern
constitution was a rifted and polarized disciplinary landscape inhospi-
table to the needs of things. At first sight, the role of poststructuralism
in countering this modernist legacy may seem heroic and promising, as
manifested by its programmatic tenets of blurring boundaries, investigating spaces in-between, and exploring intertextual networks. However,
the primacy given to language as a "model world" and the unwillingness
to acknowledge nondiscursive realms of reality and experience (cf. Butler
1993) make poststructuralism an unreliable ally in the defense of things.

4

The Phenomenology of Things

Near to us are what we usually call things. But what is a thing?

—Martin Heidegger, *The Thing*

It is hardly an exaggeration to state that much of social and humanistic research have been prone to what Ian Hacking has called *linguistic idealism* (also known as the "Richard Nixon doctrine"), in which "only what is talked about exists; nothing has reality until it is spoken of, or written about" (Hacking 2001:24). Taking this doctrine literally, an entity exists—and is thus rendered important to social analysis—only insofar as the knowing subjects are consciously aware of it and are able to discursively articulate this experience. Needless to say, our understanding of past and present lifeworlds, cultures, and societies has suffered from being subjugated to different versions of such idealism. One immediate consequence is, as Henry Glassie remarked, that "we miss the wordless experience of all people, rich and poor, near or far" (1999:44). Since this wordless experience is mostly related to people's engagement with the material world and with things, the materiality of human life has been left equally void in most social studies. Taking into consideration how often things (and tool making) are claimed to be diagnostic of humanity (rivaled only by language), the risk is, as stated by Michael Schiffer, that social scientists "may have ignored what might be the most distinctive and significant about our species" (1999:2).

While this asymmetry is clearly an outcome of a dominant thing hostile tendency in modern Western thinking (cf. chapter 5), it has not been unchallenged. From the late nineteenth century onward, there have been sincere attempts at coming to grips with this hostility and avoidance. Central among these is phenomenological philosophy, which from its very beginning, although perhaps somewhat prematurely, recommended a return "to the things themselves." Edmund Husserl's maybe too ambitious slogan notwithstanding, phenomenology may nevertheless be seen as conceptualizing the opposition against the idealist legacy in modern thinking. Thus, the main focus of this chapter is the phenomenological approach to things, especially the attempt to explore the ontology of things and, moreover, how our engagement with things is fundamental to our own being in the world. Drawing heavily upon Martin Heidegger's phenomenology, this chapter also takes some initial steps toward exploring the properties and "integrity" of things. First, however, I shall briefly outline some of the intellectual heritage as it relates to our perception of the material world.

PHENOMENAL PERCEPTION

Modern philosophical approaches to how we experience the world have been heavily affected by idealist models of mental cognition (also basic to its discursive representation). Our experience of things is by and large conceived of as a cognitive perception in which sensory images, mainly based on vision, are filtered and transformed by our mind and language. Cartesian thinking left us with a notion of matter as passive and inert, while the human mind was seen as active and creative. Matter and mind belonged to separate realms, and the widening gulf between them became a never-ending source for modern epistemological inquiries about how (and if) our conception of the world could correspond with the material reality "out there." The skeptical attitude that followed in the wake of René Descartes's "methodological doubt" placed a seemingly irretrievable wedge between the material world and the human mind. The so-called external world of matter and nature had no necessarily given or immanent existence; actually, it might all prove to be a construction in our heads. If not unreal, matter was still mere surface without any power or potential; all qualities and ideas about it had to be located in the thinking subject (ct. Matthews 2002: 8–9, 24–26; Thomas 2004).

As for much of modern thinking, Immanuel Kant's efforts to reveal the a priori structures of experience had a great impact on these issues. According to Kant, the thing in itself (*Das Ding an sich*) could not be grasped directly. Although things around us clearly exist, they are inaccessible to us as objects of experience in their own essence. Only things *as they appear*, that is, as *phenomena*, are knowable "objects of sense": "And we indeed, rightly considering objects of sense as mere appearances, confess thereby that they are based upon a thing in itself, though we know not this thing in its internal constitution, but only know its appearances, viz., the way in which our senses are affected by this unknown something" (Kant 2001/1783:53). Although phenomena are admittedly in some way related to things as they are "in themselves" (the *nomena*), things in this "internal constitutive" state are excluded from our experience because our concepts of intuition and understanding cannot grasp them. These concepts extend only to appearances, the transcendental object, and "consequently to mere things of sense; and as soon as we leave this sphere, these concepts retain no meaning whatever" (Kant 2001/1783:55; cf. Körner 1955:94–95).

Kant's denial of any face-to-face encounter with the material world meant that we understand the thing, not "in itself," but only in the way it is formed by ourselves, that is, by our own thinking or reason (Andersson 2001:81–93). Kant did not try to work out an ontology of things; his main concern was how *we* conceived of things. As noted by Graham Harman, "Kant's rift between thing in itself and thing as appearance resolves entirely around the question of *human* relevance. Nowhere does he suggest that two colliding bricks encounter each other as phenomena rather than as nomena; indeed, he is never clear as to whether they encounter one another at all" (2002:279, emphasis in original).

The phenomenological movement of the twentieth century can be seen as a radical challenge to this notion of perception. However, phenomenology started off as far less critical toward the Kantian (and Cartesian) legacy. Husserl's early (transcendental) phenomenology may actually be seen as a development of Kant's "transcendental" approach coupled with the notion of intentionality (Matthews 2002:25). According to Husserl, our conscious awareness of an object is always intentional; it exists for us as a meaningful object *of* or *for* something (Husserl 1976). This intentional object is, however, an ideal construction that does not need to correspond to any real object. (It might be an invented object, e.g., a ghost.) To further grasp the essential meaning of an object, its ordinary existence and entanglements (the way it appears to us in our "natural attitude") must be suspended. Thus, it must be "bracketed off" or reduced—what Husserl denoted as the "phenomenological reduction" (or *epoché*).

His famous example is the thought of an apple tree: even if it clearly is related to the actual tree, it is still different from the physical object growing in the garden (Husserl 1982:214–15). To bring forth the intentional apple tree, the real tree must be "put in parentheses." Whatever happens to the real tree, regardless of whether it falls down or burns, the meaning of the tree as an intentional object ("as something meant") remains. However, it may be stated that some serious problems also remain. A real tree *can* burn, fall over, be climbed, and grow apples. It also has branches, leaves, and a stem. In short, it has a physiognomy, as well as mass and

other properties. Contrary to Husserl's conception of the intentional object as the essential entity, it may be claimed that it is rather in the tree's
material heterogeneity and ability to change that its meaning and truth re-
side (Buck-Morss 1977:72). Thus, despite his slogan "*zu den Sachen selbst*"
("to the things themselves"), the materiality of the object seems trivial or
at least secondary to its transcendental existence as a "thought object,"
which was the true object of Husserl's "scientific" phenomenology. The
real world with its trivia and "noise" had to be "put in parentheses" in
order to reveal the true essence of things—that is, things as they appear
as ideal objects of our consciousness (Husserl 1976).

Husserl's later philosophy took a turn that at least partly brought it
closer to a very different and "engaged" approach to human perception,
mostly known through the phenomenology of Heidegger and Maurice
Merleau-Ponty (Husserl 1970). This "turn" implied a rethinking of his
phenomenology by introducing the concept of lifeworld (*Lebenswelt*) as
constitutive for human understanding. While his former phenomenological reduction may be seen as yet another version of the methodological
doubt of Descartes—in the sense that consciousness was the only secure
basis for knowledge—Husserl now also emphasized the importance of
our ordinary life experience as constitutive for our understanding of the
world. What needs to be "put in parentheses" is not the real world, but
rather the abstract categories and concepts of science and philosophy.
Humans are not Cartesian egos bracketed off from experience, but instead
are engaged subjects who are actively involved in the world they experience. Whereas Husserl (like Kant and Descartes) was previously preoccupied with how the world existed "in us," it was now more a question
of "how we are in the world" (Matthews 2002:28–29).

This concept of being was already a starting point for Heidegger,
as it later became for Merleau-Ponty.[1] Phenomenology was no longer
a method granting a secure knowledge of the hidden essence of ideal
things, or something to be performed by a detached subject contemplating the world from outside. Heidegger conceptually emphasized the
latter point by substituting the term *subject* (or *human*) with *Dasein* (literally, "being *there*"), a subject situated *in* the world. As also expressed by
the hyphens in his famous *being-in-the-world*, our being is an entangled
existence—we are tightly joined in the world we seek to understand. A
phenomenological understanding of this experience is to describe what
this entanglement consists of and to make manifest our relationship to
the world.

Phenomenology is thus concerned with the world as it manifests itself
to those who take part in it. It involves a "return to the world of active
experience," to "restore to things their concrete physiognomy . . . to re-
discover phenomena, the layer of living experience through which other

people and things are first given to us, the system 'Self-others-things' as it comes into being" (Merleau-Ponty 1962:57). In Heidegger's words, phenomenology is to let "that which shows itself be seen from itself in the very way in which it shows itself . . . expressing nothing else than the maxim . . . : 'To the things themselves'" (1962:58). Or, finally, as formulated by Merleau-Ponty, "It is the things themselves, from the depth of their silence, that it wishes to bring to expression" (1968:4).

This phenomenological approach to human perception implied two important insights: First, our relatedness to the world. We are entangled beings fundamentally involved in networks of human and nonhuman beings. Second, we relate to the world not (only) as thinking subjects but also as bodily objects—our *"being-in"* this world is a concrete existence of involvement that unites us with the world. Although the latter point may be claimed to be more explicit in Merleau-Ponty's work than in Heidegger's, central to both philosophers was the attempt to break down the subject-object distinction implied in previous approaches to perception. As Merleau-Ponty's latest works suggest, the thingly aspect of our own being (our common "fabric" as "flesh") is essential for our integration with the world. The ability to touch and be touched, to see and be seen, to act upon things while at the same time being acted upon by them, can only happen if there is some kinship, "if my hand . . . takes its place among the things it touches, is in a sense one of them" (Merleau-Ponty 1968:133).

MATTER AND IMAGE: BERGSON

However, to give the phenomenologists "proper" all the credit for this "tangible" turn leaves out one scholar for whom perception and matter were so close that their difference was claimed to be a matter of degree, rather than kind (Bergson 2004:291, 299). Despite his somewhat confusing and mysterious conception of matter, one basic premise of Henri Bergson's philosophy is that our knowledge of this world is founded on a practical competence acquired by constantly having to deal with things. We recognize objects by using them and by being bodily engaged with the material world. Our knowledge of place, and of how to familiarize ourselves with new places, is based on this competence, this "habit knowledge"—rather than mental representations (Bergson 2004:89ff., 112; Mullarkey 2000:48–50).

How do we perceive the material world? Trying to escape the choice between idealism and realism, Bergson introduced the concept of *image,* described by one commentator as "something more than an idealist calls a representation and something less than a realist calls a thing—image is situated between the two" (Pearson 2002:148).[2] The concept may be seen as denoting how we experience things or matter through our active and direct engagement with them. This should not, however, be confused with having a cognitive "image" of things as an ideal object of our consciousness. *Image* denotes the way things appear to us in an intimate bodily experience of them and is the product of a corporeal involvement that stems from our relatedness and kinship—from the fact that our body is an image among images (Bergson 2004:12–13). This body is capable of finding its way among other images, coordinating or inhibiting actions that are materially possible (Bergson 2004:12–13; Mullarkey 2000:152; Pearson 2002:149–50). Thus, our being-in-the-world is a relational involvement; I am a positioned and oriented image that acts upon and reacts to other images.

Bergson also introduced an important "reductionist" notion in relation to our experiencing of things. Faced with the "numberless vibrations" of the material world, our perception of it has to be subtractive (Bergson 2004:276). This especially counts for our conscious representation of it. Although far richer than cognitive representation, even our "image-based" bodily involvement cannot embrace all aspects of this materiality—by necessity, it also implies some reduction. To render the myriad of things and possible links intelligible, we have to perform an act of simplification or narrowing (see also Gibson 1986:134–35). A material object "in itself" is bound up in endless networks with other images, "it is continued in those which follow it, just as it prolonged those which preceded it" (Bergson 2004:27). By necessity, representation involves a suppression of those links, a reduction of the complexity. In other words, to "see" a thing we have to loosen it somewhat from its relational web and subject it to a "picturing." In Bergson's words, to obtain this transformation "it would be necessary, not to throw more light on the object, but, to the contrary, to obscure some of its aspects, to diminish it by the greater part of itself, so that the remainder, instead of being encased in its surrounding as a *thing*, should detach itself from them as a *picture*" (2004:28). I shall return to Bergson's work in more detail in later chapters. This brief section hopefully helps to expose some nodes of kinship with later phenomenological approaches. This relationship is obvious in Merleau-Ponty's work (cf. Casey 1984; Matthews 2002), but on several points, Bergson's notions of seeing and picturing resonate in the work of Heidegger as well.

HEIDEGGER'S TOOLS

Although Heidegger's writings are generally described as dense and abstract, they contain a long-standing concern with things (cf. Harman

2002). Actually, this is true to such a degree that he once complained that thingy trivia was all people read out of *Being and Time*: "For Heidegger, the world consists only of cooking pots, pitchforks and lampshades; he has nothing to say about 'higher culture' or about 'nature'" (Heidegger quoted in Inwood 2000:130). Challenging the Cartesian notion that our relationship to the world is mediated and orchestrated by the mind, Heidegger proposed that our being in the world involves an immediate engagement and entanglement with things. Our everyday dealing with things (*Umgang*) relates to a mode of being that is ontologically fundamental and prior to any conscious (detached) cognition of the world (*Erkennen*; Dreyfus 1991:60–61).

What does this everyday *Umgang* with things consist of? To start, we relate to things by using them to accomplish something. The fork is there for eating, the bike for biking, the bow and arrow for shooting and killing, and so on. Heidegger applies the word *Zeug*—"equipment" or "gear"—to emphasize this functionality (the "in-order-to"). Next, things are connected in a chain of references, so that strictly speaking "there is no such thing as *an* equipment"; it "always belong to a totality of equipment . . . constituted by various ways of the 'in-order-to' such as serviceability, conduciveness, usability, manipulability" (Heidegger 1962:97). The hammer relates to the nail, the nail to the plank, the plank to the framework, the framework to the house, the house to dwelling, the dwelling to the village, and so forth. In our everydayness, we are always dealing with things and beings in their relatedness as "an *assignment* or *reference* of something to something" (Heidegger 1962:97).

In this mode of dealing with them, Heidegger calls things "ready-to-hand" (*zuhanden*). In this state, we do not "see" the thing but are practically and skillfully involved with it: "The less we stare at the hammer-thing and the more we seize hold of it and use it, the more primordial does our relationship to it become. . . . If we just look at things 'theoretically,' we can get along without understanding 'readiness-to-hand'" (Heidegger 1962:98). In other words, in order "to be ready-to-hand quite authentically" (99), things have to "withdraw" from our conscious attention to them, which only happens when they are properly working as part of our everyday conduct. *Umgang* is not only utilitarian, but is also a concernful dealing, involving care for the things we relate to.

At the same time we ourselves are immersed in the situational context in which we find ourselves, we become "concernfully absorbed" in our tasks and things (Heidegger 1962:103). Driving a car unites us with the car; the driver and car act as a single unit. The functioning of the car, the movements of our arms and feet and our senses of touch, sight, and hearing all work together in a relational whole without being the object of individualized or thematic awareness. The car becomes an extension

Figure 4.1. "In this mode, we do not 'see' the thing, but are practically and skillfully involved with it." Uniting with the kayak, West Greenland, ca. 1880 (photo: M. P. Porsild).

of our body, and through the car we relate to roads, signs, other cars, and so on. This also suggests, as Harman has argued in detail, that the ready-to-hand is not something reserved for tools but is a mode of being that is also an aspect of human being (Harman 2002).

It can be argued that the ready-to-hand in Heidegger's conception is a mode primarily relating to things' *human* relevance. The spear is ready-to-hand only insofar as it conducts its in-order-to task as intended by the hunter. In other words, that this is not a mode of things' being per se but an effect of the human purposes they serve. Harman has forcefully argued against this objection. A knife does not become effective (and invisible) only because people use it; it is rather an aspect of the tool's own mode of being:

> It can only be used because it is *capable of an effect*, of inflicting some kind of blow on reality. In short, the tool isn't used—it *is*. In each instant, entities form a determinate landscape that offers a specific range of possibilities and obstacles. *Beings in themselves* are ready-to-hand, not in the derivative sense of 'manipulable,' but in the primary sense of 'in action.' (Harman 2002:21)

This is also an important argument in support of the "integrity" of things (see chapter 8) and the ready-to-hand as an integral aspect of things' being. However, it is questionable whether this complies with Heidegger's original conception of this mode of being.

Readiness-to-hand, according to Heidegger, does not render us blind to things we engage with. It involves a kind of sight which he refers to as *Umsicht*—the "look around" something or the "view beyond" (Heidegger 1962:98–99). Thus, the involvement with any equipment brings about a wider field of things related and united in an "equipmental totality." Repairing the fishing gear brings forth not only the immediate pieces of equipment (net, thread, net needle, floats, sinkers) but also the boat, fish, water, deck, winches, fishing grounds, markers, and so on. This *circumspection* is not a conscious observation of isolated objects, but rather a "knowing how" awareness of how things are in their relatedness—in other words, "our practical everyday orientation" (Heidegger 1982:163).

Apropos of what is often claimed to be a "phenomenological" dimension of archaeological experiencing, circumspection is not to contemplate what there is in sight, what can be seen from this or that point in the landscape, or to be equated with the "shifting human visual experience of place and landscape" encountered through a walk (Tilley 1994:74; cf. Tilley, Hamilton, and Bender 2000; Hamilton et al. 2006:33). As suggested by Hubert Dreyfus, if circumspection is to be conceived of as a form of "vision," it is one implied by a skilled knowledge of how to "go on" in routine action, how to cooperate with things and how to be interwoven with them (1991:66–67). Our doings and movements are monitored by this *Umsicht*—we "know" what to do next, where things are, what they offer us, how to work with them, and so on. It does not imply a view or a reflexive gaze at what there is in sight, nor is it an interpretative and holistic knowledge held together and monitored by a (moving) human subject alone. Circumspection is a "vision" emerging from the combined impact of *all* the constituents, of their efficacy (individual and combined) in sustaining and affording the accomplished tasks. In this sense, there *is* probably a great difference between the "visions" of a Mesolithic hunter stalking his prey, a Neolithic farmer working the fields, and a phenomenological archaeologist looking for views and monuments (cf. Tilley 1994:74).

INTERRUPTIONS: BECOMING AWARE OF THINGS

For things to remain in their mode of readiness-to-hand, their "unobtrusive presence" must be secured. In our everydayness, we implicitly expect that things will last, that they will work as they have done, and that the world will continue in its current state. Any interruption of the way we deal with and encounter things may, however, cause another mode of awareness: the *present-at-hand* (Heidegger 1962:102ff.). Things in this mode of being are objects of conscious concern; they "light up" and become something that might be thought of in an abstract manner as well (much in the same way as something becomes an object of theoretical concern). This also relates to Heidegger's distinction between the ontological and the "ontic." The *ontic* mode of knowing is the "scientific" way of grasping the specifics of things as they consciously "come to mind" rather than circumspectively "come to hand."[3]

Ordinary things often become present-at-hand to us by some sort of disturbance or interruption (see Dreyfus 1991:70–83). If the tire flattens, the driver soon becomes consciously aware of it and its importance to the functioning of the car; we realize, to quote Heidegger, "what it was ready-to-hand *for*" (1962:105). When there is an electricity blackout, we become conscious of all the nonworking equipment the electricity normally powers. If these things were there for us as usual—as functioning, ready-to-hand stoves, lights, and phones—we would not have paid attention to them or paid attention to their powering from the electrical network. By their malfunctioning, they become conspicuous to us. A similar awareness arises when something is missing or is in the wrong place. If we lose the key to our car, it becomes urgently "un-ready-to-hand" and thus "present" to us. Its absence makes it "obtrusive." Another way things announce themselves as being present-at-hand is by standing in our way and preventing us from conducting our daily tasks. If a gate we pass through every day is suddenly closed, we become aware of it due to this "obstinacy" (Heidegger 1962:102–3). As noted by Heidegger, "If knowing is to be possible as a way of determining the nature of the present-at-hand by observing it, then there must first be a *deficiency* in our having-to-do with the world concernfully" (1962:88).

Something more is also implied in Heidegger's exposition of the triggering of the present-at-hand: we become aware of the relational assignment and entanglement of the thing that is missing or malfunctioning (Heidegger 1962:105). The wider field (the *Umsicht*) is "lit up," and it makes us aware of how things and tasks are related. It is not only the missing key, the flattened tire, and the broken pot that are "seen." Their importance in relation to making other things perform is also revealed, as well as the wider field of collective action in which they are combined. The "in-order-to," which earlier was part of the nondiscursive circumspective knowledge, is transformed into a conscious and causal relational awareness: "The context of equipment is lit up, not as something never seen before, but as a totality constantly sighted beforehand in circumspection" (Heidegger 1962:105).[4]

This may be an appropriate point to show some points of connection between Heidegger's phenomenology and aspects of actor-network theory discussed later (see chapter 7).[5] Despite Bruno Latour's often-voiced antagonism toward Heidegger's philosophy (cf. Latour 1993:65–67, 1999b:176ff.), there are some striking similarities between Latour's network approach and Heidegger's world of relations. One particularly appropriate issue here is the link between Latour's concept of "black-boxing" and the ready-to-hand—and the way both modes call attention to themselves by some sort of breakdown or interruption. *Black-boxing* was initially used by Latour in depicting a scientific proposition or concept that has moved from being controversial and a matter of debate into something taken for granted, a matter of fact in what Thomas Kuhn once termed "normal science." Its own success has, so to say, made it "invisible." He later also used the concept in relation to technology and things that have become so self-evident in our everyday dealings with them that we no longer notice them unless there is some sort of interruption or breakdown. Consider the following (somewhat dated) example of the overhead projector provided by Latour:

> It is a point in a sequence of action (in a lecture, say), a silent and mute intermediary, taken for granted, completely determined by its function. Now suppose the projector breaks down. The crisis reminds us of the projector's existence. As the repairmen swarm around it, adjusting this lens, tightening that bulb, we remember that the projector is made of several parts, each with its role and function and its relatively independent goals. Whereas a moment before the projector scarcely existed, now even its parts have individual existence. . . . In an instant our "projector" grew from being composed of zero parts to one to many. How many actants are really there? (1999b:183)

As for Heidegger, a "breakdown" not only renders the thing in question visible, but also lights up the relational web in which it is acting (being "articulated"). Not only is its functional and mediating role in a greater "equipmental totality" brought to mind; the breakdown also evokes an awareness of the compositional complexity of the thing itself. This of course is grounded in another central commonality between the two: the shared emphasis on the relational character of things.

One differentiating aspect is that Latour's black-boxing, originally at least, was much concerned with the process of becoming ready-to-hand (the controversy preceding the black-boxing) in the specialist fields of science and technology. Heidegger is more concerned with our tacit everyday doings and ordinary things in which the entangled ready-to-handness is something we are "thrown" into. This state of being-in-the-world "is always in some way familiar [*bekannt*]" (Heidegger 1962:85), and knowing is grounded beforehand in a "Being-already-alongside-the-world" (88). As our being is always an entangled being involved in concernful dealing with the ready-to-hand, the process of becoming ready-to-hand is less interesting (see below).

AWARENESS: THE TIP OF THE ICEBERG

Those instances triggering the "coming to mind" in Heidegger's work may all be categorized as related to some type of internal deficiency, and the underlying assumption of "closed" lifeworlds is hardly sufficient to account for all such triggering instances. Our ready-to-hand dealings with the world are not only disturbed by such accidents as things breaking down, being in the wrong place, or missing. The introduction of new and unfamiliar technology, such as metal implements in a stone-tool-using society, may radically challenge established dealings not only with the affected old things but also with the wider relational field in which they were entangled (cf. Sharp 1952). Any encounter with the alien or unfamiliar may, depending on the circumstances, bring to consciousness that which is taken for granted. Arrows and bows may present themselves in ways never thought of when confronted with firearms. New materials, designs, and functions are also brought to awareness through exchange, trade, and travel and thus challenge existing and taken-for-granted ones. Form, function, and materials may be compared and evaluated, properties rejected or swapped, and new technologies learned. In such contexts, things' ready-to-hand mode may temporarily be "overdetermined" by their present-at-handness.

Heidegger's conception of present-at-handness seems to imply that this is an accidental mode of things' being. Things just momentarily light up due to some interruptions and soon return to their ready-at-hand slumber. However, some objects are "always" seen or become conscious to us in a primarily present-at-hand mode. The reasons why some things constantly show up, are selected for special care, or become "inalienable," individualized, aestheticized, or otherwise removed from the everyday taciturnity of their fellow beings are, of course, related to a number of factors (cf. Kopytoff 1986; Miller 1998a). However, whatever the specific reason may be for this attentive persistency, one should be cautious to think of this only as an effect of the needs and/or aesthetics of those humans who are involved with such things. Things also draw attention to themselves by being peculiar, different, or conspicuous in their own various ways. (See chapter 8 for a more detailed discussion.) In other words, present-at-handness as a mode of things' being also entails more than the inherent "capacity" of disturbance and breakdown.

Notwithstanding the composition of the items "consciously coming to mind" and how they may be ranked according to their present-at-hand persistency (e.g., a missing car key vs. an ancestral burial tomb), it is still the case that things in this mode will only surface as the tip of the enormous iceberg of the ready-to-hand. Ready-to-handness is always the dominant mode of things' being. Interruptions are mostly leveled out and the unfamiliar in most cases becomes familiar. After some time, the steel ax reenters the former "Stone Age" world as ready-to-hand equipment, "noticed" only as an object of circumspect concern. The constant dominance of the ready-to-hand is also a product of a certain "perceptive necessity" as proposed by Bergson. Faced with the "numberless vibrations" of myriad things and their networks, the conscious perception of the material world must by necessity be "subtractive." As also implied by Heidegger, for some things (or some aspects of a thing) to show up and become illuminated, there must be a diminishing and darkening of others.

BRINGING TO HAND

A possible field of great interest and attractiveness to archaeologists and anthropologists concerned with the phenomenology of landscape is Heidegger's discussion of the spatiality and directedness of the ready-to-hand (1962:134ff.). Although rarely explicitly referred to, his explorations of these topics clearly find resonance in various landscape archaeologies (cf. Tilley 2004:24–26). Accidentally or not, this part of his phenomenology is also among those in which the anthropocentric tendencies most clearly shine through as Heidegger, occasionally at least, assigns Dasein a too unprecedented position as master director.

According to Heidegger, space is not conceived of as measurable distances but as modes of proximity or availability. To deal with something ready-to-hand, it must be brought to hand. In our "inconspicuous familiarity," we relate to things in terms of their closeness (or remoteness), not in terms of objective measured distances. Embedded in this being is a bringing-close, and Heidegger actually defines *closeness* as an essential human tendency, as an "existential." He depicts this tendency conceptually by using unfamiliar words as *Ent-fernung*, "deseverance"—meaning to abolish a distance, the act of making something remote closer, "making the remoteness of something disappear, bringing it close" (1962:139). This is not so much about overcoming a geographic distance, at least not in any strict measurable sense but relates to a mode of becoming familiar with something. It is part of our everyday dealing with things in their ready-to-hand mode: "Bringing close or deseverance is always a kind of concernful Being towards what is brought close and desevered" (Heidegger 1962:140). Accepting new tools, techniques, and raw materials always involves this circumspective process of desevering, of "putting it in readiness, having it to hand" (140). Likewise, moving to new territories, encountering new peoples, and settling in all involve the process of bringing close, becoming familiar with.

Contained in our circumspective dealings with things is also a notion of "belonging somewhere" (Heidegger 1962:136–37). Our routine dealings with things presuppose a certain order of things, which also explains why "obtrusiveness" and "obstinacy" appear as disturbances. In our everyday dealings with things, we implicitly know that they belong to certain places and tasks structured by their involvement, or the place they occupy in the relational whole. Particular things belong somewhere and are used to conduct certain tasks, which applies as much to my own daily academic routines as to nomadic reindeer herders. The range of these related "somewheres" of things "which we circumspectively keep in view ahead of us in our concernful dealings, we call the *'region'*" (Heidegger 1962:136). Again, this should not be thought of in strict geographical terms, as Heidegger's "region" relates proximity and spatiality to concern. Thus, that which is spatially close to us, but not of circumspective concern, does not belong to the region. Moreover, objective measured distances rarely conform with "lived" spatiality (Heidegger 1962:141). Something desired but objectively distant may feel closer and shorter to travel to than something closer but less desired.

Heidegger's concepts of *Umgang*, *Umsicht*, and region (*Gegend*) are closely related. Our everyday dealing with things is to deal with things ready-to-hand. As such, they are not "objects" for contemplation or scientific gaze or something to be seen, but appear to us circumspectively through our concernful engagement with them. *Circumspection* means that they belong "somewhere" within our range and our region and that we are directed toward them. Relating to things always involves directionality (*Ausrichtung*). The human being (as Dasein) is always oriented toward something, always itself spatial. This, however, is not a spatiality that involves a positioning within an abstracted Euclidean space. It is not an intellectual enterprise, but a spatiality that is fundamentally involved in our being-in-the-world, which emerges from our circumspective encountering of this world. Circumspective dealings "always-already" imply a direction toward something: "Circumspective concern is desevering which gives directionality" (Heidegger 1962:143). In short, it is our circumspective dealings with things that orient us.

DIRECTIONALITY:
THINGS AND THE HUMAN SUBJECT

As already noted, Heidegger's writings on space and directionality, as briefly outlined above, seem to go well with general tropes in phenomenological landscape archaeologies. In particular, Christopher Tilley's various notions of somatic, perceptual, and lived space all stress space as something sensorily experienced through bodily action and daily practices. However, and despite some evident anthropocentric tendencies, Heidegger is far from seeing the "region" as a social construct or as something being created by us. The difference may be spelled out by taking a look at how spatiality and directionality are conceived. According to Tilley, somatic or bodily space is experienced through a human-centered directionality: "An understanding of this space takes as its starting point the upright human body looking out on the world" (1994:16). Directionality is thus claimed to always be relative to the position of the standing human subject (right/left, front/back, above/below; Tilley 1994:16). Although this is made explicit only for one of his various notions of space (somatic space), the directionality of the body is still claimed as a universal basis for comprehending the landscape and for our experience of space. Outlining how walking the English landscape enables you to grasp its full and perspectival richness, Tilley states, "Things in front or behind you, within reach or without, things to the left and right of your body, above and below, these most basic of personal spatial experiences, are shared with prehistoric populations in our common biological humanity" (1994:74). Ten years later, Tilley elaborates on his phenomenological body doctrine, but only in order to reconfirm the centrality of the human body for spatial experience (2004:4–10). The dimensions of the body are claimed to be imperative for how we conceive the world, which always becomes relative to the position and orientation of the body: things are in front of me, to the right, at the back, and so on. Thus, "we order places *and their significance*, through our bodies, through the articulation of the basic distinctions between up/down, front/back and left/right" (Tilley 2004:9, my emphasis).

The centrality of the body for our experience of space may seem obvious and unquestionable, although the alternative option is just as conceivable—in other words, that the directionality of our body and our experience of the world *is relative to landscape and things*. This is not just an unsupported suggestion. The common assumption that the body constitutes the universal orienting principle for our conception of space is profoundly challenged by anthropologists and cognitive linguistics (Dirven, Wolf, and Polzenhagen 2007:1212–13). For example, Balthasar Bickel's study of the Belhare community living at the southern foothills of the Himalayas in eastern Nepal provides a well-documented case of how the topography of the landscape constitutes the organizing principle for how directions and orientations are perceived and conceptualized (Bickel 2000).

Also for Heidegger, circumspective orientation does not start from the subject's position, but takes into account the entire familiar "region" (the encountering context of things and task) in which we are beings and which *orientates us*. In his criticism of Kant's proposition of left and right as a foundation for every orientation, Heidegger points to how this (and thus Tilley's) presumed a priori principle itself is based on the "*a priori* of Being-in-the-world, which has nothing to do with any determinate character restricted beforehand to a worldless subject" (Heidegger 1962:144). Thus, for the landscape phenomenologist the individual looking out on the world should *not* constitute a self-evident starting point. Such an attitude is more akin to Heidegger's late conception of the *Horizont*, which he saw as typical of the representational stance, reducing the circumscribed world of things to representing objects (Inwood 2000:100). This way of conceiving the world is dependent on our own position, seeing only "the side turned toward us," an embodied region filled with our own representational view (Heidegger 1966:63–64).

The notion of habitual and lived space being constituted through routine actions and bodily practices is frequently encountered in phenomenological and social archaeologies. Although some of this may be informed, even sometimes better informed, by Heidegger's phenomenology, it is the philosophy of Merleau-Ponty, as primarily outlined in his *Phenomenology of Perception* (1962), that constitutes the main source of inspiration (cf. Tilley 2004:4–30). Thus, this may be a timely place to leave Heidegger for a while and have a look at Merleau-Ponty's phenomenology of the body.

THINGS AND THE PHENOMENOLOGY
OF THE BODY: MERLEAU-PONTY

The central aspect of the phenomenology of Merleau-Ponty is our everyday practical experience of the world. Contrary to G. W. F. Hegel's maxim of philosophy as "thinking thinking itself" and Ludwig Wittgenstein's silencing of the unsaid, Merleau-Ponty wants to ground his phenomenology precisely in this practical, nondiscursive experience: that which is nearest in being, but furthest away in analysis (Macann 1993:164). Before any conscious, present-at-hand reflections of the world, we are already engaged in a practical, ready-to-hand dealing with it. According to Merleau-Ponty, "perception is not a matter of intellectual contemplation, but of active involvement with things" (Matthews 2002:133). Prior to the Cartesian "I think," it is necessary to acknowledge an "I can" or "I do," that is, a practical, nondiscursive consciousness that governs my relationship with the world and that is expressed in routinized practices and actions (Merleau-Ponty 1962:137ff.).

Following Bergson, Merleau-Ponty claims that the body is the site of this experience. It is through our bodies that we as human beings are placed in a world, and this bodily being-in-the world must be understood through tasks and actions that have to be carried out and through the spatial and material possibilities that are open to the body. Developing the notions of spatiality and "directedness," Merleau-Ponty introduces his "phenomenological body" in order to depict our primordial involvement with the world. The body is a matrix of habitual behavior. It acts out a repertoire of motor skills that are mostly not determined or (even less) coordinated by mindful thought (1962:102–6). This bodily knowledge of "how to go on" contains a "primordial spatiality" (Macann 1993:176) that monitors our actions and moves. As noted by Macann, "the relation of the body to the world in which it finds itself is not to be understood in terms of objective distances but in terms of a sort of primordial coincidence or co-existence of the body with that towards which it enacts itself, mobilizes itself, projects itself" (1993:176). Thus, the positioning of the body in the world (Heidegger's "somewhere") has less to do with an exact position in a Euclidian grid than with what Merleau-Ponty refers to as a "spatiality of situation" and the "laying down of the first coordinates, the anchoring of the active body in an object, the situation of the body in face of its tasks" (Merleau-Ponty 1962:100).

In *The Phenomenology of Perception*, Merleau-Ponty seems less concerned with mundane things than does Heidegger. The primary entity is clearly the human body and the way it lives, acts, and moves around the world. ("The body is our general medium for having a world" [Merleau-Ponty 1962:146].) Thus, in this respect and in this work, Merleau-Ponty's phenomenology seems more akin to the versions that have made its way into archaeology and anthropology. Still, "that towards which it acts itself" is clearly of concern, as exemplified by the following statement:

> Consciousness is being-towards-the-thing through the intermediary of the body. A movement is learned when the body has understood it, that is, when it has incorporated it into its 'world,' and to move one's body is to aim at things through it; it is to allow oneself *to respond to their call, which is made up independently of any representation*. (Merleau-Ponty 1962:138–39, my emphasis)

Merleau-Ponty's main concern with things relates to the way they orient the body, particularly their role in motor habits and the way they relate to, limit, or extend the body. I shall explore these issues in more detail later on (in chapter 7), and here just briefly refer to his notion of motor habits.

Merleau-Ponty maintains that our bodily existence is primordially embedded in space. This space is not an infinite collection of points or relations synthesized by my thinking, which then guide my movements and acts. It is something combined and included in my bodily existence

(Merleau-Ponty 1962:140): "It is already built into my bodily structure, and is its inseparable corrective" (142). He exemplifies this by typing. We know *how* to write using a typewriter (Merleau-Ponty's case) or a computer keyboard even if most of us, retrospectively and divorced from the PC, are unable to describe the configuration of letters on it. Neither do we (after the habitual skills are acquired) need to look at the keys to guide our fingers. Sitting down to write, "a motor space opens up beneath my hand," and a certain "physiognomy" comes forth that evokes a prescribed type of motor responses (Merleau-Ponty 1962:144). Needless to say, this is equally relevant to all our engagement with things such as boat building, flint knapping, weaving, and archaeological digging. It is a "knowledge in the hands, which is forthcoming only when bodily effort is made, and cannot be formulated in detachment from that effort" (Merleau-Ponty 1962:144).

Although we shall return to this later (see chapter 6), one should notice how Merleau-Ponty in his major work—and distinct from Heidegger's treatment of ready-to-hand equipment—does not give much credit to things' capacities or competence. Thus, even if insisting that every action is an *inter*action, things' share of the "inter" seems rather modest. Is it really the case that the knowledge referred to only is "knowledge in the hands"? Or should some credit also be granted to keyboards, axes and woods, flint, weaves, soils and trowels—in short, to the properties and capacities of the things? If you think such appreciation is superfluous or even wrong, I would urge the reader to try out the cleverness of the hands without keyboards, weaves, or textiles. And the experiment should not be restricted to seeing if you can perform—which you clearly cannot—but it should also explore whether you can remember in solitude, which seems equally futile. (See chapter 6.)

GOOD THINGS, BAD THINGS: CHANGING CONCEPTIONS OF THINGS

What is the thing then in phenomenological terms? Heidegger uses different notions (*Ding, Zeug, Sache*), although there is a change in the way he uses them as well as in his attitude toward "things." In *Being and Time*, the concept of thing (*Ding*—although still frequently used otherwise) is depicted as a present-at-hand category. It is something that we are consciously aware of, an "object" distinct from a "subject." Our everyday dealing with "things," however, does not involve such "objectification" or any conscious experiencing of them as separate or abstracted entities of their own. Heidegger therefore applies the word "equipment" (*Zeug*) to erase the objectifying conception implied in the notion of *thing*, that is, to render them ready-to-hand—"some-things" that are used and fundamentally involved in our everyday existence. Equipmental things do not appear to us as abstracted members of any "thinghood" distinct from our "personhood," that is, as our negativities (or others; Heidegger 1962:96ff.).

In his later works, Heidegger assigns a much more affirmative role to the concept of "thing." In a lecture later published as *The Thing*, he explores the "thingness of the thing." The thing is no longer conflated with the consciously perceived (present-at-hand) object, but rather contains its own integrity or independence, a self-supporting capacity, that allows for its existence regardless of being represented or not. He also argues that (natural) science has annihilated the thing: "The thing as a thing remains nil. The thingness of the thing remains concealed, forgotten. The nature of the thing never comes to light, that is, it never gets a hearing" (Heidegger 1971:168). Going back to its etymological roots (such as the Old High German *Thing*), he now explores the gathering or assembling function of the thing and the derived verb, *dingen*, "to thing."

Heidegger explores this "thinging" function in relation to a somewhat opaque and pretentious description of the assembling of the "fourfold" (earth, sky, gods, and mortals). This partly ridiculed, partly ignored theme in his writings (cf. Harman 2002:190ff.)[6] can be read as a statement on the nature of things "being." This being cannot be reduced to being a product, something brought about by its making or (even less) as an expression of an idea. The concept's semantics are used to manifest the way in which a thing acts: its gathering and "staying" qualities, as something evoking the "nearness" of (or embeddedness in) a world set apart, something that unites, not as a property but as a work: the thinging of the thing (Heidegger 1971:179).

In another of his later works, "The Question Concerning Technology," Heidegger emphasizes how this being-in-itself of things was cared for in premodern technology and craft. When a Greek silversmith makes a silver chalice, he "considers carefully and gathers together," first, its material "cause" (the silver); second, the chalice's design or form cause (its *eidos*—i.e., its idea, "appearance"); third, the socioreligious cause constituted by the rituals in which the chalice is meant to function; and, finally, its purpose or *telos* (1993:315). This way of making, which Heidegger found preserved in the fine arts, is to bring forth what is already in some way conveyed in the materials to "answer and respond" to the forms and capacities "slumbering" within them. This Aristotelian *poiesis* (bringing forth, making) manifests what already "dwells" in things (as also reflected in the Greek terms *techne/physis*, i.e., aided/unaided bringing forth [Heidegger 1993:317–19; Young 2002:39–41]).

This stands in stark contrast to the way Heidegger conceives of modern technology, "a monster born in our midst" (Latour 1999b:176). While ancient technology was harmoniously interacting with humans and nature, the modern *Gestell*[7] (enframing) violates this relationship. In our modern inauthentic being, things are disclosed to us only as resources—and our attitude to humans themselves mirrors this resourcelike way of conceiving things. Everything appears to us as *Bestand* (standing-reserve or supply), and the world "shows up" as instrumental and calculative, which, in short, means that "to be is to be an item of resource" (Young 2002:45). Contrasting the old wooden bridge crossing the Rhine with the hydroelectric plant set into its current, Heidegger illustrates how the river is transformed into *Bestand*. While the old bridge was joining the banks of the river, complying with its character, the modern plant changes the river, dams it, and turns it into a standing-reserve, "a water-power supplier" (Heidegger 1993:321). Although this is claimed to always have been one aspect of things' being, what is new in the age of *Gestell* is that this *Bestand* aspect becomes the dominant, even the only, mode of its disclosure: "Where this ordering holds sway it drives out every other possibility of revealing. Above all, enframing conceals that revealing which, in the sense of *poiēsis*, lets what presences come forth into appearance" (Heidegger 1993:332). What is lost is things' "own-ness," their being-in-itself, as only their manipulative being-for-us as a "standing-reserve" remains.

At this point, at least, some ambiguities become evident in Heidegger's philosophy. In saying that technology has always embedded some aspects of *Gestell* ("the hidden nature of all technology"), he comes close to saying that this attitude is part of (or even *is*) the ready-to-hand, although it is only in modern times that "this nature begins to unfold as a destiny of the truth of all beings as a whole" (Heidegger 1971:109). In his book on Heidegger's later philosophy, Julian Young makes the claim that for Heidegger "machines and tools, human artefacts in general" have no being-in-itself (2002:51). They are only being-for-us. Heidegger himself claimed that a chair only had the mode of the present-at-hand (Heidegger 1982: 166; ct. Harman 2002:34–35, 299). However, as shown by Harman (2002), he is far from consistent on this point. After all, Heidegger's preferred example in his discussion of how "things thing" (the gathering of "the fourfold") is a mundane jug. It is probably more correct to say that Heidegger, in some of his later attacks on inauthentic being, modern technology, and *Gestell*, comes to condemn all practical utility and ends up with a rude taxonomy of "good things" and "bad things" that clearly is at odds with the way ready-at-hand equipment was conceived in *Being and Time* (cf. Harman 2002).[8]

This contradiction seems to develop as Heidegger becomes increasingly concerned with art and "gentle things" (and maybe also as a response to the "mundane" readings of *Being and Time* referred to above). In his famous essay "The Origins of the Work of Art," Heidegger argues how

Figure 4.2. "Bad things, on the other hand, have no soul to lose. They never become 'homesick' since they have always been part of a serviceable *Bestand.*" Harbor installations in abandoned mining town of Pyramiden, Svalbard, Norway (photo: Bjørnar Olsen).

equipment is determined by its usefulness and serviceability;[9] it "takes into service that of which it consists: the matter" (1971:44). In fabricating a stone ax, "stone is used, and used up. It disappears into usefulness" (44). By contrast, building a temple is a "world building":

> The temple-work . . . does not cause the material to disappear, but rather causes it to come forth for the very first time and to come into the Open of the work's world. The rock comes to bear and rest and so first becomes rock; metals come to glitter and shimmer, colors to glow, tones to sing, the word to speak. All this comes forth as the work sets itself back into the massiveness and heaviness of stone, into the firmness and pliancy of the wood, into the hardness and luster of metal, into the lighting and darkening of color, into the clang of tone, and into the naming power of the world. (Heidegger 1971:44–45)

Good things are the work of *poeisis*; they allow for the gathering "function" to come forth and are there for "caring-for." The Black Forest farmhouse, the temple, the chalice, and the jug all manifest this being-in-itself of the thing. They may of course be deprived of it by being turned into a commodity on the antiques market, losing their "thingness" to the "trade of calculation" (Heidegger 1971:111). Bad things, on the other hand, have no soul to lose. They never become "homesick"[10] since they have always been part of a serviceable *Bestand*. It still remains confusing as to why the being-in-itself of the thing should "dwell" in a jug or a farmhouse and not in a stone ax, if not based on a common-sense, prejudiced divide between "artwork" (or at least "real authentic things") and "mere things" (so well problematized by twentieth-century art itself).

WHAT IS THE RELEVANCE?

In coming close to the end of this long and winding chapter, the reader may be wondering about the relevance of all this. What does it mean in terms of archaeology and material culture studies? As argued earlier, things' ontology is not something easily fleshed out in a case study, due to the concern with things' being. It is still possible, however, to indicate how a Heideggerian position may alter the way we conceive and interpret landscape and what by convention is referred to as the archaeological record.

The distinction Heidegger makes between "thinging things" and modern *Gestell* provides a convenient starting point. Although it contains some very problematic notions, as exposed above (see also chapter 5), it still reveals some significant changes that modernity has brought about in terms of both the conception of materials and the role humans have played in altering the world. Modern production implied an emerging disentanglement of the old interplay between material and form and was strongly linked to the increasing confidence in humans' power to work against the will of landscapes and material properties (Ingold 2000:341–51; Andersson 2001:32–39). This modern capacity to manipulate and alter the world was itself, of course, thing dependent, although it also rested in the modern way of *thinking* about things and the environment (see chapter 5). This human-centered ontology casted the material world as inert and passive, as something to be formed and *made* meaningful by thoughtful human intervention.

As argued earlier, this ontology still grounds much thinking about things in material culture studies (Olsen 2007; see chapters 2 and 5). To be sure, things may indeed be social, even actors, as numerous of these studies show. However, upon scrutiny, things and landscapes are rarely ascribed more challenging roles than to provide societies or individuals with a substantial medium in which they can embody and mirror themselves. Meaning is always something being mapped onto things and landscapes, which they themselves have seen drained of all significance to facilitate their so-called cultural constructions (Ingold 2000:154). Contrary to the split inherent in the notions of embodiment and representation, a Heideggerian position would rather claim that we are "thrown" into and engage with a world *already* meaningful. To create is to release or bring forth what is already conveyed in the materials, to respond to the forms and capacities "slumbering" within them (Heidegger 1993:317–19).

Interestingly, a number of studies have recently emphasized how megaliths, monuments, and rock art actually resonate with the topographical or geological capacities of the landscape. Megaliths are seen as being "inspired" by, or mimicking, natural rock formations; rock carvings are made and structured according to the microtopography of the rock surface (e.g., Bradley 1998, 2003; Hauptman Wahlgren 2002; Helskog 2004; Helskog and Høgtun 2004; Keyser and Poetschat 2004; Tilley 2004; Gjerde 2006; Jones 2007). This clearly represents a new and refreshing symmetrical attitude. As pertinently pointed out by Tilley in relation to earlier recordings of rock art in southern Sweden, "the rock surfaces have been regarded as a kind of blank slate on which the carvings are inscribed and their qualities effectively ignored" (2004:152). Scandinavian rock art provides abundant examples of how cracks and lines in the rock surface are incorporated into the designs, how depressions become dens in a bear scene, how the edge of a stone constitutes the body outline of an elk, and so forth (cf. Helskog 2004; Hesjedal 1994; Gjerde 2006, in press; Arntzen 2007). Likewise, in Paleolithic Franco-Cantabrian cave art, the interplay between figures, rock surface, cracks, and fissures is well documented, sometimes producing three-dimensional images (cf. Clottes 2007; Hodgson 2008). Some particularly pertinent manifestations of this "symmetrical" attitude are found at rock-art sites on the Columbia Plateau in Oregon (Keyser and Poetschat 2004). For example, a cracked and segmented stone column provides an already-made rattle of a rattlesnake, and a curved ridge of basalt, the backbone of a lizard waiting to be carved to completion (Keyser and Poetschat 2004:124–26).

It might well be that the rock features "gave life" to these images, contextualized them, and helped them—and the rock—in *becoming* meaningful. However, a petrified backbone, a ready carved leg, or a sculptured head already resting in the stone may also reveal a different way of conceiving of the world. They were carvings *already made*, an initial figuring slumbering in the stone. To work on the rock was not to embody oneself in substantial material or to make the rocks meaningful, but to bring forth or add to what already dwelled in them. Deep inside coastal caves in northern Norway, red rock paintings mingle on the walls with natural deposits of red iron oxide, often making the distinction between them difficult (Hesjedal 1992; Bjerck 1995). This suggests that to paint was to *add*, continue, or complete something already painted, already meaningful. This also manifests the contrast between this way of approaching

Figure 4.3. Lakes, rivers, valleys, mountains, and sea: rock surface as meaningful microtopography. Hjemmeluft, Alta, Arctic Norway (photo: Karin Tansem).

landscapes and things and the one grounding various conceptions of objectification and embodiment (see chapter 2). Human engagement with the world is not emerging from some "outside" position; it is not about embodiment, or domesticating and appropriating an alien or meaningless world. Rather, to live with and work on the landscape is grounded in an entangled ready-to-handness, a "thrown" condition. Being-in-the-world "is always in some way familiar [bekannt]" (Heidegger 1962:85); it is grounded beforehand in a "Being-already-alongside-the-world" (88).

This probably does not sound too exciting compared to the spectacular interpretative perspectives that are offered in archaeology and anthropology. Is Tilley thus right, claiming that a phenomenological approach is inadequate, a descriptive exercise that has to be fleshed out by the "hermeneutics of interpretation" involving "the exploitation of metaphoric and metonymic linkages between things" (2004:224)? Phenomenology may well be insufficient, though not necessarily on those terms. What strikes me after reading many recent books and papers on rock art is the never-ending urge to intellectualize the past: a constant search for a deeper meaning, something beyond what can be sensed. According to this unveiling mode a boat, an elk, or a reindeer can be claimed to represent almost everything—ancestors, rites of transitions, borders, supernatural powers, and so on—apart, it seems, only from themselves. A boat is never a boat; a reindeer is never a reindeer; a river is always a "cosmic" river. This is not at all to dismiss the images' potential symbolic significance. However, may it not be plausible that—sometimes at least—it was actually the depicted being that mattered?

Modern Sámi reindeer herders have hundreds of terms that relate to reindeer. This attention is not so much a symbolic attention as it is a circumspective one. It reflects a care and concern for the reindeer in its different states of being, as well as the profound significance of the reindeer to Sámi life (Demant-Hatt 1913; Turi 1987). A reindeer has value and significance in its own right, as has the herd; it should not be offended by derogatory comments or abusive attitudes but instead cared for, respected, and honored (Oskal 1995:136–38). The significance and care for these animals may not have been very different in the prehistoric past. Thus, maybe it was just the world as it circumspectively appeared to the prehistoric carver through his or her own concerned engagement with it that northern rock art "is about." This was a "meaning" that in some sense was already given, and to carve was to add to, to work on, or to supplement this latent circumspective significance. In this world, the reindeer was sufficiently meaningful by "just" being a reindeer.

CONCLUSION: HEIDEGGER'S LEGACY

Phenomenology was launched as a way of "relearning to look at the world," a return to "the things themselves," that is, to a lived experience unobscured by abstract philosophical concepts and theories. Even if the toil of actually reading Heidegger may raise serious doubts about the implementation of that thesis, his works reveal a persistent concern with things that is hardly matched by any other philosophical life projects. Serious objections may be raised against his work, but no other Western philosopher or social theorist—with the possible exception of Walter Benjamin—has been more consistently concerned with things than Heidegger. Although much credit should also be given to the other two philosophers dealt with in this chapter, Bergson and Merleau-Ponty, Heidegger differs by his genuine concern with actual things—ordinary things—and their being.

Contrary to some of the recent interest in Heidegger's thing theories (cf. Karlsson 1998), I do not consider his later works on technology, art, and "the thing" as his most important. To an archaeologist or any student of material culture, the single work of most profound significance is clearly *Being and Time*. Far from being a trivial moment to be rushed past "towards all points further south" (Harman 2002:7), the tool analysis provided here is indispensable to any phenomenology of things. The crucial question, therefore, is why it received so little attention in phenomenological archaeology and material culture studies. Given the preoccupation with the social, symbolic, and ritual in these studies, my guess is that Heidegger's detailed concern with mundane things in their everyday uses, with equipment and their referential assignment, most likely seemed irrelevant. Actually, his thing vocabulary, such as the "in-order-to," "serviceability," "usability," and so on probably sounded embarrassingly functional to scholars who had spent most of their career telling us exactly the opposite about things. The fleeing from the everyday and the ordinary constitutes another irony of the phenomenological project in archaeology. Almost all energy was spent on studying ritual monuments and contemplations of landscapes, leaving us with a phenomenological archaeology strangely alienated from the everydayness of herding sheep, clearing fields, cutting woods, building houses, or cooking and feeding.

Having said this, it should also be pointed out that there is an important turn in Heidegger's later philosophy that is very valuable for any future discussion of the ontology of things. This turn is expressed in his late emphasis on the "thingness of the thing." While Heidegger's previous concern with things to a large extent was grounded in their human relevance (Karlsson 1998), he became increasingly more concerned with the integrity of things in their own being (see chapter 8). This insight, however, was somewhat undermined by the fact that in his later works he became less concerned with mundane, everyday artifacts and increasingly more preoccupied with the distinction between real "authentic things" and mere objects (commodities, technology). As will be shown in the next chapter, this was a distinction that grew to become extremely influential in philosophy and social theory from the nineteenth century onward, which has also left its mark on material culture studies.

This distinction between authentic/inalienable and inauthentic/ alienable things has also been widely read as a reflection of, or at least accentuated by, the traditional-modern distinction and transition in which our immediate relations to things (and even things themselves) have fundamentally changed in the wake of industrialism, consumerism, and capitalism. Although some of the changes accounted for clearly took place, increasingly turning things into *Bestand*, I think the most fundamental change is located in our intellectual attitude toward things and in the way we consciously conceive of them. While it should be commonplace to attest to the fact that most of our dealing with things still takes place in a circumspective way and a ready-to-hand mode, what modernity has brought is a new way of "thinking things," making their present-at-hand mode of more concern than previously. This new and distancing awareness probably also accounts for the modern Janus-faced attitude toward things as both objects of fear *and* objects of desire. These concerns bring us to the next chapter.

5

Tacit Matter

The Silencing of Things

> The present vividly felt charm for the fragment, the mere allusion, the
> aphorism, the symbol, . . . places us at a distance from the substance of
> things; they speak to us "as from afar"; reality is touched not with direct
> confidence but with fingertips that are immediately withdrawn. . . . In
> all this we discover an emotional trait . . . the fear of coming into too
> close a contact with objects.
>
> —Georg Simmel, *The Philosophy of Money*

The previous chapter outlined how our dealings with things largely
take place in a mode of inconspicuous familiarity—how, unless broken, interrupted, or missing, things often pertain to a kind of shyness.
Being at the same time "the most obvious and the best hidden" (Lefebvre
1987:9), they largely escape our attention. It is tempting to see a causal
connection between this humbleness and things' marginal position in
twentieth-century social science research. In other words, since people's
dealing with material culture mostly takes place in an implicit and nondiscursive manner, it also escapes the attention of the "second-order ob-
server," that is, those studying human societies.

However, what people are consciously aware of in their daily life does
not normally determine the concerns of research. If so, it becomes difficult to explain why phenomena such as the unconscious, chromosomes,
grammar, social structures, or germs have all become matters of great
scientific or philosophical attraction. Thus, things' everyday reticence
is hardly a good explanation of their exile from modern social analyses.
This is not to say that the two levels of taciturnity are unrelated—the

point is rather not to confuse them. Despite the fact that both modes can be conceived of as ontologically grounded, there is still a significant difference between the way things escape our everyday attention and the way they are kept at arm's length in social studies. While things' everyday reticence stems from their embeddedness—the fact that they are "too close" to draw explicit attention—their exile from the social sciences is caused more by exclusion, an enforced boundary that dislocates things out of reach.

In the previous chapter, I dealt explicitly with the first level of taciturnity and also took some initial steps toward explaining why things seem to have vanished from the fields studied by social scientists (cf. Olsen 2007). In this chapter, I shall go into more detail on the issue of why things have been forgotten or ignored in contemporary social-science research. Another concern is to explore how modernity implied a changed consciousness or awareness of things which in and of itself—somewhat paradoxically—may have come to influence their fate in this research.

TECHNOLOGY AND EVIL THINGS

As previously argued, modern humanist and social thinking have been deeply affected by a conception of being in which things are seen as redundant and obscure. Beginning with Immanuel Kant if not earlier, this ontology denied any direct access to things, and it later surfaced as a skeptical attitude in which the material was treated with suspicion and rarely allowed more than a provisional or transcendental existence. Things-in-themselves were largely out of reach, shut off from our immediate experience and thus dispelled from the knowable world. Only in their abstracted condition, as objects of science, could they still be admitted (Andersson 2001:130; Olsen 2007).

The curious fact that things became conspicuously present in the mundane world a short century after Kant did not do much to help their reputation. To the contrary, to most philosophers and social theorists, the mass-produced, mass-distributed, and mass-consumed objects of the late nineteenth century were a sign of an illusory world, a *Schein* conveying the deceptive image of the world as thing-made (Brown 2003). Proliferating in the ruin landscapes left by the onslaught of capitalism and industrialism, things, consumer goods, machines—the cold and inhuman technology—became the incarnation of our inauthentic, estranged, and alienated modern being. Things were dangerous in their deceptive appearance; they were a threat against authentic human and social values.

Thus, whether it was intentional or not, things ended up assuming the villain's role as humanism's other, also giving their relegation from disciplines studying genuine social and cultural practices a powerful moral justification (Olsen 2003, 2007).

Heidegger's conception of modern technology and mass culture, dealt with above, clearly complies with much of the nostalgia and pessimism that modernity has given rise to. The desertion of the countryside, the vanishing of village communities, family bonds, and traditional customs and values created a sense of loss and death—also fostering historicism and projects of conservation. Losing the "nearness" of being, authentic dwelling became a nostalgic project—the caring for the heritage of *Heimat* (Heidegger 1993; Young 2002).

Philosophers, social theorists, artists, and writers of the nineteenth and early twentieth centuries grew increasingly concerned with this process of withering and change: how mass production, factories, and machines replaced craftsmanship and manual labor and how social relationships, including labor and exchange, become increasingly mediated by the "emptiness" of money and commodities. The firmly rooted and reassuring lifeworlds—by and large conceived as isomorphic with the rural worlds of the peasants—were vanishing. In the words of Heidegger, the "monstrous" being of modern technology turned the world into a "gigantic petrol station." In place of things' social or "worldly" content, "the object-character of technological domination spreads itself over the earth ever more quickly, ruthlessly, and completely" (Heidegger 1971:112).

Similar concerns were raised throughout the early and middle years of the twentieth century by thinkers as varied as Horkheimer, Adorno, Popper, and Sartre. They all shared the conviction that the technology that was supposed to be our servant and improve our lives had instead become our master, depriving us of all freedom. Science and engineering were treated with suspicion or contempt, as things that threatened humanity, and this caused social scientists and philosophers to increasingly define creativity, emancipation, and authentic being as that which escapes the material, as in Sir Karl Popper's "nightmare of physical determinism": "It is a nightmare because it asserts that the whole world with everything in it is a large automaton, and that we are nothing but little cogwheels, or at best sub-automata within it. It thus destroys, in particular, the idea of creativity" (1972:222). Paired with this technological menace was the distaste for the inauthentic and the artificial, the supposedly natural offsprings of industrialism and mass production. Mass-produced replicas and consumer goods replaced "good things"; evil things were substituted for things with "soul." This "age of mechanical reproduction" gave rise to a new and ambiguous awareness of things in European thinking, well captured in this quote from a letter by the German poet Rainer Maria Rilke (1925):

> To our grandparents, a "house," a "well," a familiar steeple, even their own clothes, their cloak _still_ meant infinitely more, were infinitely more intimate— almost everything a vessel in which they found something human already there, and added to its human store. Now there are intruding, from America, empty indifferent things, sham things, _dummies of life_. . . . A house, as the Americans understand it, an American apple or a winestock from over there, have _nothing_ in common with the house, the fruit, the grape into which the hope and thoughtfulness of our forefathers had entered. (quoted in Heidegger 1971:110–11, emphasis in original)

The mass-produced goods swarming the mundane world, providing people with affordable replicas of objects and materials otherwise reserved for the few and the rich, were read as signs of cultural decline. The new and scandalous "preference for the unreal" became diagnostic of what the Austrian culture historian Egon Friedell (1937) termed "the common and principal era of material fraud." This preference manifested itself in a wide range of fakes: "Whitewashed tin presents itself as marble, papier-mâché as rosewood, plaster as shiny alabaster. . . . A splendid Gutenberg Bible is revealed as a sewing box . . . the butter knife is a Turkish dagger, the ashtray a Prussian helmet . . . the thermometer a pistol" (quoted in Christensen 1993:27, my translation). Another symptom of this concern for the vanishing real was the aversion against new materials and designs that started to make their impact on the built environment. Iron, for example, was distrusted by nineteenth-century architects because it was not immediately present in nature; thus, when used for scaffolding, it was given a stone covering. New styles and materials became associated with the "vulgar" works of engineers, expressed in the _Gestell_ of machines, arcades, exhibition halls, bridges, hangars, and silos (Benjamin 2002:33; Buck-Morss 1999:127–29).

ALIENATION AND THE "PROBLEM OF THE FETISH"

It can be forcefully argued that the modern social and humanist turn against consumer goods and technology seriously contributed to things' "nonsocial" status. Although directed at the "evil things," that is, the inauthentic, this movement fueled an implicit suspicion toward the material and toward things more generally. A very influential—although somewhat paradoxical—expression of this modernist aversion against "evil things" originates from Karl Marx's writings on alienation and

Figure 5.1. "New styles and materials became associated with the 'vulgar' works of engineers." Glass meets iron and stone, Palace of the National Bank, Bucharest, Romania (photo: Elin Myrvoll).

reification, especially as developed in the notion of "commodity fetishism."

Fetishism is a concept that emerged in Western discourse primarily as a way of describing "primitive" religious practices in which stones and statues were worshipped and treated as "real" gods. This phenomenon, which Western travelers and anthropologists saw as a "fallacious substitution," was developed by Marxist and psychoanalytical thinking into a more general conception of fetishism as misrepresentation or displacement, a "misunderstanding" by which qualities that can properly be ascribed only to the realm of humans are attributed to things (Christensen 1993:39–41, Pels 1998).

A consistent issue in Marx's writings was how the capitalist economy fetishized the commodity by ascribing it an abstract intrinsic value (or an "exchange value"). Operating in support of a wider bourgeois ideology, this fetishism masked the "real" value of goods stemming from the social labor invested in their production. Things (as commodities) appeared to have a value of their own—purely resulting from their circulation in a market. Thus, they were alienated from their producers, divorced from human toil and the social relations involved in their production. In the capitalist economy, the social relations of productions themselves became misrepresented as a thinglike relation: "In the sphere of political economy this realisation of labour appears as a *loss of reality* for the worker, objectification as a *loss of and bondage to the object*, and appropriation as *estrangement*, as *alienation*" (Marx 1975:324, emphases in original). According to Marxism (also as developed by later theorists such as Lukács, Horkheimer, and Adorno), the "commodity fetishism" is symptomatic of a more general process of reification or objectification in capitalist society, in which human relations and cultural forms increasingly appear in the form of object relations. This fetishism was claimed to work in a dual way, by which social phenomena took on the appearance of things, as well as inanimate things being treated as if they had social qualities (Held 1980:220).

Thus, despite the notion of (historical) materialism attributed to Marxism, and the immense importance it assigned to ready-to-hand technology (as forces of production) for social change and progress, it also came to fuel the aversion for things in modern social theory (cf. Kopytoff 1986:84–85). Although intended more as a critique of how things lost their social value and human involvement in the capitalist mode of production, Marxism ended up providing social theory with a vocabulary—*objectification, reification, instrumental reason*—that strongly contributed to their stigmatization. Through these metaphors, things became symbols of the destructive and humiliating physicalism of modern society, providing their social dismissal with a powerful moral justification.

Much as a consequence, as observed by Daniel Miller, most later critics of mass culture and technology have tended "to assume that the relation of persons to objects is in some way vicarious, fetishistic or wrong; that primary concern should lie with direct social relations and 'real people'" (1987:11). Ironically, this critique joined forces with a long-held bourgeois contempt in academia (especially in the humanities) for dirt, manual labor, and working-class life in general. Academia was an arena for pure thought to be kept apart and distinct from any repugnant trivia of labor and production. Only the aestheticized material—such as fine art, the exotic, and the book—was allowed access, keeping the oily, smelly object at arm's length (cf. Beek 1989:95). The long-held aversion against technological disciplines and engineering as "real" academic disciplines is another aspect of this story.

THE LOSS OF THE "MIMETIC CAPACITY"

As already noted, the contempt that intellectuals such as Rilke and Friedell expressed toward the "unreal" hinted at a new and ambiguous consciousness of things in Western thinking. In *The Philosophy of Money*, Georg Simmel sharply identified this ambiguity by pointing at a seemingly paradoxical tendency in the modern attitude toward things: at the same time that things were losing their embedded social and ready-to-hand meaning, there was a simultaneously growing interest in and fascination for the peculiar things, the genuine object. As somehow parallel to the case of historicism, to be discussed in the next chapter, Simmel argues that it was *because* things became deprived of their implicit meaning that a substitute was consciously sought:

> Since so many objects continuously detached by money lose their direction-given significance for us, there develops . . . a deep yearning to give things a new importance, a deeper meaning, a value of their own . . . the lively motions in the arts, the search for new styles, for style as such, symbolism and even theosophy are all symptoms of the longing for a new and more perceptible significance of things . . . modern man . . . now seeks (often in problematical vacillations) in the objects themselves that vigor, stability and inner unity which he has lost because of the changed money-conditioned relationship that he has with them. (1978/1906:404)

Simmel saw this new interest in things as superficial and fragmentary, a means to escape the pestering of the present material world ("The flight from the present is made easier"). Thus the modern interest in exotic art, in antiquities, in "turning objects into art" is an act of redemption. The new obsession with the fragment, with the atomized and aestheticized thing, becomes little more than "comforting stimulation for weakened nerves":

> The present vividly felt charm for the fragment, the mere allusion, the aphorism, the symbol, the underdeveloped artistic style . . . place[s] us at a distance from the substance of things; they speak to us "as from afar"; reality is touched not with direct confidence but with fingertips that are immediately withdrawn. The most extreme refinement of our literary style avoids the direct characterization of objects; it only touches a remote corner of them with the word, and grasps not the thing but only the veil that envelops them. . . .
> In all this we discover an emotional trait whose pathological deformation is the so-called "agoraphobia": the fear of coming into too close a contact with objects. (Simmel 1978/1906:474)

Although in disagreement with Simmel on many other issues, Walter Benjamin developed a similar perspective in his writings.[1] To Benjamin, modernity also involved a change in the conception of things. His main concern was how a "mimetic" and "auratic" capacity was giving way to a sublimated and intimate attitude. While the mimetic attitude implied a respect for things in their otherness and their auratic own-ness, the modern gaze was isomorphic, subjecting them to intimacy and sameness (Benjamin 2003:255–56). While this in some respects is akin to Heidegger's criticism, Benjamin saw this change not so much located in the things themselves as in our attitude toward them. Things' capacity to affect and speak to us, Benjamin argued, rests precisely in their difference. By embodying them with human privacy and imbuing them with our own personality, things are brought to silence. If they speak, it is only our own voices that are heard (Andersson 2001:30–36). The dominant premodern attitude was to respect this otherness and be attentive to "the material community of things in their communication" (Benjamin 1996:73, cf. Benjamin 2003:338). The attentiveness to the way things express themselves was crucial to the experience of a thing's "aura." This mimetic faculty, Benjamin speculated, was perhaps the explanation of the oeuvre expressed in northern hunters' rock art: "Perhaps Stone Age man produced such incomparable drawings of elk only because the hand guiding the implement still remembered the bow with which it had felled the beast" (2002:253).

Modernity, in Benjamin's analyses, was Janus-faced. Contrary to Heidegger's mostly negative depiction, he saw it as also containing the salvaging means to destroy its own tradition. New techniques such as film and photography, as well as materials and styles such as steel and glass architecture, could bring about a disruption, a *Verstörung* that challenged the prevailing tendency of (false) aesthetization, intimacy, and the sublimation of tradition. His critical writings of the 1930s were targeting this dominant trope in the modern conception of materiality, as displayed in the *intérieur* of the late-nineteenth-century bourgeois home. Staged as inventory in this domesticated setting, things had completely lost their otherness and individuality. They were sentenced to serfdom and became nothing but labels of privacy, faithfully mirroring their owner, *"das Etui Mensch."* Controlled inside the homely theater, the *intérieur* provides the etui-man with self-confirming comfort: "The inside of the case is the velvet-lined trace that he has imprinted on the world" (Benjamin 1999a:502, 1999b:8–9; cf. Benjamin 2003:38; cf. Andersson 2001:47–48).

While things' otherness originally was the source of communication and interaction, the loss of the mimetic capacity made things' difference problematic and fearsome. Their material integrity became a threat and thus a subject for domestication through processes of privatization and intimization. In a wonderful (and Simmel-like) fragment, Benjamin expressed how modern man, "chilled in a chilly environment" (1999a:779), tries to overcome his material estrangement:

Warmth is ebbing from things. Objects of daily use gently but insistently re-
pel us. Day by day, in overcoming the sum of secret resistances . . . we have
an immense labor to perform. We must compensate for their coldness with
our warmth if they are not to freeze us to death, and handle their spiny forms
with infinite dexterity if we are not to bleed to death." (1996:453)

FORGETTING THINGS

At the same time that philosophers, writers, and intellectuals at large increasingly began to express their concern with an "objectified," monetary-
and technology-driven modern society, we began witnessing the exiling
of things as a significant source material from anthropology and the social
sciences. Although the correspondence, of course, needs to be explored
and explained in far more detail, there is a suggestive coincidence in
time between the general intellectual reaction to the "evil and alienating
machines" and the first cry against things as meaningful sources of social
inquiry (see chapter 2).

One powerful trajectory of this "turn against things" is seen in the development of British anthropology. By the 1920s, it had reinvented itself
as "social anthropology," a discipline concerned with "processes and
structures" conceived of as being impossible to be accessed by things (Kuper 1978). A very different development, but with similar consequences,
took place slightly earlier in American cultural anthropology. As a key
figure of the latter, Franz Boaz himself came to manifest this new distrust
in things. Whereas he had previously been deeply involved in collections
and museum anthropology, he began to abandon these projects by 1905.
One reason given by Bill Brown is that "he had become increasingly convinced that the most important elements of culture were irreducible to
artefacts, that anthropological facts could never become artifactual—that
the cultural Thing, let us say, was too intangible to be found in things"
(2003:118).

The outcome has already been addressed (see chapter 2): during the
twentieth century, to study "just things" became a source of embarrassment, a reactionary heritage of a mindless antiquarianism. Even if there
may have been a certain tendency to grant "too much independence to
the empirical world" over which "idealism had a nice polemical virtue"
(Latour 1999b:147; "In the past we were presented with lithic industries
which, to judge by their descriptions, were copulating, hybridizing, evolv-
ing, adapting and producing offspring" [DeVore 1968:346]), the trump card
of fetishism always seemed to be very close at hand. Thus, when Miller in
1987 found it necessary to express his moral contempt for approaches to
modern material culture in American processual archaeology, fetishism

became an argument beyond verification or explanation: "Such studies exemplify the kind of fetishism to which material culture studies are always prone, when people are superseded as the subject of investigation by objects, and become essentially labels for their movement or pattern" (143).

"SIMPLE COUNTRY PEOPLE HAVE A KIND OF FETISHISM"

The described intellectual turn against "evil things" is of importance in understanding why fetishist theories were so smoothly accepted within modern thinking and why things, more generally, could be treated with such instant distrust. However, the reaction caused by the changing political economy of things itself is hardly sufficient to fully understand the fate of things in modern social research. To take further steps toward a more comprehensive explanation, we have to respond to a few basic questions: Why is it a priori "wrong" to blur the boundary between humans and things or to ascribe personality and identity to things? What is the ontological justification for the persistent idea that action, influence, and power are capacities of which only humans hold possession?

The answers to these questions are intimately linked to a wider effective history of thing oblivion and displacement in Western thinking since the seventeenth century. As noted in the previous chapter, the skeptical attitude that followed in the wake of Descartes's "methodological doubt" gave rise to an all too significant difference between the material world and the human mind and thus between nonhumans and humans. This "significant difference" somehow predestined things to their subsequent intellectual dismissal and silencing. However, as taken for granted as the *opposition* (not to be confused with the difference) between humans and nonhumans might seem to a Western intellectual, it is nonetheless far from a universally held dichotomy. The conception of a strictly divided world was clearly not shared by those many "others" for whom the opposition culture-nature remained unfamiliar and to whom the affection for things was quite natural. Such, according to Bill Brown, is also the case for the "simple country people" portrayed in Sarah Orne Jewett's late-nineteenth-century novel *Deephaven*. Here, "the narrator's friend Kate speculates about the 'simple country people' who 'have a kind of fetichism'" because "they believe there is a 'personality' in 'what *we call* inanimate things'" (Brown 2003:115, Brown's emphasis). A closer look at this fetishism, and also the sort of *animism* referred to by earlier anthropologists, may reveal some convictions that contribute to explaining things' faith in modern social research.

More than any other discipline, anthropology has provided overwhelming evidence of societies that blur or do not recognize this boundary that modern thinking—and seemingly the discipline itself—mostly takes for granted. As discussed in detail by Tim Ingold in relation to hunter-gatherer societies, their being-in-the-world rarely involves absolute distinctions such as mind/matter or culture/nature. Neither does one find much evidence that they relate to landscape or nature as an external, "natural" world to be domesticated or embodied. In other words, most of them do not see themselves as spiritual, cultural subjects struggling with an alien object world of nature simply because a strict division between spirit and matter, culture and nature, does not have a place in their thought or praxis (Ingold 2000:42–43). A wide range of examples illustrates how peoples in different settings refer to animals as kindred or as beings with whom they can have close social relationships. Again, this is not to erase their difference, but rather to emphasize points of linkage and the possibility of interaction.

Among the Sámi of northern Scandinavia (as with most other circumpolar peoples), the brown bear was treated as a personalized being who well understood human discourse and dispositions. Conceptually, it was sometimes addressed as a relative or in human terms, and the killing and consumption of the bear involved elaborate rituals terminating with a humanlike burial (Fjellström 1981/1755; Myrstad 1996). To the Sámi reindeer herders, the reindeer was a fellow creature. Both man and animal contained their own will and shared the capacity to teach each other. Mountains, pastures, trees, and dwelling places were greeted and conceived of as communicable (Turi 1987:41, 75–76). Returning from the mountains to the winter pastures in the northern Swedish forest, the ethnographer Emilie Demant Hatt observed a young Sámi girl hugging a big tree trunk, saying, "Good day pine, I greet you from the mountain willow" (Demant Hatt 1913:84, my translation). As also exemplified by their drums (which were assigned life-cycle rituals) and their "fetishized" stone "gods" (*sieidis*; Kalstad 1997; Price 2002; Hansen and Olsen 2004), personality, identity, and the capacity to act were not conceived as characteristics reserved only for people. Although clearly different, humans and nonhumans were not considered to occupy two oppositional spheres.

Numerous examples from other contexts provide more evidence of this "fallacious" blurring. Investigating Viking Age burials in Iceland, Þóra Pétursdóttir shows how horses are both included in human graves and given separate, even elaborate, burials. Without excluding the possible symbolic significance of the horse as a means of traveling to the world of the dead, the fact that these horses were buried as humans, she argues, is also due to the fact that "they were considered as fellow social beings—not as humans in disguise but as different but still equally potential subjects of a less compartmentalized cosmos than we are used to today" (2007:75). This complies well with how the Vikings also ascribed

Figure 5.2. Already blurred? Sámi sacred site, Seitjaur, Kola Peninsula, Russia (photo: Bjørnar Olsen).

personality, intention, and "being" to things such as their boats and weaponry. Swords, for example, could have reputations and were given names, such as *Tyrving, Kvernbit, Gram,* and *Skrep* (Gansum and Hansen 2002:16–17). Such attitudes were not only reserved for pagans. In medieval Europe, church bells were named and treated as individuals—possessing their own will of how to be rung (Berger 1992:28).

Anthropologists, historians, and social scientists of course acknowledge these attitudes as expressions of native beliefs and affirm this cultural "otherness." Interpreting this otherness, however, nearly always implies the application of some sort of "hermeneutics of suspicion" by bringing it to court against a preconceived (modern) ontology of how the world "really is"—that is, divided. Analysis thus becomes an act of "purification" (Latour 1993), a sorting of the muddled worlds into the appropriate categories. The Icelandic Viking Age habit of burying horses in humanlike fashion must be due to their symbolic or economic significance, not because the horses themselves were conceived of as deserving a burial on par with those of humans. Statements involving the blurring or crossing of the dividing line are interpreted as "metaphorical," as symbolic appropriations of nature. Rock art depicting elks, bears, boats, and humans in compositions that blur the divide are read as the embodiment and negotiation of human social relations (Tilley 1991; see chapter 4).

Following Ingold, these demystifying analyses usually involve arguments such as the following: "primitive people" make sense of their relation with things and the natural world by drawing on metaphors from their social life and their capacity as humans (cf. Godelier 1977). They use their social experience to "model" their relation with the nonhuman world, whereby ecological or "thingly" relations "appear" as social ones (Ingold 2000). Simple people themselves are unaware of this and have not realized that their social relationship to nature is based on an illusion. However, as noted by Ingold,

> the entire argument is predicated upon an initial ontological dualism between the intentional worlds of human subjects, and the object world of material things—or in brief, between society and nature. It is only by virtue of holding these to be separate that the one can be said to furnish the model for the other. The implication, however, is that the claim of the people themselves to inhabit but one world, encompassing relations with both human and non-human components of the environment on a similar footing, is founded upon an illusion—one that stems from their inability to recognise where the reality ends and its schematic representation begins. (2000:44)

Anthropologists hence have to draw the line, start purifying, and sort out the categories for them. On the other hand, no suspicion arises when people establish intimate relations among themselves. These are "only" social (or subsocial, e.g., economic, sexual, political). So we have one set of relations that are taken for granted as real, authentic, and honest, and another set that are false. This falseness seems to arise when we transgress a certain border between the "us" and the "it," projecting relations prescribed for one realm onto another. This raises the question of why this boundary has become so obvious and ontologically secure that analyses can be grounded on it a priori.

THE GREAT DIVIDE:
BECOMING MODERN BY DISTINCTION

In his book *We Have Never Been Modern*, Bruno Latour argues how modernity institutionalized a "Great Divide," two completely distinct ontological zones that became constitutive of its social and philosophical conduct. By this split, the power, interests, and politics of humans came to be placed at one pole, while knowledge about objects and the nonhuman was placed at the other. While modernity has been celebrated as both the origin and the triumph of humanism, as well as the birth of the human being and the subject (cf. Foucault 1989), there is less talk about its less desired offspring: the simultaneous birth of "things" and "nature." The construction of the human thus presupposed the construction of—and simultaneous separation from—the nonhuman. From this moment on, the human and nonhuman were delegated to different ontological and disciplinary zones—on the one hand, those concerned with the humans-among-themselves, and on the other, those studying the things-in-them-selves (Latour 1993:13ff.; cf. Kopytoff 1986:84ff.).

According to Latour, this first great divide caused another significant distinction, namely, that between us (i.e., the moderns) and the others (i.e., the nonmoderns or premoderns). The premoderns did not under-stand the first distinction but mixed everything together in an appalling stew of people and things, culture and nature. It is because we are able to distinguish between people and things, culture and nature that we differ from them (Latour 1993:97–103). Or do we? Following Latour, our entire existence is founded on overlapping relations and translations between the human and nonhuman and on hybrids that preserve and mediate these relations (Latour 1993, 1999b, 2005). Our society is based on such mixings of culture/nature. If truth be told, the mess has never been greater! Despite all curses and denouncement of things among Western intellectuals, their own writing, teaching, and living have become ever-more enmeshed with the very beings they denounce: more and more of their actions are delegated to things. Thus—and this is the very paradox of this trope—we have never been modern (Latour 1993:46–48).

Still, the distinction between nature and society persists, not because it "dwells" as an ontological constant according to which knowledge or the sciences are differentiated, but because modernity and the various sci-ences continually create, maintain, and defend the opposition. Scientific practice is thus also a "purifying practice" in which everything that ex-ists has to be placed within two distinct ontological spheres, categorized either as culture or nature, subjects or objects. As noted by Latour (2003), the true originality of the moderns was not a doing away with things and hybrids, but rather their estrangement from their own practices—which allowed them to do the exact opposite of what they were saying: it is only when you are so convinced that nature and society do not mix that you can mix them so thoroughly as to produce the mess that we are stewing in today. This "discrepancy between self-representation and practice" (Latour 2003:38) was only possible by applying the same acts of purifica-tion that social scientists have used to cleanse the illusions of those "oth-ers" who claim to inhabit but one world—encompassing relations among humans, animals, and things on an equal footing. In other words, the modern attitude consists of splitting the mixtures apart in order to extract from them what came from culture (the social, the episteme, the *Geist*) and what came from nature (Latour 1993:78).

This desire for a divided world emptied of its mediators assigned things an ambiguous position within the modern constitution. They are located outside the human sphere of power, interest, and politics—and still are not properly nature. Although prescribed for the nonhuman side, material culture ended up occupying neither of the two positions prescribed by the modern constitution (culture and nature). Although this is a somewhat speculative suggestion, I think it brings us to the core of things' exile from the social sciences: being a mixture of culture and nature, a work of translation and itself increasingly mediating such relations, material culture, quite literally, became "matter out of place"—in other words, part of the "excluded middle" (see Grosz 2002:91–94). In this sense, we may also relate this exclusion—and the associated "dangers of fetishism"—to the concept of the "abject" (Kristeva 1982). The *abject* is associated with the ambiguous border zone between the "me" and the "not-me," a sign of ourselves as composite beings (or cyborgs), and thus something that the subject seeks to expel in order to achieve an independent identity (Brooker 1999:1; Butler 1993:243, 3). Things may be seen as typifying this conception of the abject, although not in a literal sense, and only as indicative of a very localized and historically situated discourse rather than one psychologically given.

"ANTHROPOLOGY" VERSUS "PHILOSOPHY"?

There is a defensive argument often used to counter the line of reasoning put forth here. Reviewing recent approaches to materiality, Daniel Miller (2005a) argues against the claim that the dualism witnessed in many anthropological analyses should be seen as an outcome of their ontological grounding or as resulting from any processes of "purification." Rather, such claims are indicative of the opposition between an abstracted philosophy ("doomed to reinvent a particular philosophical wheel") and down-to-earth anthropological research that just reflects vulgar reality as it truly is (Miller 2005a:14–15, 43–44). In contrast to "philosophers,"[2] Miller argues that anthropologists are concerned with practice and with real people to whom any talk about transcending the dualism of subjects and objects must seem "mystificatory and obfuscating":

> Anthropology always incorporates an engagement that starts from the opposite position to that of philosophy—a position taken from its empathetic encounter with the least abstracted and most fully engaged practices of the

various peoples of the world. In this encounter we come down from the philosophical heights and strive for the very vulgarity that philosophy necessarily eschews. We may often find ourselves conducting research among people
for whom "common sense" consists of a clear distinction between subjects
and objects, defined by their opposition. . . . As part of our own engagement
we will necessarily attempt to empathize with these views. Furthermore, we
will strive to include within our analysis the social consequences of conceptualizing the world as divided in this way. (2005a:14)

What Miller seems to be saying is that the empathy embedded in the
anthropological approach ensures a harmony between analytical representations and everyday experience. In short, anthropology reflects what
people are doing. The generality of this sympathetic argument however
is hard to sustain. If true, how should we explain the remarkably heterogeneous portfolio of analytical positions proposed in anthropology over
the last eighty to ninety years? Are all these "paradigms" grounded in the
sensitivity to the way *people* act and think? Moreover, is it the "empathetic
encounter with the least abstracted and most fully engaged practices"
that has led anthropology to dismiss and ignore things for so long?

Miller takes his argument even further. He claims that anthropology's empathetic sensitivity also involves an ethical concern not shared
by "those who strive for more abstract resolutions" and who tend to
"denigrate others as deluded, vulgar, or simplistic in their preference
for more pragmatic and less abstracted perspectives" (2005a:114–15). For
some reason Miller does not mention those numerous groups of people
studied by anthropology whose "common sense" does *not* inform them
about a clear distinction between subjects and objects and especially not
as something defined by their *opposition*. One may rather ask how many
people have been mystified and obfuscated by persistent anthropological attempts to draw the dividing line, to purify the entangled mess, and
to reassemble the entities by placing them in their "proper" places. It is
hard to see that these skills of suspicious hermeneutics are achieved only
through empathetic encounters. Maybe it is not just philosophy that can
become "simply a tool for describing others as false or stupid" (Miller
2005a:15)?

CONCLUSION: ALLOWANCE AND DIASPORA

In the last two chapters I have conducted a long and somewhat rhizom-
atic travel from things' taciturnity in their "everydayness" to their ontological diaspora within the modern intellectual constitution. This chapter
has largely been devoted to understanding things' bad reputation and

why they have been omitted to such an extent from studies of social and cultural practices.

Some qualifications are however needed. It is not true that academia—and public discourse in general—have forgotten things altogether. Some objects have always been allowed to dwell and perform well within these discursive formations. With some notable exceptions, however, they only accept allowance for objects of a certain kind, which are usually objects that are emancipated from the networks of everyday trivia, dirt, and work. Thus, and although the opinions on their capacity to inform social science and humanistic discourses may vary greatly, objects of art—conspicuous objects—have always been welcomed, talked about, and discussed. En passant, it is curious to notice how this effective history of "selective object allowance" continues to influence not only public discourses but even the core of material cultural studies. Even though that realm is clearly more liberal and inclusive, also allowing space for the trivial and mass-produced, the conspicuous object, the singularized artifact, and the unusual still seem to be greatly preferred over the bulk of the materials we live with.

Simmel's diagnosis, that the attraction for these decontextualized and aestheticized objects reflected a fear of coming into too close contact with our (common) things, might be too harsh. Still, there is little doubt that the "materialist" changes brought about by modern technology, by mass-produced goods ("empty indifferent things") swarming the mundane world, and by cityscapes more and more formed by iron, glass, and concrete provided little relief to intellectuals and "etui men" alike. Being perceived as *Gestell*—as the monstrous Being of alienation and estrangement, modern material culture came to assume the villain's role in academic and public discourses from the late nineteenth century onward. Stigmatized as humanism's other, things seemed utterly unfit to inform the disciplines studying genuine social and cultural practices.

Their exiling, however, was based on a more profound and grounding othering of things and nature. The "Great Divide" launched by the modern thought regime created an abyss that things were assumed never to cross. Social relations were, per definition, relations among human subjects, and any attempts at including things, animals, and nature were seen as highly suspicious. Such inappropriate attitudes were either condemned as an expression of fetishism or were to be purified as primitive metaphorical statements and symbolic appropriations of nature. Despite the proliferation of hybrids in its midst and all nonhumans being enrolled into the very fabric of society, the modern regime came to properly acknowledge only those entities that could be firmly situated—in other words: as dwelling either in culture or in nature (Latour 1993). Things thus became an utterly problematic and ambiguous entity within modern thinking, an abject category that blurred the boundary. Not properly situated either in nature or culture, they became matter out of place, doomed to their exile. This prescribed the fate for an entity that was given the unfortunate but pertinent hybrid label: *material culture*.

6

Temporality and Memory

How Things Remember

To write history means giving dates their physiognomy.

—Walter Benjamin, *The Arcades Project*

In his essay "The Temporality of the Landscape," Tim Ingold writes about the landscape as a network of interrelated times and time rhythms. It cannot be ascribed any particular age or subsumed to any single rhythm (such as the seasonal cycle), but instead is a complex composition of concurrent cycles and chronotopes. Ingold illustrates this differentiated temporality by discussing a Renaissance painting by the Flemish artist Pieter Bruegel, known as *The Harvesters*. Drawing our attention to selected components of the painted landscape, Ingold effectively brings out the various interweaving temporalities and historical references simultaneously present in it: the (relative) permanence of the topography of hills and valleys; the cycles of movements and activities and arrivals and departures associated with paths and tracks crisscrossing the landscape; the growth life and annual cycles of the old pear tree under which the harvesters rest; the coevalness of the wheat field depicted in the process of being cut (thus also marking a seasonal rhythm); the "pastness" and biography of the stone church (also scheduled to announce calendrical and human cycles by its bell); and, finally, the rhythms and cycles of people of different ages (not only the harvesters), engaged in different tasks and relations (2000:201–7).

Far more entities contained in the painting contribute to the complex network of interweaving durations and time references, such as the village houses, distant churches, harvest tools, cloths, sea, drifting skies, and

107

so on, and we do not need to consult a Renaissance painting to let this "mixing" of times and time rhythms occur to us. A quick view around us anytime, anywhere will suffice. Our material and temporal being-in-the-world is always-already a hybrid experience of different temporal references. At every moment the materials of the world confront us with a great patchwork of coexisting temporal horizons that create networks and connections between different times, different pasts. It is not only a network that interweaves and draws together different pasts and presents, but one that, by its very "nature" and its durability, is also projected ahead of itself toward the future.

This is as much an inescapable truth for past lifeworlds as for those we are currently dwelling in. Still, as archaeologists and culture historians, we often tend to think of the past as a series of enclosed temporal horizons to be identified and purified through strategies of careful sequencing. Laurent Olivier has made a well-founded point about this encapsulation of time and how he himself for a long time imagined that Iron Age people lived in some kind of Iron Age environment, in Iron Age buildings, working with Iron Age tools, and burying their dead according to Iron Age funeral practices: "All that seems obvious, all of that seems natural: all archaeological chronologies, all archaeological reconstructions of the past, are based on that basic assumption, according to which any age of the past bears in itself its own temporal specificity" (2001:64). But, as he adds, "things do not work like that" (64). Reflecting on the time when his writing takes place (1999), he notes the "invisibility" of the 1990s in what he sees from his window. What he sees are houses and constructions dating back to the seventeenth, eighteenth, and nineteenth centuries. The late twentieth century seems reduced to details in the material surroundings. Thus, the present is not comprised of things belonging to the same age, but takes the form of a multitemporal field in which the past has accumulated itself (Olivier 2001:66–67). Drawing on Henri Bergson's concept of duration, Olivier's general argument is that any present can be conceived of as a material recording of the past: "The current state of the present . . . basically consists of a palimpsest of all durations of the past that have become recorded in matter" (2001:66; see Olivier 2008).

These initial remarks set the agenda for this chapter. It is written as a critical commentary to the prevailing disciplinary and popular conceptions of history as inevitably successive, of the past as gone and of memory as only a recollective capacity that might be activated in search of this lost time. My most important objective, however, is to highlight the crucial role that things play in upholding the past, thus enabling various forms of memory. Things are not just traces or residues of absent presents; they are effectively engaged in assembling and hybridizing periods and epochs. As durable matter, things make the past present and tangible;

they constantly resist the regime that has subjugated time to the prevailing image of it as instantaneous and irreversible.

The very etymology of the word "thing" precisely suggests such a transcending or gathering function. As noted by several authors (cf. Heidegger 1971:172; Glassie 1999:67–68; Serres 1987), the Old Norse and Old English word *þing* meant "assembly," as did the Old High German *Thing*. However, it is less widely known that a possibly older etymological root (*tenku*) suggests an additional temporal dimension: "duration," or, literally, "extended" or "stretched time" (Falk and Torp 1994/1906:903; Bjorvand and Lindeman 2000:939ff.).

ARCHAEOLOGIES OF MEMORY

We have recently witnessed a considerable interest also in archaeology in regard to memory and the enduring past (cf. Rowlands 1993; Olivier 2001, 2008; Alcock 2002; Bradley 2002; Williams 2003; Van Dyke and Alcock 2003; Meskell 2004; Lucas 2005; Jones 2007; Naum 2008). One widely shared assumption in these studies, if not an uncontested one (e.g., Olivier 2001, 2008), is of memory as a "recollective" faculty. By this I mean that memory is seen as a conscious and willful human process of recalling or reconstructing the past, most eagerly emphasized in relation to the creation of selective and hegemonic accounts. For example, in the important volume *Archaeologies of Memory*, all contributors are said to engage "with the twin, inter-related themes of authority and identity, and the role memory plays in their creation, defence and possible transformation" (Van Dyke and Alcock 2003:7). Moreover, when the editors present their four "materially accessible media" through which social memories are constructed and observed (ritual behavior, narratives, representation, *and* objects and places [Van Dyke and Alcock 2003:4–5, my emphasis]), they seem little concerned with what memory-preserving qualities things *qua things* have to offer. Objects are pertinently mentioned only as *representative* expressions (paintings, figurines, rock art, etc.) that possess commemorative functions, while places "are spaces that have been *inscribed* with meaning, usually as a result of some past event or attachment" (4–5, my emphasis).

This resonates well with a general concern in historical and cultural studies with how memory crystallizes into sites or places of memory, locales of collective remembering (Nora 1984; Assman 1992). Despite the eventual presence of inscribed monuments or memorials, the materiality of the *lieu de mémoire* itself is normally not considered to be decisive. The crucial issue is the past event, a gone past, and the will to remember it through site embodiment. In related studies in archaeology, things also primarily achieve their mnemonic significance from being a medium, something that allows memory and meaning to be recorded and codified for later recollection (Bradley 2003:222; Joyce 2003:108). Andrew Jones rightly asserts that collective remembrance is not so much a social interplay between people as it is an "interplay or dynamic between people and things" (Jones 2003:84). However, also to him the "social" has the final say:

> Although the material world provides a framework for remembrance, it is the social practices in which artefacts are engaged which determines how remembrance is socially experienced and mapped out. In this sense we can consider the material world as a kind of "distributed mind," not only spatially distributed, but also temporally distributed. (Jones 2007:225)

The studies referred to all expose relevant and important aspects of social memory. However, to different degrees they seem to underrate the role things themselves play in enabling remembering and in upholding the past, a role that is not primarily consciously driven but also relates to the intrinsic gathering and enduring capacities of materials. For example, when Richard Bradley writes that more than ever it is important "to understand why particular versions of the past were captured in a permanent form" (Bradley 2003:223), he seems to suggest that the endurance of the past is mainly a result of the willful processes of human selection.

There are clearly processes of selection involved, with many of them related to human choices and ideological interests. However, the past still evidently present is at any moment far too varied, complex, and comprehensive to be seen as representing particular "captured versions" or as an edited or censored text. The past also sediments in unpredictable ways and according to material trajectories that are beyond, or unrelated to, human control and intervention. This present past constitutes a reservoir for different memories and mnemonic practices and also brings about involuntary and abject memories (see chapter 8).

THE PAST AS GONE

Despite the inevitable presence of the past in our lives—and the seemingly obvious fact that things and entities can exist at different times, and thus what is past can also be present—it is still common to claim that the past is "gone," leaving us with a void that only can be filled by our historical reconstructions and imaginations: "The actual past has gone. . . . The presence of the past is manifested only in its historicized traces. . . . Such traces signify an absent presence" (White 1990:174). This conception of the past as gone, that we are living in a new time that radically breaks with the past (accessible only through the fragmentary traces it has left behind), rests on several partly (but not necessarily) interrelated premises. Some of these are well known, others deserve more careful attention.

The first is the common conception of time and history as something that passes as an irreversible series of discrete moments, a line of instants (cf. Lucas 2005). For this to be true, as argued by Latour (1993:72–73), history has to be made up of a series of presents in which all elements at each point are aligned and made "contemporary." These elements must further be conceived of as moving in step and being replaced by other systems of things equally aligned. "Then, and only then, time forms a continuous and progressive flow" (Latour 1993:73). Despite the massive criticism raised against this conception of "instantaneous" and spatialized time, it has proved remarkably persistent, which of course is an effect of its constitutive role for modernity and all notions of evolution, progress, and historicism (Fabian 1983). Our historical and archaeological divisions of the past into clear-cut periods and epochs were made possible by this epistemic imperative. In fact, this synchronization of the past also contributed to the spatial image of time as exemplified by the alignment of artifact and monument types made "present-at-hand" in museums and textbooks from the mid-nineteenth century onward. Figures, tables, and showcases located artifacts and monuments in a hierarchical and efficiently visible spatial organization of continuities and discontinuities—that is, in a matrix of finely gradated and measurable intervals that revealed their typological and chronological identity (Foucault 1979; Olsen and Svestad 1994). The "order of things" created by this regulatory ideal thus gave reality to the serial image of time as moving between discrete immobile states.

This way of disciplining things into clients and servants of spatial, divided, and linear time is becoming ever more evident. The modern feeling of living in a temporally labile time, of time as shifting—actually as moving faster and faster—is to a large extent orchestrated by things, mainly ephemeral consumer objects mobilized in support of this regulatory ideal of progressive time (cf. Attfield 2000:76–84). This is perhaps most conspicuously and illusively seen in the fashion industry, where segments of our material life are prescribed to be renewed in what Roland Barthes once termed "an annual potlatch" (1985:xii; cf. Appadurai 1986a:32). This "instant" conception of time was strongly linked to the new capitalist consumer society that emerged during the nineteenth century. In his unfulfilled *Passagen-Werk*, Walter Benjamin depicts how the once-modern nineteenth-century Parisian shopping arcades were becoming ruins, ending up as the stranded relics of the consumer capitalism that soon made them extinct (Benjamin 1999b). The rapid cycle of modern material replacement made even the novelties of one's parents' youth outdated

(Benjamin 1999b:461–62): "For the first time, the most recent past becomes distant" (Benjamin quoted in Buck-Morss 1999:65). Today, Benjamin's observation is becoming ever truer: new retrospective visual media help to create this image of time as moving irreversibly, of the past as black and white, outdated and replaced—by depicting the velocity of changes, revealing how ridiculously old-fashioned our clothing and haircut were far back in the 1990s.

A second premise for conceiving the past as gone is the common attitude of associating society and culture with the nonmaterial, with the thoughts and actions of living people. The past is gone since the human subject is gone—leaving us only with traces or epiphenomena of their thoughts and actions. This brings in an absoluteness (at least beyond the oldest living human) that allows for no partial or relative existence of the past, letting it exist "somewhat" through its surviving material constituents (cf. Latour 1999b:156). Thus, the Renaissance is an absent past, a time to be recovered, despite the abundance of paintings, texts, music, buildings, and dead bodies still present. Likewise with other pasts, since the minds, relations, and actions of the living subjects are vanished; "what we simply have left are their things, the physical reminders and instantiations of the greatness that was Egypt" (Meskell 2004:219). According to this premise, history and historicity are limited to thinking and living subjects and banned for nonhumans and dead bodies.

The third premise is subtler, as it claims that an absent past—the conception of the past as gone—constitutes a necessary epistemological and ontological foundation of the modern historical inquiry—that historical remembering is possible only as a mode of forgetting. The past becomes a challenging problem, a mystery to be solved because it is hidden to us in the present. As Michael Shanks and Christopher Tilley have remarked, "the distance, the other-ness, the absence of the past is postulated as a condition of the challenge" (1987:9–10). Thus, it can be argued that the modern concern with the past requested a certain attitude of "forgetting"—a "blindness" toward the temporality and "pastness" of the "present" material world (cf. Casey 1987:2–7). As an outcome of this attitude, which Friedrich Nietzsche once denounced as the "illness of historicism," the past becomes something to be restored only because it is lost (Latour 1993:69). This point, however, needs to be explored further.

THE FORGOTTEN PAST:
HEIDEGGER ON TEMPORALITY AND HISTORICITY

In *The Order of Things*, Michel Foucault made the seemingly paradoxical claim that the rise of modern historicism in the early nineteenth century emerged as an outcome of a "break" in which humankind found itself in a dehistoricized condition: "The imaginative values then assumed by the past, . . . the consciousness of history of that period, the lively curiosity shown for documents and for traces left behind by time—all this is a surface expression of the simple fact that man found himself emptied of history" (1989:369). This curiosity and historical consciousness was in fact a sign that "he was already beginning to recover" (369), and the new interest in monuments and antiquities in the early nineteenth century may be seen as directly related to this recovery. Material remains became both witnesses of a lost past and the promises of its reconstruction (Olsen and Svestad 1994; Svestad 1995; Olsen 2001). As noted in the previous chapter, there is a close connection between this loss and recovery of history and the changing attitude toward things (cf. Andersson 2001:17).

Foucault's claim that our modern historical consciousness was conditioned by our "emptiness of history" may be traced to Martin Heidegger's notion of "forgetting" (1962:388–89; Macann 1993:102; Inwood 2000:155–56). Heidegger coined this term to describe a certain attitude toward the past, characteristic of our modern being. He contrasts this "ontic" mode of being with "repetition" (*Wiederholung*), which refers to an authentic "reliving" of the past in which the past lives on in our present, in our careful concerns and ready-to-hand dealing with things ("Being alongside what is ready-to-hand . . . *temporality reveals itself as the meaning of authentic care*" [Heidegger 1962:374, emphasis in original]). The past is not an "object" of conscious consideration, something Dasein explicitly remembered but is embedded in our very being-in-the-world.

"Forgetting" (*Vergessen, Vergessenheit*) is an inauthentic way of relating to the past (and present). We forget that the past is part of our present being and, by doing so, open up the past as "a field of recollectables" or as something to be consciously reenacted (Inwood 2000:156; Andersson 2001:17). It makes the past *past*—the very condition for remembering it: "Only on the basis of such forgetting can anything be *retained*. . . . Just as expecting is possible only on the basis of awaiting, *remembering* is possible only on that of forgetting" (Heidegger 1962:389, emphasis in original). As noted by Macann: "What Heidegger intends by this seemingly strange conjoining of forgetting and remembering is the insight that, when we 'remember' the past, in the typical mode of 'gone forever,' we are 'forgetting' that we *are* our past, that we are haunted by our past, that our past lives on in our present" (1993:102).

So far, so good. However, when Heidegger more explicitly discusses time and historicity, the past still present is primarily argued to be a mode of *human* temporality and historicality. The ontological basis for this "historicizing" is the human subject's temporal "connectedness of life"—"that is to say, the stretching-along, the movement, and the persistence which are specific for Dasein" (Heidegger 1962:427). As mortal beings, our lives are essentially temporal, stretched between birth and death, also grounding the concern or care that defines Dasein's being. It is this temporality, mediating past, present, and future, which makes Dasein historical. Thus, the past "itself" is not constitutive of our historicality, "entities do not become more historical by being moved off into a past . . . so that the oldest of them would be the most authentically historical" (Heidegger 1962:433). It is an effect of our existence as temporal beings (unifying the future and past in the present).

Contrary to what was argued by theorists such as Benjamin, Heidegger did not conceive of things as historical or as making any contribution to human "historicality." According to Heidegger, things are at best "secondarily historical," as revealed in his discussion of museum objects:

> The "antiquities" preserved in museums (household gear, for example) belong to a "time which is past"; yet they are still present-at-hand in the "Present." How far is such equipment historical, when it is *not yet* past? Is it historical, let us say, only because it has become an *object* of historical interest, of antiquarian study or national lore? (1962:431, emphasis in original)

According to Heidegger, to be proper historical objects the things themselves must be historical and must "in themselves" have "something past" (1962:431). He indeed acknowledges that museum objects do show the wear and tear of time, that some of them become fragile, worm-eaten, and so on. This *Vergänglichkeit* (transience), however, is not part of the past, but something that goes on in the present:

> What, then, is the past in this equipment? What *were* these "Things" which today they are no longer? They are still definite items of equipment for use; but they are out of use. Suppose, however, that they were still in use today, like many household heirlooms; would they then be not yet historical? All the same, whether they are in use or out of use, they are not longer what they were. What is "past"? Nothing else than that *world* within which they belonged to a context of equipment and were encountered as ready-to-hand and used by a concernful Dasein who was-in-the-world. That *world* is no longer. (Heidegger 1962:432, emphasis original)

Thus, for Heidegger that past world is gone. The only being that can transcend this pastness is Dasein itself. Things receive their historicality by being the concern of the only being that is primarily historical: Dasein, which is rendered historical by its own temporal mode of being. Things thus become epiphenomena or "derivatives" of the world and of Dasein's historical being.[1] In Heidegger's argument about past things (or equipment), there is a strange and constraining dichotomy: they are *either* past and ready-to-hand *or* present and present-at-hand. Even if the past object is used in the present, it consciously *occurs* to us as past, for example as a present-at-hand heirloom. Consider how this point is explained by one of his commentators, using an ancient dinner plate as an illustration:

> The dinner plate belongs to the past because it belongs to a past world. It constitutes a trace of a particular conceptual and cultural framework within which it fitted as one element in a totality of equipment. . . . It remains present to us as an object within our world, and—whether used to serve food or displayed in a cabinet[2] . . . it is still an heirloom, still an historical object, because it is marked by the world for which it was originally created and within which it was originally used. Even for the family for which it is an heirloom, it is not used for serving food in just the same way their contemporary dinner service is used—the heirloom is for special occasions. (Mulhall 1996:168)

There are several problems with this argument. First, there is no recognition of the multitudes of degrees of duration in the material world, ranging from the momentary piece of bread to a stone ax or a city. While some objects must be replaced many times during a work task, a season, or a human life cycle, others can slumber as contemporary ready-to-hand items for several human generations without ever drawing attention to themselves as present-at-hand historical objects. In fact, it may be argued that what turns them into historical objects is a "forgetting" of them as present items of use. Second, and using Heidegger's later philosophy against himself (cf. Heidegger 1971; Young 2002), a house treated with care, for example a Black Forest farmhouse, will live on, offering "dwelling" for repeated generations, helping to create their *Heimat*. Thus, the life history of the house may help disclose the full "thingness" of it (that which "gathers"), which has been threatened or obstructed by the calculative tendency to see it only as useful and utilitarian (as *Gestell*; Young 2002:44ff.; see chapter 4). Last and most seriously, Heidegger (and Stephen Mulhall) seem to fall back on a conception of history as a series of synchronous and homogenous states of lifeworlds. To each such state there corresponds a unique "equipmental totality," which is replaced by another "world" (or *Umwelt*) equally well united and close-knit. No entity can exist at different "times"; overlapping and enduring durations are ruled out. The web of relational assignments so constitutive of Dasein's being-in-the-world (Heidegger 1962:91–148; cf. chapter 4) seems operational on a purely synchronous, spatial level, rendering the human subject as the only temporal being able to transcend its confined momentary historical location. It may rather be argued that this network of assignments or references creating links between things, and between people and things, also enables a historical linking (or "gathering") of different historical horizons.

BERGSON AND HABIT MEMORY

Heidegger's initial distinction between "repetition" and "forgetting" (and "remembering") can be further illuminated by taking into account Bergson's work on time and memory (Bergson 2004; Mullarkey 2000; Pearson 2002). As did Heidegger, Bergson conceived of our day-to-day dealings with objects as referential assignments—the isolated object is a fictional assumption (Pearson 2002:145). They also shared a conception of human involvement with things as nonrepresentational, a relation Bergson explicitly stated as a bodily relationship (Bergson 2004:86–87, 111–13).

Crucial to Bergson was that the difference between matter and perception should be erased: "Let us place ourselves face-to-face with immediate reality: at once we will find that there is no impassable barrier, no essential difference, no real distinction even, between perception and the things perceived" (2004:291). This relation should be conceived of as one between part and whole—we are part of what we perceive, an image among images (Pearson 2002:160; see chapter 4). Our perception of matter (or aggregates of things), Bergson further asserted, is intimately related to the potential of actions (and reactions) created by the interface between bodies and things. Things act on us, they "indicate at each moment, like a compass that is being moved about, the position of a certain image, my body, in relation to the surrounding images" (Bergson 2004:10). Herein also lies the potential for a different kind of memory, not related to mental representations and conscious recalling. In our "average everydayness," we repeat certain actions by habit or by prescribed "instructions" for motor skills provided by the things themselves: "Our daily life is spent among objects whose very presence invites us to play a part" (Bergson 2004:113). This enmeshment produces a material habitual competence and spatial knowledge, a "knowing-your-way-around-somewhere" (Casey 1984:283). It is this competence acquired by iterative practices, rather than mental representation, that helps us navigate; in other words, it produces knowledge for "how to go on" in a landscape, a city, or a house: "In fact, we commonly act our recognition before we think it" (Bergson 2004:113).

The outcome is habitual schemes of bodily practices that constitute the basis for a particular kind of memory, a *habit memory* (Bergson 2004). In contrast to *recollective* memory, which involves a conscious gaze at a particular past (the searching for unique, dated recollectables), habit memory is a bodily memory preserved by repetitious practice. The past continues by being relived in our routines and ways of dealing with things so that "it no longer represents our past to us, it *acts* it" (Bergson 2004:93, emphasis in original). Our referential involvement with objects, organizing various bodily movements into relational wholes, makes us "remember" sequences of bodily practices when encountering one (Mullarkey 2000:49).

Opposing idealist conceptions, Bergson maintained that this memory did not consist of a regression from the present to the past, "but, on the contrary in a progress from the past to the present" (2004:319). The past was not recalled; instead it lived on, making itself present. In Bergson's formative conception of habit memory, this prolongation was a function of adaptive value: only those aspects of the past that were useful or compatible with our present conduct were "remembered" in habit memory. It is a memory that is not concerned with origin (such as our nutritional system remembering our pre-Neolithic past) but can rather be seen to be directed ahead of itself, committing itself to becoming (i.e., as something to be actualized, accomplished), whereas recollection by definition is exclusively directed toward the past (a "looking back"; Casey 1984:281).

This relates to another characteristic of habit memory, which is the difference between its actual and "virtual" level. As exposed earlier, our perception of things by necessity is subtractive. Faced with the "numberless vibrations" of the material world, we need to subtract or shadow substantial parts in order to make some of it appear (see chapter 4; Bergson 2004:27–28, 276). Actual memory involves such a reduction or suppression of the vast virtual level, bringing forth what is situationally relevant. According to Edward Casey, the virtual is a kind of potential or hidden reservoir of action, a *Parathaltung* (holding-in-readiness), which may be activated spontaneously: "It is precisely because of this marginal-yet-available position that so many of these memories arise in an unrehearsed way; we simply snatch them out of the pool of our immediate accessible resources for being-in-the-world in a fully functional way" (1984:283). This larger field is also related to Bergson's somewhat ambiguous conception of a "pure memory" and a "pure past," which condition both recollection and habitual memory (Mullarkey 2000:52). This "pure" past may be regarded as an all-embracing past, the real reservoir for the selective fragments consciously recollected or living on in our practical comportment. These fragments constitute "the tip of an enormous pyramid whose total bulk is the past itself" (Casey 1984:293). Despite the fact that much of it may have ceased to be useful, and maybe never will be actualized as recollections or in habits, it has not ceased to be (Pearson 2002:158, 173–74).

INVOLUNTARY MEMORIES

Another term used by Bergson to describe and define habit memory is "inattentive" recognition, as opposed to the attentive recognition related to "recollective," representational memory (Bergson 2004:89ff.). In much the same way as things withdraw from our attention in the ready-to-hand mode, we are not aware of this memory because it is so embedded in our habitual practices. Habit makes us inattentive to the common world that is simultaneously stored up (cf. Benjamin 1996:468). However, and in a manner similar to Heidegger's description of how the ready-to-hand becomes present-at-hand (cf. chapter 4), attentive memory can be evoked when our routinely based involvement with things is disturbed (Edensor 2005:143ff.; Jones 2007:56–61; Bergson 2004:113). In other words, these are not exclusive forms of memory, but possible modes of remembering (see Joyce 2003:107–8). The memory filling the gap caused by our interrupted programs of action may be conceived of as the virtual or "pure" past actualizing itself (Mullarkey 2000:50–52), reconquering "the influence it has lost" (Bergson 2004:169).

Such interruptions make us aware of experiences forgotten; they accidentally bring back elements of past habitual living. The smell, sound, or touch of a thing may trigger an abrupt flash of memory, a déjà vu, in which the past is revealed to us (cf. Benjamin 1999b:473–76). The difference between this kind of actualization and conscious recollection is its "involuntary" character. It occurs when our habitual, ready-to-hand routines are disrupted, as opposed to willful "voluntary" remembering (the conscious recalling of the past). Such incidences, in which the virtual is made actual, are unpredictable and always involve elements of chance and surprise: "The past is situated somewhere beyond the reach of the intellect and its field of operations, in some material object. . . . And whether we come upon this object before we die, or whether we never encounter it, depends entirely on chance" (Marcel Proust, quoted in Benjamin 2003:315).

This kind of *mémoire involontaire* is masterfully narrated in Proust's work *In Search of Lost Time*, described by Benjamin as the one that puts Bergson's theory "to the test" (2003:315). In the famous madeleine scene, a piece of cake (a *petite madeleine*) and a cup of tea suddenly bring to the present the narrator's childhood in the village of Combray (of which he consciously held only very indistinct memories): "No sooner had the warm liquid mixed with the crumbs touched my palate than a shiver ran through me"(Proust 2003:60). Unable to locate the origin of the sensation felt, the narrator strains his senses recalling it (and also repeating the act), and suddenly the memory reveals itself: his Aunt Léonie offering him tea-soaked madeleine on Sunday mornings. In that very moment all of his childhood's Combray is revealed to him: "The good folk of the village and their little dwellings and the parish church and the whole of Combray and its surroundings, taking shape and solidity, sprang into being, town and gardens alike, from my cup of tea" (64). Later the narrator recalls how

Figure 6.1. "Despite the fact that much of it may have ceased to be useful, and maybe never will be actualized as recollections or in habits, it has not ceased to be." Window ledge assemblage in the abandoned mining town of Pyramiden, Svalbard, Norway (photo: Bjørnar Olsen).

two uneven paving stones trigger the memory of Venice, a napkin reminiscent of Balbec: "I experienced them at the present moment and at the same time in the context of a distant moment, so that the past was made to encroach upon the present and I was made to doubt whether I was in one or the other . . . because they had in them something that was common to a day long past and to the present" (Proust 1999:262).

DURATION AND HABIT MEMORY: RE-MEMBERING THINGS

Central to this theme, of course, is Bergson's conception of time as *duration* (*durée*). Opposing the dominant view of time as the succession of instants, he asserts that the past (and time) appears to us as duration—as sediments constantly piling up (and gradually eroding): "Duration is not merely one instant replacing another; if it were, there would never be anything but the present—no prolonging of the past into the actual, no evolution, no concrete duration. Duration is the continuous progress of the past which gnaws into the future and which swells as it advances" (Bergson 1998:4). Duration may be seen as the material, physical, expression of memory (Olivier 2001:61). The past endures, it accumulates in every becoming "now," making these presents polychronical by definition. As noted by Gilles Deleuze in his *Bergsonism*: "The past and the present do not denote two successive moments, but two elements which coexist: one is the present, which does not cease to pass, and the other is the past, which does not cease to be but through which all presents pass" (1991:59).

In Bergson's exposition of duration, the past is "pressing against" the present, "gnawing" and "swelling" into the future. As noted, this layering of the past in the present is hard to conceive of without things. In the same way as habit memory must be conceived of as a material memory, the duration of the past and the "physiognomy" and reality it thereby acquires in the present is a function of material duration. Duration is the material expression of habit memory. Strangely, though, with the notable exceptions of Proust and the closely kindred project of Benjamin, things themselves seem to be of little explicit interest to those concerned with habit memory. In his discussion of how an organist encounters a new instrument, Maurice Merleau-Ponty relates such memory entirely to the "instantaneous" power of the body, a habitual cultivated potential for movement and actions that can also be rapidly modified to accommodate new (but related) situations (1962:145–47). Even to Bergson, most honor seems ascribed to the motor skills of the human body, thus enabling it to "store up the action of the past" (2004:87).

The body as a matrix of habitual action is clearly decisive for habit memory—in other words, for making the past immanent in the present. However, the whole point is that habitual action would be impossible without things and their facilitating capacities and arrangements. Despite Marcel Mauss's insistence on the pure "techniques of the body" (1979:104), very few techniques or habitual actions unfold or are learned and remembered outside an active engagement with things. Things are fundamentally involved, not only as a means for the action to be completed, but also in making the action and material experience familiar and predictable. Things themselves also assign or "instruct" a certain bodily behavior. They require certain formalized skills to actualize *their* competences (cf. Johansen 1992:112–19). A spear, whether a javelin or hunting spear, sets up its own rules for successful use, although in cooperation with the spear thrower, the prey or target, the ground, the weather, and so on. In Merleau-Ponty's example with the organ player (1962:145–47), it is, of course, not only the trained and clever hands and feet of the organist that matter. His skill can only be implemented by interacting with an organ that is actually *there* and possesses the same familiar qualities as those on which he obtained his skills, to make his actualization and remembering possible.

Neither can the tacit, existential assurance of the past as "incontestable" (cf. Merleau-Ponty 1962:19 and below) be facilitated through bodily dispositions alone. The enduring past is anchored in the accumulating bedrock of materials, in artifacts, streets, and monuments, and in architecture—what Benjamin called "the most binding part of the communal rhythm" (1996:418). This bedrock constitutes a fundamental condition for the repetition and continuation involved in habit memory and is of vital importance to the ontological security that any social being is based on. Contrary to actions, performances, and speech, things *last* (cf. Olivier 2001:65). There are, of course, differences in their duration, but the past still present cannot be accounted for without the lasting and gathering quality of things. Despite temporary discontinuities in human involvement, things *are* and can be approached again and again to be constitutive of new actions and memories (cf. Edensor 2005:150–59). Due to their persistence, the (past) material world is always directed ahead of itself into our present and future. Thus, every becoming present receives a greater share of the past. Also in this sense things are historical.

HOW SOCIETIES REMEMBER

In his book on social memory, Paul Connerton (1989) has convincingly demonstrated how habit memory is an essential aspect of "social memory." Connerton's book became immensely popular in archaeological and anthropological studies of memory and commemorative practices, in part because his notion of incorporating practices fitted well into the emerging discourses on the body and somatic experiencing. Still, as argued throughout this book, the reinstallment of the body in social discourses did not necessarily attest to a more material approach, and the question is if Connerton makes an exception.

Connerton bravely criticizes what he terms a "cognitive imperialism," which has had the dual effect of, on the one hand, privileging inscription and text over habitual memory and, on the other, reducing habitual bodily practices to language and signs (1989:94–104). In historical interpretation, "inscribing practices have always formed the privileged story, incorporating practices the neglected story. . . . The primary objects are canonic texts, and the life of human beings, as a historical life, is understood as a life reported on and narrated, not life as physical existence" (Connerton 1989:100–101). Connerton asserts the importance of bodily practices for memory: "Habit is a knowledge and a remembering in the hands and in the body; and in the cultivation of habit it is our body which 'understands'" (95).

Connerton coins a distinction between two "fundamentally different" ways in which societies "remember," *inscribing* and *incorporating* practices, which are clearly related (but not identical) to the duality of habit memory and recollective (or representational) memory. Inscribing practices are mostly intentional and consist of storing (inscribing) information in a lasting medium such as text, images, and other memory-storing devices from which the past may be recalled. Incorporating practices are both intentional and nonintentional and consist of bodily practices in which cultural norms are *acted* rather than inscribed. This memory is related to bodily performances (he also uses the term "performative" memory), in which "the past is, as it were, sedimented in the body" (Connerton 1989:72). He briefly acknowledges that objects and material structures are also involved in incorporating bodily practices, asserting that "patterns of body use become ingrained through our interaction with objects" (94).

In Connerton's own analysis, things and materials mostly become epiphenomenal to bodily practices (which themselves seem subsumed to cultural norms). In fact, there is an ironic similarity between the way Connerton treats things and the way he claims historical interpretation has treated habit memory. Consider his argument on how the natural sciences have "abducted" the body from hermeneutics and the social sciences:

> The mechanisation of physical reality in the exact natural sciences meant that the body was conceptualised as one object among others in an object-domain made up of moving bodies which obey lawful processes. The body was regarded as a material thing: it was materialised. Bodily practices as such are here lost from view. (1989:101)

Although there may be some truth to this (see chapter 5), Connerton does not extend his concern to the "material thing," which obviously is properly located where he ascribes it (in the "natural" world) and is thus in no need of repatriation. Objects may contribute to the physical scene and setting, but are not "incorporated" themselves into the act of remembering. Connerton continues by arguing the well-established case that habit memory is largely inattentive and based on repetitive (mnemonic) and persistent practices. By contrasting this to inscribing practices, which "by the fact of being inscribed" demonstrate "a will to be remembered," he states, "It is equally true that incorporating practices, by contrast, are *largely traceless* and that, as such, they are *incapable of providing a means by which any evidence of a will to be remembered can be 'left behind.'*" (102, my emphasis). Neither properly inscribed nor properly incorporated, things become insignificant for "how societies remember."

Figure 6.2. **"Things themselves also assign or 'instruct' a certain bodily behavior. They require certain formalized skills to actualize *their* competences." Music studio in the abandoned mining town of Pyramiden, Svalbard, Norway (photo: Bjørnar Olsen).**

Of course, Connerton is right in that habit memory needs to be actualized, practiced, or performed by acting bodies. It is, however, as much a fact that without material spaces, objects, and equipments, the possibility of repetitious action will be erased. It is quite remarkable how little attention archaeologists have paid to this material aspect of memory since, as noted by Lynn Meskell, "this ideally should be our sphere of expertise" (2004:62). Instead, Connerton's utterly problematic notion of incorporation practices (and thus habit memory) as "traceless" seems widely accepted. Ruth Van Dyke and Susan Alcock, for example, claim that "it is easiest for archaeologists to access the inscribed, material end of the spectrum of memory practices" (2003:4), while incorporated practices "are more difficult," leaving at best only "footprints" (4). This acceptance clearly hinges partly on how memory is conceived but also on the common conception of bodily practices, including "techniques of the body," as somehow self-governed and self-sufficient (Connerton 1989:101).

As outlined in this chapter, this asymmetrical conception is hard to sustain. This does not only relate to "simple" techniques and habit memories such as biking, in which the body needs a bike as much as the bike needs a biker. Elaborate political and ritual performances are also always enmeshed with materials enabling the performed conducts, their organization and their (eventual) public reception (see Connerton 1989:86–87; Meskell 2004). Without such "mnemonic" devices, it is hardly conceivable how any incorporating habitual memories could be actualized and remembered. Moreover, the persistency of the material world during periods of discontinuity of human bodily action is also a holding-in-readiness, a material *Parathaltung* for recovering or reenacting bodily memories and the "communal rhythm" (*pace* Benjamin). In other words, incorporating practices are actually as "trace-producing" as inscribing practices—or rather, the "traces" are the material constituents of the bodily remembered.

MATERIALIZING MEMORY

Compared with a conscious recollection of the past, habit memory has formed the neglected story, thus sharing a fate with things, one of its primary constituents. For our day-to-day lived experience, habit memory is probably far more "effective" and often more significant than recollective, attentive memory (cf. Ingold 2000:147–48). Of particular importance is the ontological or existential security that emerges from this memory. As pertinently observed by Merleau-Ponty:

> If the past were available to us only in the form of express recollections, we should be continually tempted to recall it in order to verify its existence; and thus resemble the patient mentioned by Scheler, who was constantly turning round in order to reassure himself that things were really there—whereas in fact we feel it behind us as an incontestable acquisition. (1962:418–19)

This "incontestable acquisition" is manifest in the layers of pastness that make up the present: the landscapes, streets, buildings, interiors, artifacts, and all material surroundings that we encounter every day in a circumspective way. To live with this past and to enact the habit memories it facilitates is an inescapable part of our existence. It is actually a materially "thrown" condition shared by all people throughout history.

The way in which habit memory actualizes the past as something combined and included in my present being-in-the-world may in some sense be compared to Hans-Georg Gadamer's notion of how tradition and "effective history" influence our present horizon and our interpretation of the past (cf. Johnsen and Olsen 1992). In much the same way as the "effective historical" has been of little concern to historians and archaeologists, habit memory also appears to most as "more an obstacle than a resource" (Casey 1984:283)—perhaps obviously, since by resettling the past into the present, it challenges or bypasses the epistemological (and ontological) foundation of historicism and the modern historical inquiry: that of an absent past, the past as gone (Olivier 2008:86).

Defending memory as habit memory is, of course, not a denouncement of other forms of memory. Neither should habit memory be conceptualized as the antithesis of recollective memory, with one excluding the other. As with the relationship between inscribing and incorporating practices, this relationship is intricate and interactive. Moreover, and despite their constitutive role for habit memory, things are also essential to other—conscious—memory practices. The differentiated qualities offered by things are always mediating between customary habits and conscious recollection. In other words, acknowledging the incorporating, habitual significance of things in social remembering by no means denies them a role in aiding cognitive memory. In all societies, there has probably been an ongoing tension or resonance between the inattentive material totality and those features of it that "occur" or "light up" as historical symbols (while simultaneously being a present past). Old buildings, cities, monuments, and rock art may form part of our inattentive, ready-to-hand "world" but may also more or less occasionally call attention to themselves as "signs" of the past—as symbols of ancestors, cultural origins, mythical heroes, and so forth—in short, as "heritage." There is always a potential for attentive recognition in that which is ready-to-hand (cf. Joyce 2003; Edensor 2005:148).

The opposite process is also possible, though far less common. Certain objects or monuments (such as burials and memorials) may have been consciously intended as inscriptions of memory from their very creation, at least as *part* of their rationale. However, even being a product of such inscribing practices does not exclude these things from having or achieving an incorporating role. War memorials are clearly the results of conscious inscribing practices, manifesting a "will to remember," while at the same time clearly facilitating ritualized behavior and repetitious, incorporating practices. Furthermore, the role that things serve in inscribing practices is not entirely prescribed by human purposes and intentions. By their very solidity and enduring nature, materials such as stones call attention to their own potential as an *aide-mémoire*—they "afford" inscribing practices and have throughout history offered their competence as a memory storing device to humans. This mnemonic importance of things is also recognized in classical rhetoric (Yates 1966) and in cabinets of curiosity, as well as in modern museums—which probably represent the utmost technology for such inscribing practices (while increasingly—and in different ways—also acting as instruments of incorporation; cf. Crane 2000).

The materiality of memory is well understood among ordinary peoples as reflected in their care and passion for objects, places, and monuments. It is also evident in the deliberate "care" devoted to destroying and erasing materials associated with "the other" in war and ethnic conflicts (Layton, Stone, and Thomas 2001; Rowlands 2002). This importance of materials for individual and communal memories is clearly recollective in character, although this recollection is mostly (if not always) grounded in a lived, habitual engagement with them. Among modern and "critical" anthropologists, archaeologists, and political scientists, this passion for materials and places is poorly understood (Rowlands 2002:126–31). It is mostly doomed and ridiculed as a reactionary view of culture, at odds with their taken-for-granted celebration of it as extramaterial, fluid, and situational. Within the new master doctrine, such attachments to a past still present become impossible to adequately analyze due to the a priori refusal of the very materiality that this type of social memory is based on (cf. González-Ruibal 2008:254).

CONCLUSION: THE PAST EVER MORE PRESENT

The main thing lesson of this chapter is that the past is not left behind but gathers and folds into the becoming present, enabling different forms of material memory. One effect of the "illness of historicism" is that it made us blind to this very effective history and the potential it constitutes for genuine remembering. Cultural memory is not only an intentional process of recalling a specific past or, even less, of inventing that past. Memory is also habitual and material, a constant act of re-membering embedded in our very being-in-the-world. The past lives on, making itself present. In its "raw" mode, it presses against the present, "gnaws into the future and . . . swells as it advances" (Bergson 1998:4). This past does not comply with the constructivist idea of representing selective or particular versions "captured in a permanent form" (Bradley 2003:223). It accumulates and sediments also according to material trajectories that are beyond human control and willful selection, creating the enormously rich and palimpsestal present we encounter every day.

Maybe more than any other discipline, archaeology has the potential to cure the illness of historicism. Contrary to the popular romantic trope, archaeologists do not discover the past, but rather work on the past that *is* in the present (Shanks 2007:591). This material past does not manifest itself as linear texts or historical sequences. As Colin Renfrew rightly argued, the archaeological site is truly *mixed*, "consisting of a palimpsest of structures and rubbish pits, constructed and deposited at different periods" (1989:36; see chapter 3). What the *excavating* archaeologist encounters is always a set of hybridized conditions such as mixed layers, superimposed structures, artifacts, stones, soil, and bones mixed together—in short, sites that object to modernity and historicism's wished-for ideal of completeness, order, and purified time. However, rather than actively using this material record to challenge historicism, the opted-for solutions have nearly always been to purify this entangled mess and to reassemble the entities to conform to the expectation of linear time and narrative history. Time is not allowed to be mixed and hybridized but has to be cleansed and sequenced, in short, "unlocked." Through ever more fine-grained dating methods and advanced stratigraphical and typological sequencing, prehistoric settlements and sites are cut into increasingly thinner slices of time, cleansing them from the historical conditions that grounded these presents.

It may be argued that this purifying practice is nothing but a necessary reversal of the destructive transformational process that the archaeological record has undergone. Thus, what we have left is the distorted impression of "compressed" time; that beyond and prior to the exposed entangled mess, there is a historical order to be restored, a pure temporal specificity. This argument may sound convincing but should be tested by exploring how it plays out in its own time. How would such temporal slicing work when applied to sites such as London, Rome, or Tromsø? To which age does Rome belong? How do we identify the *contemporary* London, the present? By excluding all entities that are more than ten, fifty, or one hundred years old? What would be left of this site, in fact any site, if we applied such a rigorous chronological approach? In any case, what we would have lost is that which makes these sites what they are: the outcome of a gathering past constantly conditioning the conduct of the present. In this sense, the palimpsestal archaeological record is providing a far more realistic and accurate image of the past than any historical narrative. As argued by Laurent Olivier: "Each of the moments of the past is indeed necessarily multi-temporal, since the present spontaneously becomes fossilised in being transformed; at any time, the present is made up of an accumulation of all the previous states whose successions have built this present 'as it is now'" (Olivier 2001:66). In order to realize the potential of this "thinging," past things themselves must be emancipated from their synchronous imprisonment, allowing for the "monstrous" thought, "that things themselves have a history" (Latour 1993:70). This is just another way of saying that we must release them from the conceptual stepladder of disconnected historical worlds, the monotemporal imperative based on the seductive idea that what is rendered contemporary by the calendar necessarily belongs to the same time (Latour 1993:73). In their own being, things are "polychronic, multi-temporal, and [reveal] a time that is gathered together, with multiple pleats" (Serres 1995b:60).

The past superimposes itself on the present as things, bodies, habits, and thoughts, as "incontestable acquisitions" that (*pace* Merleau-Ponty) prevent any desire to constantly "look back." Thus, history is not a projected stream leaving the past behind but bends and twists in a disorderly manner, interrupting the expectations of the "have been" and the becoming. The past proliferates more than ever in the present. It sediments and swells more and more, and if there is a distinction between the historical "rootedness" of previous pasts and the present, it is, as Bergson would have said, one of degree (or scale) rather than of kind. We repeat the past differently by making our collectives larger and more inclusive than ever—in other words, by receiving an increasingly greater share of the past; a difference created by the intrinsic capacity of the material world to *tenku* and *þinga*.

7

Living with Things
Matter in Place

> As soon as you believe social aggregates can hold their own being propped up by "social forces," then objects vanish from the view and the magical and tautological force of society is enough to hold *everything* with, literally, *no thing.*
>
> —Bruno Latour, *Reassembling the Social*

We are often met by anthropological—and archaeological—claims asserting that the world is "culturally constituted," that the meanings of things are always "culturally relative," and that variations in material culture itself stem from things being imbued with this cultural difference. Such claims seem grounded in a notion of culture as somehow "prior" to or detached from matter, that cultures and peoples "already different" approach the material world in unique ways, causing the variety of material expressions and meanings. Clearly, people around the world relate to materials in different ways and ascribe specific meanings to things, and myriads of material realities are being produced. The question, however, is whether this difference is a product of different mentalities, ideologies, or "cultures" that approach the material world in "culturally" specific ways (cf. Hodder 2004:36; Meskell 2004:2–3; Preucel 2006:257). Or is it, rather, a question of different ways of living with things, of linking (or combining) humans and nonhumans in countless hybridities without assigning any a priori precedence to who—to what—causes this difference?

The latter position is being explored in this chapter, which deals specifically with this linking: how human life is "always-already" blending with things, forming innumerable interacting hybrid units and collectives.

Here I shall discuss various theoretical approaches that deal with this blurring, focusing on the work of various scholars but with a particular emphasis on actor-network theory (cf. Latour 2005). I shall use some of these insights to explore alternative ways of understanding our living with things. Although closely related to chapter 4, this chapter is more "analytically" concerned with *collectives* (societies, cultures) and what things actually contribute to such formations. First, though, I shall once more return to phenomenology and the work of Maurice Merleau-Ponty to briefly explore an important turn in his thing-body ontology.

MERLEAU-PONTY ON THINGS AND THE LIMITS OF THE BODY

Despite the fact that things play a rather subordinate role in most of the works of Merleau-Ponty, they increasingly became a matter of more direct concern to him. In *The Phenomenology of Perception*, the thing-body theme is given a somewhat brief and straightforward consideration, possibly because the primacy of the human body is taken for granted. Things emerge as an elaboration, perfection, or extension of bodily functions, that is, as artificial substitutes. While "the body is our general medium for having a world," it cannot accomplish all desired tasks: "Sometimes, finally, the meaning aimed at cannot be achieved by the body's natural means; it must then build itself an instrument" (Merleau-Ponty 1962:146).

Discussing the way we "instinctively" adjust our actions to create a "fit" between our body with its adjuncts and the material world, Merleau-Ponty uses the well-known example of the blind man's stick (cf. Malafouris 2008). The stick becomes an extension of the body, not an object in and of itself. By being used, this instrument has become an extrasensory organ that extends the radius of the blind man's touch. To familiarize oneself with such instruments or items "is to be transplanted into them, or conversely, to incorporate them into the bulk of our own body" (Merleau-Ponty 1962:143).

In his last, unfinished work, *The Visible and the Invisible*, Merleau-Ponty develops this theme by taking a more radical ontological position. Theoretical thinking and philosophy, including his own phenomenology, had long taken for granted a radical distinction between the experiencing self and the experienced world. They had attained a spectator attitude of which the "transcendental subject" was the quintessence (Merleau-Ponty 1968:200; Matthews 2002:161–65). He now insists that even to speak of "subjects" and "objects" implies a gap between them, such that the relation between them can only be that of contemplation. The concept of being-in-the-world has more radical implications: it is not at all talk of a relation between ourselves and our world, since our own being cannot be separated from that of the world we inhabit (Matthews 2002:160–61). Resembling Henri Bergson's postulate on the kinship between matter and perception (their difference is only a "difference of degree and not of kind"), Merleau-Ponty now brings out a notion of "inter-subjectivity" and claims a "coincidence" between the perceiver and what we perceive. Seeing is possible because I have some kinship with what I see; the "visible" is a common property to us, making me both something seeing and something to be seen:

> He who looks must not himself be foreign to the world he looks at. As soon as I see, it is necessary that the vision . . . be doubled with a complementary vision or with another vision: myself seen from without, such as another would see me, installed in the midst of the visible. . . . He who sees cannot possess the visible unless he is possessed by it, unless he *is of it*. (Merleau-Ponty 1968:134–35, emphasis in original)

En passant, it can be noticed that the ontology of reciprocity grounding this conception of the visible provides a rarely noticed link between Merleau-Ponty's work and that of Walter Benjamin. Benjamin's notions of the aura of things and the ability to relate mimetically to things were grounded in a view that involved both a respect for things' difference and the acknowledgement of them as fellow beings with their own "integrity" and intrinsic capacities. Quoting from one of his rare attempts at actually describing aura and what the auratic experience consists of gives an idea of how well Benjamin's conception complies with Merleau-Ponty's late thing ontology: "To experience the aura of an object we look at means to invest it with the ability to look back at us" (Benjamin 2003:338). In other words, relating to things in a mimetic way is to expect the return of your gaze and to acknowledge the symmetry of the experience.

According to Merleau-Ponty, the mutual "presentness" of people and things is grounded in our common being as tangible, as "flesh":[1] "the thickness of the flesh between the seer and the thing is constitutive for the thing of its visibility as for the seer of his corporeity; it is not an obstacle between them, it is their means of communication" (1968:135). As a carnal being, my body is what connects me with things; it is the means by which I grasp and affect the world and the way I myself can be grasped and affected. As beings of a tactile world, there must be a close relationship and correspondence between my body, my movements, and things:

> This can happen only if my hand, while it is felt from within, is also accessible from without, itself tangible . . . if it takes its place among the things it touches, is in a sense one of them, opens finally upon a tangible being of which it is also a part. Through this crisscrossing within it of the touching and the tangible,

its own movements incorporate themselves into the universe they interrogate, are recorded on the same map as it; the two systems are applied upon one another, as the two halves of an orange. (Merleau-Ponty 1968:133)

Heidegger once asked if the thing "never yet had come near enough for man to learn how to attend sufficiently to the thing as thing" (1971:169). Merleau-Ponty's last work can be seen as responding to this claim to "nearness" by exploring the "crude" experience of being in direct contact with things—a wild, uncultivated, and barbarian experience. We can touch and be touched, see and be seen, act upon things and at the same time be acted upon by them. Being flesh among flesh, the limit between the body and the world breaks down: "Where are we to put the limit between the body and the world, since the world is flesh?" (Merleau-Ponty 1968:138). Similarly to Benjamin, Merleau-Ponty talks about "the pact" between us and things, the *intertwining* and the *chiasm* (the intersection or crossover):

This bursting forth of the mass of the body towards the things, which makes a vibration of my skin become the sleek and the rough, makes me *follow with my eyes* the movements and the contours of the things themselves, this magical relation, this pact between them and me according to which I lend them my body in order that they inscribe upon it and give me their resemblance. (1968:146)

According to Merleau-Ponty, the experience of things is a "full," bodily experience that cannot be accomplished by contemplation or by putting in parentheses our ordinary and entangled cohabitation with them. Through our shared "physiognomy," our body brings us in direct contact with things; it "bring[s] us to the things themselves, which are themselves not flat beings but beings in depth, inaccessible to a subject that would survey them from above, open to him alone that . . . would coexist with them in the same world" (Merleau-Ponty 1968:136). Although in many respects very different, here one can also see a link between Merleau-Ponty's thing ontology and the "direct perception" proposed by James Gibson (1986). To Gibson, things present themselves to us in an unmediated way and "to perceive the world is to co-perceive oneself" (141).

Merleau-Ponty's late phenomenology was an attempt to explore the "inter-subjectivity" between humans and things as an ontological grounding for experience itself. Our being in the world can never be purely cognitive or contemplative; it is a situation of active involvement with things as well as with other human beings. By necessity, our bodily dealing with things is a situated experience that is both positioned and directional. This, however, does not lead to the conclusion that our experience of place is necessarily relative to the position and orientation of the body (cf. Tilley 1994; Casey 1998:237; see chapters 2 and 4). Things appear to us not only from where we are but also from where *they* are and from *what* they are (e.g., as stones, cars, mountains, prisons, refugee places, and so on). Things' positions, importance, and power are thus not only relative to our own being in the world. Our "inter-subjectivity" is precisely that—inter-subjective—distributing responsibility and significance far more evenly among humans and nonhumans.

PEOPLE WITHOUT THINGS

Despite always-already being "thrown" into direct and entangled co-habitations with things, our intellectual life is characterized by totally opposite forces of gravity struggling to pull us apart. This ontological "fission" of the world is justified by insisting that beneath the messy surface the old divide still rules, that every hybrid is "a mixture of two pure forms" (Latour 1993:78). Moreover, it is justified by insisting that by applying sufficient amounts of suspicious hermeneutics, this authentic rifted bedrock will shine through. As argued above (see chapter 5), these processes of distancing and purification have stigmatized our thingly life as primitive, fetishized, and constrained. Defining freedom and emancipation as that which escapes the material, modern ideology and morality effectively obstructed a sincere concern with matter. Actually, as claimed by Bruno Latour in one of his vivid moments, many seem to think they would be better off without it: "Without a body they would roam through the cosmos with better ease . . . without instruments and artefacts, colleagues and laboratories, they would know more; without prostheses and machinery they would be freed and emancipated—soul, only soul" (2002:140–41; cf. Latour 1993:137–38).

One outcome of this purifying process is that the subject matter of the social sciences has largely become cleansed of nature and things. People, at least under their ideal "social" condition, largely come unequipped. In "agency theory," methodological individualism, and various "objectivist" social theories, the agent that constitutes such an essential component of social life is rarely supplied with more than intentions and a rather unspecified capacity to "act." Regardless of creating, opposing, or being determined by "structures," the proposed dichotomies between actor and structure, individual and society, facilitate this purification. There is no room for composite beings *already* mixed and networked, since such hybrids would blur the regime of oppositional distinctions.

Likewise, the craving for the subject, the individual or the "self," as witnessed frequently in archaeology and anthropology, seems grounded in the assumed existence of monadic and noncyborgian historical agents.

From this zero-degree position as naked hominids, they *enter into* relationships with things and each other. Personhood, selves, or collective identities never emerge *from* mixtures. (See Thomas 2000:148–52 for a critical discussion.) In this scenario, things are somehow prelocated on the "other side" as something the intentional subject relates to, becomes engaged with, or "brings close" through the processes of objectification, embodiment, sublation, and so forth. Thus, it follows logically that the claimed core activity of archaeological interpretation, the "getting at people" (Gamble 2001:73), is to reach the Indian *behind* the artifact (cf. chapter 2). As John Barret has argued, within this ontology agency is reduced "to an isolated being whose actions are *represented* by the archaeological record. That is to say, archaeology seeks the individual whose actions have *resulted in a material trace*" (2000:61, my emphasis).

Needless to say, within their respective "natural" fields of scientific inquiry, nature and matter are produced in a similar vein without any social and human dimension (Lee and Stenner 1999). This regime of split knowledge, as evidenced in (and reproduced by) the prevailing linguistic repertoire of binary oppositions (nature-culture, technology-society, body-soul, matter-mind, human-machine, etc.), still constitutes the major principle facilitating our academic division of labor. Through its own peculiar sedimentation and very effective history, it constantly produces self-justification by separating the natural from the social, the social from the natural. As Knut Sørensen remarks, "there is nothing innocent with these dichotomies. They produce fences between different forms of knowing and enforce on the social sciences a kind of collective amnesia in relation to nature and things" (2004:21, my translation).

To be sure, technology and nature are not absent in social discourses and theory. However, when paid attention to, it is mostly through some prescribed arrangement of antithesis or opposites—such as technology versus society, nature versus culture, or objectification versus humanism—that invites thinking in terms of simplistic cause-effect relationships, determinism, constraints, and so on (cf. chapter 5). Things, technology, and nature oppose, determine, or enclose the social world; they are not integrated parts of it. (cf. Lee and Stenner 1999:94–95). As claimed by Joerges: "The social sciences have no concepts for dealing with technology because they have no concepts for things and tangible events in general. They have left the world of matter and tissues . . . to the natural and engineering sciences, and they have constructed themselves a world of actors devoid of things" (1988:220). Although Joerges's assertion in some respects still holds water in terms of the general attitude in mainstream social science, approaches that account for a more liberal and inclusive conception of society and agency have emerged. In what follows, I shall explore what they have to offer.

EXTENDED PERSONS, COMPOUND INTERACTORS

A much-referred-to approach is to be found in the writings of art anthropologist Alfred Gell, especially in his posthumously published book
Art and Agency (1998). Here he boldly speaks against the canonized
conception of art as a system of signification to be approached through
textual or linguistic analogies. He rejects the idea that art and things in
general should be conceived of as a means of communication—as a way
of expressing meaning. A purely aesthetic, "appreciative" approach to
art is also denounced as "an anthropological dead end" (Gell 1998:5). All
material expressions, art objects included,[2] are rather about *doing*, and we
should be concerned with "exploring the domain in which objects merge
with people" (Gell 1998:12; N. Thomas 1998:ix). Despite traditional claims
to the opposite, things and works of art are never individual: "They come
in families, lineages, tribes, whole populations—just like people. They
have relations with each other as well as with peoples who create and
circulate them as individual objects. They marry, so to speak, and beget
offspring which bear the stamp of their antecedents" (Gell 1998:153).
Contrary to mainstream versions of action theory based on the intentionality of *agency* (in other words, the idea that agency is reserved for intentional human beings while things can only exercise physical causation),
Gell is concerned precisely with *things'* agency: how things affect and
relate to people as well as mediate relationships between people (Gell
1998:19). By redefining agency as "relational and context-dependent," he
attempts to emancipate the concept from any classificatory and essentialist grounding (22). Agency is about *doing*—the interactive relationship
between entities—and not a rare commodity of which only humans have
possession. This relational and transitive character of agency is opera-
tionalized through what Gell calls a "patient." Every agent relates to a
"patient," and this relationship delegates and defines agency. A car can
be my patient, responding to my will and intentions, while at the same
time the operation of the car turns me into a patient of the car. Thus, a
patient is a potential agent that can turn the former agent into a patient. It
follows that things, humans, gods, animals, and so on all have the capacity of agency (Gell 1998:21–22).

Even if human agency is "primary," it is always carried out within a
material world; intentional action would be impossible without things. It
can only become effective by delegating tasks to material operators. With
the exclusivity of agency removed, the sovereignty of the human subject
itself cannot be sustained. Relating his claim to Wagner's (1991) notion of
"fractal personhood" and Strathern's (1988) "partible" or "distributed"
persons, Gell maintains that the organic confinement of the human subject has to be blurred. Using the example of Pol Pot's soldiers, he shows

how their personhood or identities were extended or "distributed" to domains outside their bodies. Mines, guns, and instruments of torture were as much a part of their identities as soldiers as the emotional hate and fear that inspired their actions:

> A soldier is not just a man, but a man with a gun, or a case with a box of mines to sow. The soldier's weapons are *parts* of him which make him what he is. We cannot speak of Pol Pot's soldiers without referring, in the same breath, to their weaponry, and the social context and military tactics which the possession of such weapons implies. . . . Pol Pot's soldiers possessed (like all of us) . . . "distributed personhood." As agents, they were not just where their bodies were, but in many different places (and times) simultaneously. (1998:20–21)

Using a more trivial example, a fisherman is not just a person, a human body equipped with a mind. Using his boat, sonar, and instruments, he places his nets at many locations along the seascape. The boat, nets, and other gear, as well as the waves, seascape, and fish, are all components of his blurred identity. The nets continue to act—to fish—without his presence, as do the traps for the hunter and the fields and herds for the farmer. Identities and personhoods are dispersed in time and space, and the exercise of agency is also dispersed and cannot be confined to one privileged category of actors. This also puts into question the nostalgia of getting at the people behind things. People, the Indians included, do not occupy positions *behind* things (through which they may be accessed). People become human by living with and uniting with things. Their identity emerges from mixtures to which, of course, they bring their share, but that according to Gell cannot be accounted for in isolation.

While this aspect of Gell's work is well-known in archaeology (cf. Meskell 2004; Knappett 2005; Jones 2007; Knappett and Malafouris 2008), the fact that a closely related conception of relational (and extended) agency is developed within the discipline itself seems actually less acknowledged. Even if cast in a very different intellectual and conceptual environment, Michael Schiffer's notion of *compound interactors* (1999) can be treated as being akin to Gell's distributed persons (in addition to aspects of network theory discussed below). Defining *material* as all phenomena exhibiting materiality, three major families are recognized by Schiffer: people, artifacts, and "externs," the latter defined as "phenomena that arise independently of people, like sunlight and clouds, wild plants and animals, rocks, landforms"[3] (1999:13). More original however is his conceptual (and ontological) treatment of these categories. Rather than starting from the traditional ontology emphasizing their difference, Schiffer is concerned with their similarity, particularly their shared capacity for interacting. Thus the term *interactor* is used to denote them collectively. Additionally, these interactors gather and combine "in various ways to form *compound*

Figure 7.1. "A fisherman is not just a person, a human body equipped with a mind." Cod fishing, Lofoten, Norway, 1956 (photo: NTB/Scanpix).

interactors, which tend to interact as a single unity" (Schiffer 1999:13, emphasis in original). A factory, a farm, or a fishing boat with its crew of humans and gear are all examples of such "compound interactors."

The notion that each compound interactor acts as a single unit is of course just a partial truth. Even the framing of such mixed and distributed unities are blurred, as there are always "leakages" and points of transmission to other units that create long and complex networks (cf. Callon 1999). Opening up to heterogeneous networks, the interacting unit is not only the boat, the crew, the gears, the water, and resources—it is also other crews, economies, exports, legal sanctions, national and foreign politics, bilateral agreements, researchers, research funding, and so on (Holm 2000). These networks and possible links in principle are infinite, which at the same time forces us to create some graspable analytical units to avoid being swallowed by a totalizing, invisible world system of relations (cf. Harman 2002:32–34).

ACTOR-NETWORK THEORY

This seems to be an appropriate time to bring in the approach or theory known as *actor-network theory* (ANT).[4] One of its goals is to address the fallacies of the oversocialized conception of man and society. Technology, things, science, and nature are not "extra" to society—that is, they are not elements of an outside reality that causes something to happen in this authentically pure social environment (or vice versa). Neither is society itself an embracing container or structuring a priori to which all individual actions may be anchored (and projected toward). A society is rather a complex fabric of intimate relations that link and associate people and things—in short, a collective in which humans and nonhumans cohabitate and collaborate. As noted by Latour, "society is not what holds us together, it is what is held together" (1986:276).

According to John Law, network theory may be understood as "a *semiotics of materiality*. It takes the semiotic insight, that of the relationality of entities, the notion that they are produced in relations, and applies this ruthlessly to all materials—and not simply to those that are linguistic" (Law 1999:4; Latour 1987, 1993, 1999b, 2005; Callon and Law 1997; Law and Hassard 1999; Law and Mol 2002; Sørensen 2004). Instead of reducing the world to a regime of the two opposed ontological realms of culture and nature, this approach claims that nearly everything happens between the two extremes by way of mediation and translation and by heterogeneous networks linking all kinds of materials and entities. Reality is not to be found in essences, but rather in imbroglios and mixtures, the seamless and rhizomelike fabrics of culture and nature that link humans and nonhumans in intimate relationships. It is a democratic and inclusive regime, in which everything can become actors (or *actants*[5]) by being included in a network and assigned properties to act. It is a regime that cares for hybrids and those hybrid relations that other systems (be it social or natural) have largely ignored. Thus, humans and things are not defined by oppositions, by dualities or negativities, but by their relations, collaboration, and coexistence. They exchange energy, properties, and competence, and the functioning of what we call "society" depends on this interaction.

ANT approaches differ from social-constructivist and essentialist thinking (and their epistemologies and ontologies) by rejecting any a priori precedence given either to the social (or cultural) or to the natural (or material). As noted by Bendik Bygstad and Knut Rolland (2004:70), they instead may be characterized by their attempts at developing concepts and interpretations that acknowledge an analytical share of significance and influence between humans and things. Paying much more attention to things than was hitherto common does not leave us with an antihuman perspective. Rather, it may be seen as a way of bringing back a more complete human, an impossible task unless the "other part of itself, the share of things, is restored to it" (Latour 1993:136). However, as little as we are dealing with people in the normal humanist conception of them (as safely placed at the cultural side of the great divide), are we dealing with an object-world placed at the other extreme as "hard" nature. Neither do things conform to the revisionist conception of them as always transcendent and plastic, as nothing but culturally constituted sites of inscription.

According to ANT, what we are living with are rather *quasi-objects*, hybrids of cultures-natures produced by and within networks of relations. Things conceived of in this way actually recall the assembling and "thinging" quality assigned to them in the late works of Heidegger (1971:179; cf. chapter 4). Precisely because they gather and link, things are hybrids, or quasi-objects, which makes them feel alien in the rifted topography of Cartesian thinking. Thus, caring for their hybrid and mediating identity implies avoiding the common temptation of trapping them into the either/or logic of modern scholarship:

> Quasi-objects are much more social, much more fabricated, much more collective than the "hard" parts of nature, but they are in no way arbitrary receptacles of a full-fledged society. On the other hand, they are much more real, nonhuman and objective than those shapeless screens on which society—for unknown reasons—needed to be projected. (Latour 1993:54)

STABILIZATION AND TRANSLATION

Things play an immensely important and indispensable role in making society possible as a relational and hybrid collective. Without them, institutions and structures would simply not exist; *then* Marx's diagnosis of modern society as a society in which "all that is solid melts into air" would have come through. Things enable and *stabilize* society (Johansen 1992). When we wake up the next morning, we do not have to start all over again, redoing all arrangement, reinventing communities, or worrying if the world is there. Everything is (normally) there as an "incontestable acquisition" (*pace* Merleau-Ponty). In other words, we rely upon things, "taking them for granted as that naïve landscape on which even our most jaded and cynical schemes unfold" (Harman 2002:20). Imagining a social world beyond things is just that—imagination.

What we refer to as *social structures* and *institutions* are products of a continuous interchange and mixing between humans and nonhumans; and for structures to become structured, institutions to become institutionalized, a means of stability and solidity is needed (Latour 1999b:198, 2005:35, 67–70). Michel Serres catches this point in his characteristically vivid and uncompromising way:

> The only assignable difference between animal societies and our own resides, as I have often said, in the emergence of the object. Our relationships, social bonds, would have been airy as clouds were there only contracts between subjects. In fact, the object, specific to the Hominidae, stabilizes our relationships, it slows down the time of our revolutions. For an unstable band of baboons, social changes are flaring up every minute. . . . The object, for us, makes history slow. (Serres 1995a:87; cf. Latour 2005:69–70)

Thus, the emergence of a recognizable structure or institution requires not only a network of relations between entities, but also qualities of stability, concreteness, and security—in other words—things. Through our interchange with things, our habits and actions become standardized and predicable, producing what we like to think of as (social) structures and institutions. Without the tangibility and persistency of things, these structures will erode (Sørensen 2004:10; see also Durkheim 1951:313–14; Arendt 1958:137).

Consider the example of the nation. This is often referred to as an "imagined community," a social construction based on an imagined bond or communion living in the minds of a vast number of otherwise unrelated individuals (cf. Anderson 1983). Even if undoubtedly a *construction*, both the construction site and the building materials are far less porous and airy than previously imagined. The nation and the nation-state could not have been invented or constructed without the hard work performed by innumerable nonhuman agents such as print machines, newspapers, telephone and railroad lines, roads, coastal steamers, geological surveys, post offices, national museums, stamps, maps, trigonometric points, border fences, and custom points. Without the help of these nonhuman volunteers, these imaginations, ideas, and institutions would, to requote Serres, have been as "airy as clouds."

To the degree things are paid attention to in studies of nationalism and nation building, they are primarily as symbolic representations (flags, maps, costumes, songs, parades, museums, monuments)—in other words, as sites of inscription and embodiment. Akin to the dominant trope of conceiving of artifacts within consumption studies (cf. chapter 2), the importance of artifacts derives from their eventual suitability for external- izing and objectifying the nation. In short, similarly to the way people ap- propriate things to create a sense of individuality, the nation uses common symbols to carve out its own collective identity. These representational objects (and associated practices) are, however, only credited a derivative or residual role in this activity. As with other notions of embodiment (see chapter 2), the primacy of the social (and the social/material split) seems to be taken for granted. However, as noted by Latour:

> If religion, art and styles are necessary to "reflect," "reify," "materialize," "embody" society—to use some of the social theorists' favorite verbs—then are objects not, in the end, its co-producers? Is not society built literally—not metaphorically—of gods, machines, sciences, arts and styles? . . . Maybe so- cial scientists have simply forgotten that before projecting itself on to things society has to be made, built, constructed? And out of what material could it be built if not out of nonsocial, nonhuman resources? (1993:54)

More attention thus needs to be drawn to the concrete and steel, the nuts and bolts involved in a nation's construction, the brigades of nonhu- man actors that constitute the very condition of the possibility for such large-scale social institutions to be imagined, implemented, reproduced, and remembered. Even if purely an imagination initially, the imagined bond—in other words, the distribution and transport of imaginations and feelings—would have been impossible without things, not to mention the subsequent implementation of the nation-state. Thus, the imagination of the nation and the later *stabilization* of it as a structure and institution would be "unimaginable" without such *translations* and translators. Ideas, thoughts, feelings, and actions are translated, distrib- uted, and mediated. In accordance with Gell's and Marilyn Strathern's suggestions, social relation and actions involve a vast amount of human and nonhuman interactors that work together in a coordinated or pro- grammed way (Sørensen 2004:16). To study "social relations" is to inves- tigate what happens within such heterogeneous networks, a work that cannot be conducted if society is purified as idealized relations between peoples-without-things.

COOPERATION, OR YOU'LL NEVER WALK ALONE

Even if one accepts that humans are prime movers in action, that axes are made by people while people are not made by axes, the implementation

Figure 7.2. "To act is to mobilize an entire company of actors." Launching a small actor company, West Greenland, ca. 1906 (unknown photographer; Heims's collection).

of their will and goals could not happen without the delegation, transformation, and swapping of properties with nonhuman actors. To act is to mobilize an entire company of actors in which "the prime mover of an action becomes a new, distributed, and nested series of practices that may be possible to add up but only if we respect the mediating role of all the actants mobilized in the series" (Latour 1999b:181).

In many ways, ANT involves a decentering that is more radical than the poststructuralist slogan (confining the leveling mostly to humans). As argued by Nick Lee and Paul Stenner, it avoids the mode of analysis that, given the observation that "something is done," immediately starts the inquiry "who did it." Such centered approaches seek to identify some responsible figure(s) or cause(s): "he did it"; "the drought did it"; "the new world view did it" (Lee and Stenner 1999:92). Even if network theory is capable of giving an account of how centeredness may arise (i.e., by processes of black-boxing and translation, see below), it does away with the origin-of-action trajectory. Also, in cases in which a "prime mover" is identified, "the centeredness of agentic responsibility is distributed into a dispersed network of interdependencies and co-responsibilities" (Lee and Stenner 1999:93).

The urgent need for bringing in the "missing masses" (Latour 1992) may be illustrated by this trivial but still axiomatic example: Some years ago a Norwegian adventurer who had skied across the Antarctic published his account as "Alone to the South Pole" (Kagge 1993), vigorously advertised as the story of "the first solo and unsupported expedition to the South Pole." When you start to ponder these claims to sovereignty and mastery (Alone? Solo? Unsupported?), you soon discover that it actually was a whole company of actors crossing the Antarctic. Skis and a sledge were delegated the task of helping him move and carry his other indispensable equipment; producers of extreme-condition clothing had provided him with wind-proof and warm clothes, sleeping bag, and tent; his need for high-protein nutrition was covered by his carefully selected freeze-dried food; and sponsors and the media had given him the ability to obtain all this. And how could anyone unsupported and solo navigate across the vast interior anyway? Generations of mapmakers, former explorers, satellites, and navigators all helped him along the way.

When all the honor and fame is once again claimed by a single actor, it also illustrates another, paradoxical, finding of ANT: when networks stabilize—in other words, when their thingy components become massive and indispensable—important parts of their functioning become hidden ("black-boxed"), and the focus is directed toward one or a few actors that receive all the rewards and fame for the work done by those sweating on the assembly lines (Latour 1987, 1999b). What happened on the Antarctic ice shelf was in fact a typical example of collective action, "an action that collects different types of forces woven together because they are different" (Latour 2005:74). What Erling Kagge should actually be credited for, apart from his stamina and strength, is his ability to translate and delegate and thus uniting the different forces into a well-travelled collective—in other words, into a "compound interactor" (*pace* Schiffer). Thus, even in the Antarctic, you'll never walk alone.

IN SMALL THINGS FORGOTTEN?

Let us consider a well-known archaeological example. In his famous book *In Small Things Forgotten*, James Deetz discusses important changes that took place in the colonies along the eastern seaboard of North America from the second half of the eighteenth century onward. In his masterful dealing with material culture he shows a clear tendency: the communal, common, and heterogeneous were losing ground to the individual and ordered. This production of a society that increasingly cared for personhood, privacy, purity, and order is identified in a number of changes taking place in burial practices, architecture, furniture, ceramics, and eating habits. For instance, the communal infrastructure of eating was replaced by individual plates and cutlery and by individual chairs for people to sit on around the dinner table. As this took place, congested communal burial grounds were gradually replaced by small, individual family graveyards. Increasingly, houses were symmetrically organized and divided into separate rooms, with public and private spaces separated. Bunks were replaced by beds. Clothes became increasingly differentiated as people acquired personal effects, chamber pots, musical instruments, books, and so on. Deetz nicely summarizes: "Gone now is the older, corporate emphasis, wherein sharing of technomic objects was the norm. In its place we see a one-to-one match, with each person probably having his own plate and chamber pot. . . . Balance and greater importance of the individual characterize this new view of life" (1977:59–60). These material changes reflect an accommodation to a new conception of the world and the individual's place within it, "an expression of a newly emergent world view characterized by order, control, and balance" (Deetz 1977:60).

Deetz saw this as an *idea* of order, individuality, and privacy being carved out and embodied in solid materials—in other words, he believed that a mental concept existed prior to (and consequently was the cause for) its material realization. As he outlines in relation to housing in a later work (with Patricia Scott Deetz), "Vernacular architecture is not made with plans, but is rather the idea of what a house should be like that is carried in the minds of the people and passed down through the generations by word of mouth and by example. . . . Houses don't change, but ideas do" (Deetz and Deetz 2001:173; cf. Deetz 1977:36, 43, 127). Thus, what the changes in burials, houses, refuse, ceramics, cutlery, and furniture really tell us, "in ways great or small," is about a change in the American way of thinking. This change, Deetz asserts, "must have been at a very deep level of the Anglo-American mind, since it is so abstract as to manifest itself on the surface in so many different ways. The entire social order must have been similarly affected" (1977:127). From its deep cognitive location this originary force of change subsequently migrates to things and practices on the surface. In this scheme, things become *intermediaries* that faithfully execute this change, and as such constitute trustworthy sources to recall it, but are themselves assigned little causality or effects on "what happened" (cf. Latour 2005:39–40).

Deetz's identification of a founding level (the Anglo-American mind) is an example of the way archaeologists and scientists themselves conduct *translation* in a very specific way, how science creates its objects (Callon 1986; Latour 1987). This is a work that transforms heterogeneous relations and hybrid materials into a few situated and acting agents that cause and explain whatever happens (Johnsen 2004:50–51). Drawing on the vast resources provided by an effective history of dual thinking (including depth-surface models; cf. Thomas 2004:149ff.), complex and interacting networks are transformed into a relationship between mind (active, prior, depth) and material (passive, residual, surface). One telling expression of how this works is Deetz's assumption that the more widespread the changes are and the more heterogeneous the materials involved in them, the deeper in the mind we have to dig to find the originating and structuring *langue* (1977:127). Deep down, a hidden center (the Anglo-American mind) is conducting "action at a distance," affecting the shape and being of another punctuated agent, the social order, and in turn the material residues of this order.

Within an actor-network perspective, the emphasis on a "prior" mental template or worldview becomes far less important than the "how to." How could a subject-centered society emerge? How could a new order become effective and stable? How many different types of actors were gathered and what culture-natures were mobilized in creating this new order? Instead of any central hero subjects—human, worldview, mind—we should envisage a brigade of actors: plates, forks, gravestones, humans, garbage pits, houses, food, chamber pots, law books, musical instruments, and so on acting together. In each settlement these entities joined forces, acting as "compound interactors." While things in Deetz's scheme act as intermediaries, which obediently transport meaning without transformation, they should rather be conceived of as *mediators*: as innumerous interactors that transform, translate, distort, and modify (Latour 2005:39–40). Through processes of delegation and translation forming many and complex hybrid relations, these mediators effectuated and over time stabilized a new social configuration. They made new bodily practices necessary and prescribed new programs of action. Any mental conception of the individual, the private, and the pure may as well be seen as the outcome of these programs rather than their cause (cf. Olsen 1997:211–16). In any event, such conceptions would have been "airy as clouds" without the collaboration of material actors, creating innumerous webs also ranging far beyond each local community. Thus, and not without a certain irony, the individual was made possible by the collective work of a brigade of actors.

WHERE DOES SOCIAL SIGNIFICANCE DERIVE FROM?

The commonplace assumption that the meaning or social significance of things primarily derives from outside has two problematic consequences. First, it denies things any constitutive role in generating meaning; and, second, it reduces them to loyal messengers transmitting meanings and phenomena that exist more or less independently of them. However, as argued above, it should not be taken for granted that painted canoes, fur coats, Cartier watches, bell beakers, forks, teacups, and Kobe beef conform to such servile actions. Thinking of them as members of a large company of *mediating* actors actually assigns them a far more essential role. This generating and constitutive role involves more than serving as "motivated signs" or material metaphors (Tilley 1999); things possess real qualities that they offer to social construction and entrepreneurship. Walls dividing a house into rooms or compartments create boundaries and confined spaces that, whether it's intended or not, make an important difference to social perception and behavior. In this fashion, the new Georgian architecture of the late eighteenth century represented a *real* difference from previous housing: "The change for the person crossing the threshold was great, for he was standing in a dark, unheated hallway, not within the hearthside glow. . . . In the new house the most public room was only as accessible as the most private room was in the earlier buildings" (Glassie 1975:121). Privacy, for one thing, would be hard to exercise without the help of walls or shelter.

Moreover, how could social distinctions actually become and stay meaningful without the help of things and their real and intrinsic differences? An example used by Latour illustrates this point well. A common interpretation of the social distinction between silk stockings (highbrow) and nylon stockings (lowbrow) would be that this is a social difference being expressed in fashion. The difference between silk and nylon is, for several reasons (price, marketing, effective history), convenient for *representing* the distinction between those well-off and those not so well-off. However, this ready-made material distinction itself is rarely considered as significant to the existence of the social difference. It is "mobilized purely for illustrative purposes" (Latour 2005:40) to express a difference socially defined in advance. However, Latour notes that "if, on the contrary, the chemical and manufacturing differences are treated as so many mediators, then it may happen that *without* the many indefinite material nuances between the feel, the touch, the colour, the sparkling of silk and nylon, *this* social difference might not exist at all" (40). Likewise, as argued above, cutlery, Georgian houses, and tombstones were not merely expressing or—even less—symbolizing a new American mental template created in advance. They were also actively involved in creating and "ontologizing" the new social schisms and thoughts, which without them might have never existed.

Things' ability to act, and their work as mediators rather than intermediaries, is also central to Gibson's concept of *affordance*. In his ecological theory of "direct perception," Gibson maintains that landscapes—things— offer their properties and ready-to-actness in a direct, unmediated way

(1986:127ff.; see Knappett 2005). Thus, the cup affords drinking, the bridge a river crossing, the ax cutting. Flint affords blade production and fire making. Things, materials, and entities provide us with a wealth of affordances that help, permit, direct, prevent, and otherwise influence our day-to-day activities. Despite providing us with an enormous reservoir of differentiated affordances, they also join forces in offering common properties that act together. Things' persistence and durability, as discussed in the previous chapter, may be seen as a common affordance that through a wide range of individual entities facilitates certain actions, attitudes, and meanings. In other words, they cater to both widely shared and more specific purposes. The eighteenth-century New England dinner plates, chairs, beds, and chamber pots afforded people the opportunity not only to eat, sit, sleep, and urinate, but also to become individual.

CONCLUSION: REMEMBERING THINGS

In this chapter, I have considered various approaches that all express an urgent need to acknowledge that things have a far more vital role in what we like to think of as *human* society. The exclusiveness and pivotal position of humans, not only as thinking subjects but also as acting bodies, is being destabilized and decentered through concepts such as chiasm, distributed personhood, hybrids, and actor networks. Adding a Heideggerian term to that repertoire, we may say that a "thrown" condition of human life—now and forever—is to "blend with things." Thus, this *condition* is not an occasional or spatiotemporal enveloped part of our living, something that we switch to and from, decide on or deliberately accept or reject, but an always-already imperative of human life. The building of a society and the making of social change cannot and have never taken place outside the embeddedness of being, and if there is one predictable historical trajectory, it is that of increasing entanglements and delegations.

Living with things is not of course a static involvement. Things transform our life and are themselves, to some extent at least, transformed by this mutual engagement. An Inuit hunter becomes a very different actor when united with his kayak and thus with the kayak's attached repertoire of lines, spears, and so on, and at the same time the kayak is transformed into something more. They are both turned into someone/something else—in other words, into a specific hybrid actor, cyborg, or compound interactor (Latour 1999b:178–83; Schiffer 1999:19; cf. Gell 1998:20–21). Again, this should not mislead us into assuming that mixing and "compoundness" are situational, that is, reserved for special situations. The same Inuit hunting on ice during winter and spring interacts with other assemblages (dogs, sledges, whips, etc.) that create other hybrid and

Figure 7.3. Man, kayak, and hunting gear, Narsaq Kujalleq, Nanortalik, West Green-land, 1911. The man's kayak suit (*tuilik*), made of softened, water-resistant seal skin, was sewn as a hooded jacket with drawstrings. These secured the suit around the face and wrists and fastened the bottom opening tightly around the coaming of the kayak cockpit (see figure 4.1). When the man was seated and strapped in, he and the kayak operated as a unit, with all hunting gear (weapons, float, lines, etc.) mounted within easy reach (photo: John Møller).

interacting units. Just as Kagge never crossed the Antarctic alone, hunting is not an individual exercise. A complex flock of actors was involved, united by a skillful combination of the power and properties afforded by each of them. In other words: "Action is . . . not a property of humans *but of an association of actants*" (Latour 1999b:182, emphasis in original).

Needless to say, to separate a material world from a social or cultural world and to insist that the latter somehow should exist "behind" the former becomes utterly problematic. As confirmed by all daily observations, people are not actors without things, and to split the mixture apart in order to present us with a human society devoid of things actually renders us with a rather strange *prehuman* image of that society (Serres 1995b:165–66, 199–200). As argued above, however, the effective history of the conception of things as "bracketed off" from society and culture is strong and actually very effective and has to a large extent become "ontologized" by its own materialization into books, university buildings, museums, and educational programs. These Janus-faced sediments act as a means of purification that paradoxically provide stability to the modern wish image of a divided world.

Backed by this effective history, it still seems self-evident that archaeologists should "transcend the merely manifest in the objects which they uncover and see through these fragments to the reality of the social and cultural lives of which they are mere remnants" (Miller 2005b:212). Thus, when Lynn Meskell claims that "we cannot privilege the material world alone *since materiality is ultimately bound up in creative cultural contexts*" (2004:13, my emphasis), the material-cultural split and its hierarchy seem to be taken for granted. Needless to say, questioning the cultural prior is not a matter of giving priority to "the material world alone." Rather, it is a claim to do away with such hierarchies or centers, to thus acknowledge things not as a backdrop to, or embodiment of, remnants of societies and cultures, but as an inseparable part of their very constitution.

The social and cultural field is not an invisible realm to which things relate in an epiphenomenal or residual way. Societies have always been reified, and although the surviving material components of past societies are fragmented, they are no less social or cultural than those less tangible entities that have not survived (cf. Leone 2007:206). If in doubt about this materialist opinion, one should explicitly direct one's suspicion to the things *we* perceive, experience, and mix with in our own present living. Are the buildings, streets, power stations, satellites, cars, airports, electricity, computers, and food and drink the remnants—the residues—of our own culture or society? As all laypeople living and toiling below the "philosophical heights" (*pace* Miller) can confirm, things are genuine and constitutive elements of the collectives to which we add such names. As much as these collectives depend on us, they depend on things. Thus, the crucial issue is not so much to move from the latter to the former as it is to try to understand how we are combined to make society possible.

8

In Defense of Things

Endowed with a persistence which echoes with obsessiveness, things
saturate the world with their presence. Wherever the I turns, there are
things, and when it closes its eyes, they still haunt its imagination with
the presentation of odors, sounds, tastes, almost imperceptible sensations through which things still pulse their vitality.

—Silvia Benso, *The Face of Things*

Throughout this book I have presented and discussed fragments of
various assemblages of thing-theory that have surfaced under labels
such as poststructuralism, phenomenology, and actor-network theory
(ANT). These may be seen to be more or less diverse, as might indeed the
works of the individual authors normally associated with them. While
some scholars conveniently serve as totems for strong theoretical lineages, others, such as Henri Bergson and Walter Benjamin, occupy more
ambiguous positions within the theoretical landscape. In my dealing with
these theories and theorists, I have tried to avoid a "developmental reading" (Harman 2002:7) both within and between scholarships. Without
denying sympathies—or antipathies—I have tried to let myself be guided
by the declared *bricoleur* attitude, searching around for usable bits and
pieces that may be reassembled with other appropriate spare parts (cf.
chapter 1).

So far, much time has been devoted to this reconnaissance work and the
immediate evaluation of the usefulness and quality of the various finds. I
regard this task as temporarily accomplished, although much may be said
about the actual finds and their treatment. In any event, such work has

151

a pragmatic aspect; it is relative not only to availability and immediate needs, but also to the eyes and skill of the collector. Bricolage as an actual work process, however, is not only to gather bits and pieces but also to creatively reassemble them—using those parts to construct something usable. This is the more difficult and challenging part, and I have only partially attempted to pursue this goal through the thematic reassembling in the previous chapters. Much more work of course is needed, and in this final chapter I shall start this work by addressing some issues that run across the previous chapters and trying to build some main arguments from these partial encounters.

Before embarking on this final journey, I would like to emphasize the kinship between bricolage and archaeology, beyond the obvious common toil of collecting. The *bricoleur* and the archaeologist join forces in working on what there actually *is*—which often is the fragmented, the discarded and abandoned. Both also share the dubious fate of having the name of their craft appropriated by anthropologists, philosophers, and literary critics in their search for something sufficiently metaphorically material to buttress and concretize their abstract conceptions. Thus, writing this work as an archaeologist may also be seen as involving an act of theoretical repatriation, that is, reclaiming a concept.

DEFENDING WHAT THERE IS

For the student of material culture familiar with the debates that have circulated since the 1960s, this book must be seen as missing some vital components. What about the debates on style, about how things are shaped and selected as part of a meaningful process of creating individual or collective identities? How can one possibly talk about the way things are formed and changed without taking into account the thoughtful historical agent, the toolmaker, the consumer? To some extent, my opinion on these issues has already been addressed (cf. chapters 1–3), and it is tempting to refrain from further arguments due to the fact that this book explores thing-territories that these debates have largely avoided. However, a few additional comments seem pertinent at the beginning of this final chapter.

While recognizing the importance of the various perspectives that have been advocated, I also find their general outcome unsatisfactory in several respects. One reason is the widely shared assumption that the sexiest significance of things always lies in their symbolic and representative functions, while their habitual everyday uses are trivial and of interest only to old fashioned "folk" studies. As argued above (see chapter 4), habitual use is not "trivial," in the derogatory sense of the word; it implies knowledge, care, and respect for what objects are in their own being. The significance of a boat, for example, is not primarily a function of the symbolic role it potentially may serve in transitional rituals, by acting as an embodied sign of power or by communicating individual or group identity. What seems forgotten in the vast majority of material culture studies is that the boat is mostly significant for what it *is*—that is, a boat. It is significant because of the knowledge and skill it assembles, the capacities it possesses in terms of speed, stability, mastering of winds and waves; the practices it affords such as transport, fishing, hunting, and so on. In a similar way, an ax is significant due to its ax qualities, and a reindeer due to its reindeer qualities. Whatever symbolic roles they may play are residues of the primary significance of their own being.

There is another, closely related, asymmetry written into these numerous texts: the focus is almost entirely on how things are creatively used by people for their various purposes rather than on asking what things afford or have to offer us. Thus, in most debates about things' "meaning," the material qualities of the objects in question actually seem rather irrelevant to this meaning or to their own "cultural construction." As with the "readerly" text (*pace* Barthes), the transformation is always supposed to involve the hierarchical and unidirectional move from signified to signifier, from content to form, and from idea to expression (cf. chapter 3). Beyond being a concrete and visible medium for inscription and embodiment, things' integrity has been sacrificed or subsumed to the dominant social and humanist trope in which their role is to always represent something extramaterial else.

To make myself clear, I am not at all disinterested in things' meaning and share the concern with the significance of things. However, I think we need to pay far more attention to the questions of why and how things are significant. What difference do *they* make in making the world meaningful? Clearly, things are also being made and formed with human intentions in mind and for an infinite number of purposes. Rather than thinking of this as a process by which a human idea is being implanted into something raw and meaningless, we should think of design as also emerging from the materials and the practices that are intimately involved with them (see Lemonnier 1992, 1993; Ingold 2000). The qualities that "slumber" in the material used, the equipment involved in the processing, the "ready-to-hand" knowledge of the human producer, the effective history of former things and their production are all affecting the outcome, thus making this a far more complex and entangled process than suggested by the old style-function debate (Sackett 1982, 1985; Wiessner 1983; see Boast 1997). Even today, when technology is supposed to have enforced its power on nature, when "making" is supposed to have replaced "weaving" (to use Tim Ingold's terms), when nature and materials seem reduced to *Bestand* (*pace* Heidegger), design is not liberated from

Figure 8.1. "Habitual use is not 'trivial,' in the derogatory sense of the word; it implies knowledge, care, and respect for what objects are in their own being." Persistent tools at Lyngmo farm, Arctic Norway (photo: Bjørnar Olsen).

these enabling and constraining forces. Actually, the constant urge to invent new materials with different qualities may be seen as a confirmation of the intimate link between design and materials. Thus, the remaining part of this book will be devoted to the material properties of things: what is their significance, and what difference do they make?

THINGS MATTER—ALSO BY THEMSELVES

Most of the theories addressed in this book can be described as *relational*, emphasizing the significance of context, interaction, linkage, and difference. This may be seen as a diagnostic feature of modern interpretative and social theories at large. In hermeneutics, the parts receive meaning from the textual whole; structuralism stresses difference and opposition; and from Heidegger we learn how tools always belong to a set of other equipment, an equipmental totality. Marxism, structuration theory, and system theory, to mention a few other programs, are no exception to this general rule. It is no surprise then that this is a dominant theoretical trope in material culture studies as well. For example, one assumption of the contextual approach was that "an object out of context is not readable" (Hodder 1986:141), and while the poststructuralist counterclaims denied the very possibility of being "outside" context (and the play of difference; Yates 1990:270–72), relationality is nevertheless the unchallenged key to understanding (cf. chapter 3).

In other words, meanings are produced in relations, and much of the recent explicit inspiration for this thesis is of course found in structuralism and semiotics. In John Law's definition of ANT referred to in the previous chapter, a central feature is "that of the relationality of entities, the notion that they are produced in relations"; ANT is a "semiotics of materiality" and "applies this ruthlessly to all materials—not simply to those that are linguistic" (Law 1999:4; Latour 2005:153). Importance and significance are products of the difference between entities, rather than inherent qualities of the entities themselves.

Moving from the meaning-constitutive qualities of language to a "semiotics of materiality" has, in some respects, been a worthwhile exercise (see chapter 3). However, as repeatedly argued throughout this book, this transformation is hardly as smooth as is often portrayed. Indeed, something rather crucial about things' being may actually be lost if the principles of semiotics (and relational theories at large) are "ruthlessly applied" to them. Relationality may be a principle less imperative to things than to words.

To be sure, things clearly attain their relative importance through their position within a relational web. A petrol station is utterly marginalized without roads, cars, pipelines, oil wells, petroleum plants, oil fields, and so on. A hammer without nails, hands, and planks would be rather useless (although "parat" for future actions). The point therefore is not to discard relational (or contextual) theory; quite the contrary, the insights that have emerged from such varied sources as structuralism, hermeneutics, Heideggerian phenomenology, and poststructuralism are all very valuable indeed. But perhaps, as pertinently observed by Graham Harman, the case is that "relational theory has already performed its historical mission, and is now burdening us with its own excess" (2002:24; cf. Latour 2005:131–32). Although one may have some doubts regarding the subsequent claim that a "theory of substance is inevitably reborn from the ashes" (Harman 2002:24), the univocal stressing of the relational may have caused us to lose sight of the individual qualities of things, their intrinsic power, and the way they actually *therefore* work as mediators in collective action. Thus, it may be time to take one step back.

A house, a mountain, a bridge, or an oil reserve all have intrinsic qualities that seriously restrict their exchangeability. A kayak or an ax does have a competence that cannot be replaced by just any other signifier. They are not merely "enslaved in some wider system of differential meaning," but are defenders of their own private terrains, masters of their own castles (Harman 2002:280). Moreover, contrary to the linguistic sign, the reality of these entities is experienced directly, through themselves; they come to us—also—in an unmediated way (Gibson 1986; cf. Hacking 2001:10). In other words, despite being enrolled to serve in a network and achieve a large part of their meaning from it, "the elements of the world do retain individual integrity" (Harman 2002:294). They are important because each of them makes a difference to the world, not in a negative manner for the sake of the difference itself, as in Saussurian semiotics and poststructuralism, but because of the *positive* difference they make due to their irreplaceable uniqueness. As acknowledged by Bruno Latour, an actor "is exactly what is *not* substitutable" (2005:152, emphasis in original).

Even when removed from their original contextual setting and dislocated, things retain some of their integrity. A Neolithic pot used for storing food, left behind in an abandoned settlement from where it is recovered six thousand years later, retains some of its uniqueness and autonomy. Even when put on display in a faraway museum it is still a pot, not only holding in reserve its affordances and "pot properties" for eventual (if unlikely) future actualization, but also persistently offering them for direct perception. Thus, when dealing with things we should actually acknowledge that there are qualities immanent to the signifiers themselves, properties that are not accidental or only a product of their position in a relational web. What we are dealing with are not "empty signifiers" but real entities possessing their own unique qualities and competences, which they bring to our cohabitation with them—competences that also facilitate the "weaving together of difference" that is constitutive of collective action (Latour 2005:74). Their efficiency and usefulness stem not only from their human use, but also from the fact that they are *"capable of an effect*, of inflicting some kind of blow on reality" (Harman 2002:20, emphasis in original).

Things' inherent and varied properties are also decisive even (and not without a certain irony) when their "serviceability" is extended to the symbolic and linguistic sphere as objects "good to think" and "speak" with. Linguistic metaphors are actually ready to be picked from this repertoire of material difference and are somehow preselected for appropriate uses (cf. Tilley 1999; Renfrew 2001:127–29). Thus, "soft as steel" is *not* a metaphor we live by. In other words, even when things join language and participate as signs in a system of communication, their actual form or material substance is far from an arbitrary quality; their very significance actually depends on their intrinsic characteristics. In this way, they also carry with them an iconical or indexial weight that makes their pure symbolic role (in the Peircian sense) very limited (Preucel 2006).

THE PROPERTIES OF THINGS: DIFFERENTIATING AND SHARING

Things are often lumped together linguistically as "things," an attitude facilitated by their convenient common noun. As indicated by the previous section, things are not a homogenous category displaying similar characteristics. In this way, things are not only different from words and language but also differ almost infinitely among themselves. We differentiate between things according to features such as form, scale, texture, durability, color, and density—which in itself makes defining "what is the thing" so difficult and largely futile, if exact and univocal definitions are called for. Things include big objects (trains, cities, planets), soft things (butter, cotton, sponges), small artifacts (coins, pearls, microchips), durable matter (stones, rocks, irons), and perishable goods (bread, leaves, dew). Things may serve specialized functions (as arrows, lightbulbs, cameras); others may be deliberately multifunctional (Swiss Army knives, hand axes, houses); while others again (although prescribed primarily for the first category) may be flexible enough to allow for different uses (pots, knives, pyramids). These different properties are constitutive and imperative for their incorporation into collectives and networks. Thus, rather than thinking of them as produced in relations, we may think of them *as what makes relations possible.*

Many of these properties are contained in the very material which a thing is made from, properties that allow for different uses or processing (cf. Ingold 2007b:33). The texture and density of flint and obsidian afford systematic chipping and fractioning, allowing for slender blades to be produced as well as sharp and strong edges for cutting and perforating. These qualities are not found in stone materials such as slate or granite, despite their linguistic bonding as *stones* or *rock*. These "stones," however, offer themselves for other purposes and handling, such as slate for ground or polished tools (knives, axes, arrows) and granite as building materials. In a similar way, oak differs from spruce, birch from pine, and larch from willow, allowing for different uses as building materials, as utensils, in paper production, or as fuel. Other materials, such as steel, plastic, bronze, and glass, can only be artificially made, which allows for more things with more properties. Pottery unites clay, water, and fire, which in combination "afford" ceramics making. Artificial or not, the various qualities somehow "slumber" in the material and are brought forth "mimetically" by the skilled maker in partnership with his or her skilled equipment.

Things' differences are also caused by their size, mass, and physiognomy. While the human body is relatively homogenous, despite variations due to age, sex, inheritance, and nutrition, things come to us infinitely more differentiated. Some we move and carry with us, others we move with, while others again make us move, defining material programs of action monitoring and disciplining our everyday life. Some things draw attention to themselves, some create fear or pleasure, some enable views, while others block views. In other words, different materials and different things offer different uses and different meanings. Thus, to draw a first conclusion: what we are living with are not "things" or "material culture," as a homogenous or univocal category opposed to us, but a differentiated mass, heterogeneous matters, whose accelerating difference affects us in increasingly different ways. It is within this differentiated mass, as a part of it, that human life unfolds.

There is another side to this, though, which is as important and real: *similarity*. Stressing or acknowledging things' differences does not prevent us from realizing their shared properties. There is no either/or. Things—at least as normally conceived of—*do* also have features in common (and this explains, at least in part, the persistency of the appellative). They have substance and surface, and they are tangible. In short, they are *material* and thus perceivable by a wide range of senses (sight, smell, touch, sound). Moreover, if we avoid the absolutism of having to choose between the always and the never—that is, if we perceive the world in the reductive way we normally do (*pace* Bergson)—the shared properties of things become even more explicit. Things are more persistent than thought. They evidently last longer than speech and gestures. Things are concrete and offer stability, although to a varying degree. It is from these simple and naive facts that I shall now proceed.

IN THINGS WE TRUST

Things are normally in place, at least enough of them to make our existence predictable and secure. When we wake up tomorrow, the bed, room, and house are still there. So are our private belongings, other houses, the streets and pipelines that connect them, buses and cars, shops and factories, gardens, mountains, and trees. They constitute our incontestable acquisition. We do not wake up to a completely new world every morning, having to start all over again from scratch. Despite what some liberal thinkers want us to believe, the material identities of things do not change "quickly and without warning, right in front of our eyes"; they are not part of "a magician's show" (Holtorf 2002:55). Quite the contrary, things are overwhelmingly *there*, and we expect them to be in place. They are the real Dasein. Streets, buildings, airports, boats, tents, fireplaces, quartz quarries, and reindeer fences are situated, they are *in place* and they manifest themselves to us as familiar, as known. Being in place, of course, does not imply that they are immobile, but that they appear where we expect them to be. The seal-hunting gear, the strike-a-light, the lasso, the yurt, the iPhone, and the memory stick are all within reach.

This "belonging somewhere" is part of our circumspective dealings with things: we expect them to be within our "region" (Heidegger 1962:136–37). And again, this region is not isomorphic with the catchment area of the rural *Heimat* ridiculed by globalization theorists and cybernomads. Familiarity and situatedness are as much an apriorism of the supermodern nonplaces (Augé 1995), such as shopping malls and international airports, as of a Black Forest farmhouse or Sámi reindeer camp. The existential importance of this entire field of ready-to-handness, of the being-in-place, becomes evident in those cases in which it is disturbed or lost. It is well known that any dramatic changes in the thing environment, by war or environmental catastrophe, have traumatic consequences. Losing your belongings, house, city, farm, or hunting ground creates a loss that cannot be easily mentally settled. Everyone that has experienced such traumas can confirm how the existential and mnemonic importance of things lost suddenly becomes manifest (cf. Parkin 1999:214–15; Naum 2008:278–80).

Throughout human history, this reassurance of stability as the normal state of things can hardly be overstated. Even if far from being exhaustive of their qualities or equally true for all things, solidity and permanence are thing properties that make a vital difference to human life: not only to society and social bonds, but also to our existential security. The vital importance of things to this aspect of human existence was actually recognized by another sociologist pioneer, August Comte, who saw "things in place" as a grounding constituent for our mental equilibrium: the stability of the things we interact with on a daily basis provides human life with an immediate and fundamental impression of permanence (Connerton 1989:37; see also Durkheim 1951:313–14; Arendt 1958:137 for similar recognitions). Likewise, the socializing effects implied in Pierre Bourdieu's early conception of habitus, "understood as a system of lasting, transposable dispositions which, integrating past experiences, functions at every moment as a matrix of perceptions, appreciations, and actions" (1977:82–83), can of course not be implemented (or understood) without the brigades of lasting things in place, including those constituting the "region" of the Kabyle house (Bourdieu 1973; see Johansen 1992; Meskell 2005:3).

Figure 8.2.   The existential importance of things is most dramatically disclosed in those exceptional cases in which entire thing environments are lost or disturbed. The ruined fishing village of Berlevåg, Arctic Norway, after the German withdrawal in 1944 (photo: Krigsarkivet/Scanpix).

Thus, despite the unquestionable variation among things, I will claim durability and "in-place-ness" as probably the most important culturally constitutive and socially constructive qualities of things. This lasting quality of "being there, being operational" affords security and prediction (Gaver 1996:119, cf. Norman 1988) and is probably also the primary "existential affordance" of things. This trusted durability, which also includes a "holding-in-readiness" for future interactions and reenactments, however, also allows for another intimately related effect: the gathering or sedimentation of the past. As we shall see, this gathering itself allows for processes and outcomes that, to some extent at least, are unpredictable and subsumed to material trajectories that create their own statements of crucial significance for how the past is conceived and remembered.

SEDIMENTATION AND CHANGE

In *The Eighteenth Brumaire of Louis Bonaparte*, Karl Marx wrote his deathless dictum that people make their own history, not as they please, "but under circumstances directly encountered, given and transmitted from the past" (1968:96). The past not only burdens the brains of the living ("like a nightmare"), but the very material circumstances under which people live, which they directly encounter and which they are conditioned by, are inherited from the past.

Marx thus opposed, at least for the time being, the common idea of modern society as "liberated" from the bonds of the past. As noted earlier, it is a widespread assumption that so-called traditional societies, that is, the "premoderns," were closer to their past than we are. Contrary to the situation in these societies where the past was supposed to live on in "real environments of memory," *milieux de mémoire* (Nora 1984, 1989), the accelerated history of the modern is claimed to have left the past behind, leaving a void that only can be filled by our recollective memory and historical reconstructions.

A number of theorists, however, ranging from Marx, Bergson, and Benjamin to Serres and Latour, have all countered this modernist leitmotif. Their claim is rather that the past proliferates more than ever in the present—or, as Benjamin would have said, that nothing is less ended than the past. Each generation is actually receiving an increasingly greater share of it. This is not primarily due to deliberate practices of recollection in terms of books, museums, and disciplinary knowledges, the consciously developed *aide-mémoires* for storing and transmitting information about the past (cf. Huyssen 2003). A more fundamental cause for this gathering has to do with the durable qualities of things that make us live in an environment increasingly conditioned by the structures and residues of the past. In different shapes and in various conditions, this material gathers and thus constantly sediments into potentially new environments of memory. Most obvious of course, is the ongoing layering of all working and useful matter, such as roads, bridges, tunnels, buildings, monuments, and so on, which continues to constitute a taken-for-granted part of our "contemporary" lifeworlds. As previously argued, what we conceive of as our contemporary world is not made up of entities originating from the same age, the "present," but instead takes the form of a "flattened" multitemporal field (cf. Lucas 2008), the complex and dispersed stratigraphy of accumulated pasts. The present "basically consists of a palimpsest of all durations of the past that have become recorded in matter" (Olivier 2001:66; cf. chapter 6).

The notion of sedimentation clearly begs for a number of comments and the pertinent question, what about change? If materials sediment and solidify this way, preserving and objectifying society, do they always come to counteract change? (See Lucas 2008:62–63 for a related discussion.) Is there a creative, innovative aspect of humans that is somehow combated or calmed by the slowing, sedimenting materiality? (cf. Bergson 1998). An adequate response requires that we recognize the varied affordances and capacities of things—in short, and to put it in the most trivial terms possible, that they are capable of more than one historical effect. On the one hand, there is undoubtedly a leveling of instability, of "noise," through objectification. Materials and the historically effective past that "swells in our midst" facilitate society with the necessary stability and solidity, the pillar and bolts that prevent our social bonds from being "airy as clouds" (Serres 1995a:87). These firming things clearly have a preservative function; they arrest action and "slow down the time of our revolutions," to borrow another of Michel Serres's formulations (cf. Serres 1995a:87ff; Serres 1995b:199–202). There is an explicit, even banal, aspect of this "slowing down," although of course not exhaustive of its operation. The very scale and mass of society's material reinforcement, in other words of the things mobilized and assembled to make it work and stay together, *will* under certain circumstances slow change, preventing flexibility and forming a basis for the impression that the past weighs heavier on some societies than others (cf. Lucas 2008). The stones, iron, and concrete used in the massive construction of some past and present empires are not only burdening the *brains* of their inhabitants; they left a thick and sticky heritage of materials that to some extent, at least, explains their continuous, effective history.

On the other hand, things are also what makes change possible and it is hard to conceive how human creativity and agency can be realized without these very beings (cf. chapters 4 and 7). Moreover, by the physiognomy they add to history (*pace* Benjamin), things also constitute the key device in helping us to recognize historical changes. In order to adequately address the question of change we therefore need to move beyond the dominant humanist trope of creative (but unequipped) historical agents rendered *opposed* to materiality. Moreover, we also need to refrain from conceiving stability and change in oppositional terms: these are rather complementary phenomena. To recognize change there must be something preserved, something to recognize, that is, some still-effective history that makes the novelty in the change stand out as new (Mullarkey 2000:135). Exploring things' role in historical change we thus have to mediate between repetition and novelty, stability and change; in other words, to avoid the trap of the either/or. In this sense (and rephrasing Bergson liberally), history also becomes a record of how the past is repeated differently, a repetition of difference.

WHY DO THINGS CHANGE?

This does not, however, bring us very far in understanding why things, and materiality at large, change. There are, of course, gradual shifts and variations that are always involved in human and nonhuman existence. (We never step into the same river twice.) Chopping a tree, knapping a scraper, building a motorway, and driving a car all contribute to a "process world" that is always in transformation. Also contributing to this are the forces and rhythms of nature, which slowly or more abruptly are changing the physiognomy of the landscape in addition to the conditions for human life. Things themselves change, age, and wither, as the material world is also subject to the process of ruination (see below). Thus, notwithstanding the solidity of the material world, there is a multitude of changes within this mass operating at different scales and different paces, always-already in action.

Change, however, is often conceived of as "episodic" (Giddens 1981), something (at least retrospectively) conceived of as bringing something new to things themselves or society at large. In Marxist social theory, these are brought together in a causal link. Things, as productive forces (technology, raw materials, and work organizations), are accredited a crucial role under certain historical conditions by being developed to a scale and organizational level that causes an interstructural contradiction with the social relations of productions. (Related conceptions can be found in different versions of systems theory.) The reasons why things (technology and the associated organization of production) develop are largely located outside the things themselves, such as in "social needs" or contradictions within the social relations of production. These may be valid parameters, and it is not my aim here to do away with notions related to human or "systemic" motivations or "movers." My ambition is more to ask if there is something in the material itself that contributes to its own transformation. I have already addressed the various "affordances" of the raw materials themselves and shall briefly point to some other aspects.

In his important book on the materiality of social change, Norwegian sociologist Tom Johansen writes about how the potential for transformation—as improvements—is somehow embedded in the materials themselves:

> Since the material manifestations are of such a solid and persistent character they become a "concrete memory of the acquisitions of the past." But precisely because of this, they lay the groundwork for improvements, developments and refinements of this memory. Moreover, they also remind us about the deficiencies of the past—as a constant challenge to the present to extend the ploughshare, improve the dwellings, refine the ornaments, etc. Because of the exteriority of the past, it enables an enduring criticism. (Johansen 1992:30, my translation)

Clearly this is not to say that the materialized past has been subjected to such an enduring criticism, nor have the materials consciously been posing a constant challenge. However, the important issue here is their potential for doing so—in other words, the fact that their "being-in-readiness" for such criticism and reworking is constant and enduring.

Crucial here are the two modes of tool-being explored by Heidegger (see chapter 4). According to him, we normally deal with things in their ready-to-hand mode, encountering them in their "unobtrusive presence." They are not objects of conscious concern, subject to criticism or posing any serious challenges. They are, in short, absorbed by the "in-order-to" and black-boxed by their own successful operations. However, when malfunctioning, encountered in the wrong places, or lost, these very objects "light up"; they consciously "come to mind" rather than circumspectly "to hand." If the fridge stops working, we realize *what* it was ready-to-hand *for*" (Heidegger 1962:105, emphasis in original). By their very malfunctioning, things become "conspicuous" to us (Heidegger 1962; cf. Harman 2002; chapter 4).

Hubert Dreyfus has isolated three modes of "coming to mind" in Heidegger's work and has ranked them as increasingly more serious disturbances: conspicuousness, obstinacy, and obtrusiveness, of which the latter or "total breakdown" is most effective (1991:70–83). While small disturbances are normally leveled out in order for life to go on in its practical attitude, some interruptions prevent us from going on as usual. When a tool is missing/lost and our work permanently interrupted, "we can either stare helplessly at the remaining objects or take a new detached theoretical stance towards things and try to explain their underlying causal properties" (Dreyfus 1991:79).

This gradation of "the coming to mind" is a useful one, as it modifies the usual oppositional conception of these two modes of tool-being (i.e., the ready-to-hand and the present-at-hand) as mutually exclusive modes. Moreover, things' present-at-hand mode is not activated only by their obtrusive and absolute malfunctioning ("total breakdown"). Although Dreyfus may be correct in stating that this may be the most imperative case, the options he proposes for how we handle such collapses seem somewhat limited. For a philosopher, the choice may be restricted to either "staring helplessly" at the objects or taking a new "detached theoretical stance" toward them. For others, probably the vast majority of past and present people, there may be other and more viable choices for how to go on. These will all involve practical action: to repair, improve, or even invent new tools.

Far more common disturbances than "total breakdown" are things' minor or partial deficiencies, and contrary to what Dreyfus seems to assert, these are not necessarily leveled out. By not working properly and causing minor disturbances, things themselves may initiate a growing concern about their functioning. Becoming aware of something activates the potential for improvement and change. Normally, things are brought back to their original state of being through repair, replacement, or return. However, the interruption caused by malfunctioning may also cause an awareness or doubt about its original functioning, thus stimulating improvement or refinement. A boat that behaves in an unruly manner under certain wind and wave conditions will be examined, discussed, tested in an attempt to improve it. Changes to the sail or keel may be made, and, if successful, they will be translated and eventually black-boxed into future vessels. This process, however, does not include a "new detached theoretical stance towards things"—it is actually grounded in the knowing how of the skipper, the sailor, and the boat builder. This knowing how, irrespective of whether it involves a cutter, kayak, or long ship, always involves a sensibility for the "tuning" of the vessel at sea, a bodily felt awareness of how it works and how it may be improved. Thus, in this sense the ready-to-hand knowledge of things is crucial for their improvement and for the way they eventually "come to mind" and their treatment in a present-at-hand mode. As a result of this, there is always a latent criticism involved even in habitual living.

It may be argued that the modern conditions have changed all this, and that the accelerating turnover time for consumer products and technology reflects the loosening grip of the ready-to-hand; also a condition for change. That our "ontic" and rational attitude makes us far more conscious about things and increasingly renders them in a reflexive present-at-hand mode. Also due to the rationales of capitalist economies, the calming and slow rhythms of ready-to-hand trajectories, which primarily were related to practical need, are replaced by a constant and deliberate urge for instant changes. Although there is some truth to this, the picture is far more complex. For example, the vast majority of "new" things offered to us still contains and preserves their own ready-to-hand affordances, tuned in by their own effective history of being "capable of action." The knifelike quality of the knife and the shoelike quality of the shoe are not replaced or seriously modified by new styles and designs. The effective history of functional success is evident in forms and materials that have survived throughout the millennia, adding yet another dimension to how the past settles in the present.

This may also serve as a timely reminder that the ready-to-hand is *not* an endangered mode. Beyond the things we consciously notice slumbers the enormous and effective bedrock of ready-to-hand things. Although the state of "coming to mind," in terms of how we deal with things, might be seen as a relative increase, especially when entire industries today are devoted precisely to creating new designs and equipment, the material bedrock is now and always constituted by the ready-to-hand. Even the design industries and their conscious designers are situated firmly and dependently within this everydayness of inconspicuous materials, which enables them to devote their time to the tiny and often quite marginal portion of that which makes society possible.

SEDIMENTATION AND DIFFERENTIATION: RUINS AND THE DISCARDED PAST

There is a distinctive kind of disturbance or tension embedded in the notion of the sedimenting and gathering past that deserves more attention. This tension is created by its differentiated mode of acquisition: the gathering not only of the useful and feasible but also of the ruined and discarded. As we have seen in Bergson's formative conception of the term *habit memory*, it was largely conceived of as a function of adaptive value: only those aspects of the past that are useful or compatible with our present conduct are "remembered" in habit memory. Likewise, a substantial share of the accumulating past consists of surviving materials still useful and still functional, although mostly inconspicuously embedded in the ready-to-hand of our daily doing and existence. This is not restricted to what we usually think of as "old things" still in use, such as buildings, streets, bridges, but in fact includes *every* thing we use, ranging from that bought yesterday to the medieval foundation of the town we live in. It is this predominantly reassuring past that we feel as an "incontestable acquisition" that prevents (or rather makes redundant) a recollective "looking back" to make us sure that it really is there.

As discussed previously, the habit memory intimately related to these aspects of the "pure" past is normally contrasted and subordinated to "recollective memory," which by definition is conscious recovering and exclusively directed toward recalling the past (Casey 1984:281; see chapter 6). However, this dualist conception of habit versus conscious or recollective memory is complicated (and perhaps strangely mediated) by another component of the sedimenting past: the ruined and the stranded, a component that although marginal still swells, so to speak, in the spaces left open by the habitual and the recollective.

Despite the fact that things clearly do age differently and that their expected life lengths also vary greatly, there is a certain egalitarianism associated with their aging. Thus, given that persistency can be listed among their qualities, things do not discriminate among themselves in their duration. This means that in addition to those "unbroken" things that facilitate smooth or "good passages" (cf. Moser and Law 1999), there is a survival of the outdated and stranded. This is the material past that persists despite being discarded, ignored, and made superfluous—in short, the surviving material redundancy of the past. (Cf. Edensor 2005 for an

Figure 8.3. "Even when things are discarded, destroyed, and demolished, something is nearly always left—in other words, gathered." Lyngmo farm, Arctic Norway (photo: Bjørnar Olsen).

excellent discussion.) The survival of these things is, of course, threatened, not only by their own aging and withering, but also (and probably more so) by neglect and destruction (González-Ruibal 2008). However, even when things are discarded, destroyed, and demolished, something is nearly always left—in other words, gathered. Thus, in the notion of a past that sediments and swells in our midst, there is also a component of the neglected, the unwanted.[1]

Discussing the "mission" of these outdated things of the past, "freed from the drudgery of being useful" (Benjamin 2002:39), it is pertinent to pay a final visit to the project of Walter Benjamin. In his theses on history, Benjamin brings attention to a picture by Paul Klee called *Angulus Novus*. This shows an angel with its wings wide open being blown backward while his gaze is fixed on a heap of rubbish growing at his feet. The "angel of history" is staring at the past, and despite his wish to stay and heal, he is blown away. Unable to close his wings, the storm of progress "drives him irresistibly into the future, to which his back is turned, while the pile of debris before him grows towards the sky" (Benjamin 2003:392).

This picture illuminates two central themes in Benjamin's historical writings. First, as noted by Dag Andersson (2001:15), the angel's frozen

Figure 8.4.   Stranded Skoda in the field, Lyngmo farm, Arctic Norway (photo: Bjørnar Olsen).

stare at the accumulating debris of the past counters the conventional historicist gaze, which seeks to plot history as a chain of completed events unfolding within a continuous narrative. The picture challenges the idea of historical linearity in which the past is always left behind. History is topological and accumulative, not linear or biographical. It decomposes into images and historical objects, not into narratives or biographies. Things in their accumulative bonding object to the pace and linear irreversibility of continuous history. Second, and apart from the critique it also entails of the modern conception of progress and utility, the depiction of the past as an accumulation of debris, as heaps of rubbish, pertinently captures Benjamin's concern with the "other" past, the discarded, the wrecked, the "at once scattered and preserved" (Benjamin 1996:169). This rubbish, this discarded past, serves a crucial critical historical mission.

Nowhere is this more conspicuously manifested than in the ruins of modernity itself, in our own marginalized pasts. Since the nineteenth century, mass production, consumerism, and thus cycles of material replacement have accelerated; increasingly larger amounts of things are, with increasing rapidity, victimized and made redundant. At the same time, processes of destruction have immensely intensified, although they are largely overlooked when compared to the research and social significance devoted to consumption and production (González-Ruibal 2006, 2008). The outcome is a ruined landscape of derelict factories, closed shopping malls, overgrown bunkers, and redundant mining towns—a ghostly world of decaying modern debris normally left out of academic concerns and conventional histories (Edensor 2005; DeSilvey 2006; Burström 2007; Gonzáles-Ruibal 2008; Andreassen, Bjerck, and Olsen 2010).

These ruined things were once useful and thus embedded in repetitious practice and infused with habit memory. When discarded and outmoded, their habitual mnemonic significance is lost while their physical presence, albeit ruined, continues. As such they survive and gather as the material antonyms to the habitually useful, creating a tension-filled constellation that carries the potential of triggering a particular kind of *involuntary memory* (Benjamin 1999b). As debris and as a component of the "other past," things may be actualized as "dialectical images," a term Benjamin used to denote instances or moments where the past comes together with the present—not in habitual (or ideological) harmony but as an unreconciled constellation, a charged force field. In their residual state these othered things bring to attention the tensions between their own pre- or *ur*-history (of uses, success, hopes, and wishes) and their after-history, their fate as stranded rubble in the present (Benjamin 1999b:473–76; Buck-Morss 1999:110ff., 219–21).

Thus, the tension-charged constellation, "the petrified unrest" that Benjamin located in the "dialectical image" is primarily activated by the "other" and discarded past: the abandoned farmhouse, the one-eyed doll in the garbage pit, the wrecked Skoda in the overgrown field. The past that is not only blasted out of continuous history (as narrated and conceived), but that also exists in suspense to the past still present but absorbed into our habitual schemes of action. While the latter may be seen more as conforming to a Gadamerian fusion of horizons in its ready-to-handness, the mnemonic of the former consists precisely in *actualization* "flashing up in the now of its recognizability" (Benjamin 1999b:473). Reverberating against the taken-for-granted materiality of habit memory, these ruins become potential agents of disruption; they actualize the forgotten or unwanted. In other words, the duration (and sedimentation, although in different proportions) of the outdated and nonuseful alongside the habitually (and sometimes also politically and ideologically) useful, causes tensions that allow for alternative memory practices unfolding between the habitual and the consciously recollected. By definition, this memory is genuinely involuntary and acts in this respect as a device of *Verstörung*, something that interrupts and disturbs both the habitual and the recollective.

Decay is usually understood in a purely negative way; things are degraded and humiliated through material alteration, while the information, knowledge, and memory embedded in them become lost along the way (DeSilvey 2006). However, central to Benjamin was also the idea that things may actually *release* some of their meaning or generate a different kind of knowledge precisely through processes of decay and ruination (Benjamin 1999b; Andersson 2001). Experiencing a working, populated city or a complete building may not reveal much about the way it actually works, the diversity of materials and technologies that are mobilized to construct and operate it. These comrades tend to be cunningly hidden or disguised by design and smooth architectural form. Ruination disturbs the taken-for-granted; in the destruction process new layers of meaning are revealed, meanings that may only be possible to grasp at second hand when no longer immersed in their withdrawn and useful reality. Ruination can thus be seen also as a *recovery* of memory (DeSilvey 2006): a slow-motion archaeology, or self-excavation, that exposes the formerly hidden and black-boxed. The masked object is unveiled, inside is turned out, privacy revealed (Andreassen, Bjerck, and Olsen 2010). As expressed by Tim Edensor:

> Ruination produces a defamiliarized landscape in which the formerly hidden emerges; the tricks that make a building a coherent ensemble are revealed, exposing the magic of construction. The internal organs, pipes, veins, wiring and tubes—the guts of a building—spill out . . . The key points of tension become visible, and the skeleton—the infrastructure on which all else hangs—the pillars, keystones, support walls and beams stand while less sturdy materials—the clothing or flesh of the building—peels off. (2005: 109–10)

The things left, in their general accumulative bonding but most pertinently as announced by the discarded and stranded, may thus be seen as serving a double historical mission. First, they reveal the gaps in the construction of history as progress and as continuous narrative. Second, they rescue a forgotten past, not as heritage, at least not in any ordinary sense, but as a special kind of involuntary memory. This memory illuminates not only what conventional cultural history has left behind, but also what is made redundant by habitual memory. These things bring forth and actualize the abject memories that both the recollective and the habitual have displaced. Moreover, one may also speculate as to whether it is in this state of abandoned being, "freed from the drudgery of being useful" (Benjamin 2002:39) and released from the chains of relations they have been enslaved in, that aspects of things' ownness and integrity most immediately are made present.

In Benjamin's work the ruined gives face to that which is discarded and outdated, bringing forth what is fragmented and lost in conventional history. Interestingly, it is also in this field—in this borderland—that much

Figure 8.5.   Revealed privacy, Lyngmo farm, Arctic Norway (photo: Bjørnar Olsen).

archaeological work has taken place—not only when conspicuously explored in its marginal and postcolonial fields, but also in its everydayness of bringing to light those mundane things that cultural history has ignored (cf. Lucas 2004; Gonzáles-Ruibal 2008:248, 261–62). The potential significance of this merging is great, as the work of a number of scholars has already explicitly shown (cf. Burström 2007; Deetz 1977; Shanks 2004; Gonzáles-Ruibal 2006, 2008; Andreassen, Bjerck, and Olsen 2010). As argued by Michael Shanks, to do archaeology is to work on what there is and on what is left (2007:273)—in other words, things in their duration (see Meskell and Joyce 2003).

CONCLUSION: HOW ARE THINGS?

"How are things?" asks Roger-Pol Droit at the outset of his fascinating book whose title asks the very same question (2005). And although the answer is necessarily somewhat inconclusive, his mundane inquiry into the being of things reveals their profound significance in all aspects of our everyday life. My main inquiry in this book and this last chapter has been to explore the question of how and why things are significant. To accomplish this task, I have found it appropriate and necessary to pay less attention to things' "meaning" in the ordinary sense—that is, the way they may function as part of a signifying system, be involved in material semiotics, and so on. Although by no means dismissing this communicative and representative role of things (see Preucel 2006 for an excellent overview), I do not conceive of it as a primary aspect of their being (cf. Gell 1998:6). It is in any case well explored, even perhaps overemphasized, leaving us with a somewhat biased conception of things in material culture studies (cf. Ingold 2007a). My focus has therefore been the less explored facets of things' being. What is the significance of things "in themselves"? What is their *integrity*, so to speak?

The answers given start from the simple fact that things are not words, nor are they primarily signs to be read or products ready to be consumed or "sublated." Things possess their own nonverbal qualities and are involved in their own material and historical processes that cannot be disclosed unless we explore their integrity qua things. Things come to us primarily as ready-to-hand equipment: as chairs, beds, stoves, axes, kayaks, fridges, houses, cars, roads—in other words, as things that work, not as symbolic consumables. Contrary to the linguistic signifier, the tasks they fulfill are primarily due to their irreplaceability or superiority in conducting precisely these tasks and to their nonarbitrariness in significant operations such as shooting, boating, traveling, bridging, sitting, housing, and so on. In conducting these tasks, things normally come to us as reliable and familiar. We can trust them. They are in place, and they last. Not without exception, of course, but as the normal state of their being—in other words, the overwhelming majority of everyday instances.

Thus, it is hard to conceive of society and culture without the durability and "in-place-ness" of things. These are probably their most important general, culturally constitutive and socially constructive "affordances" (in addition to their specific task value). Apart from the solidity this brings to all we have learned to think of as social and cultural, it also allows for another intimately related effect: the gathering or sedimentation of the past. The past is not left behind, but patiently gathers and folds into what we conveniently term the *present*. While we have become familiar with Gadamer's notions regarding tradition and how effective historical consciousness affects us as scholars and laypeople, the way we are influenced by this very effective material past is far less acknowledged and far less frequently discussed. However, contrary to Gadamer's harmonious fusion of horizon (including the surviving "authority of tradition") and Bergson's conception of the habitual useful, this enduring materiality is—by itself—largely indiscriminate, also caring for the traces of the discarded and what is made redundant and "othered" in history. Thus, sedimentation not only "makes history slow," it also rescues that which is untimely and displaced, creating the potential for involuntary and possibly disturbing memories of this forgotten past. It is also the very same affordance that allows archaeology to be conducted and which also points to the great, critical potential of the discipline known by that name (cf. González-Ruibal 2008).

How are things then? Well, despite their marginalization and stigmatization in much of modern Western social and political thinking, they are doing pretty well, which is probably just another reminder of the discrepancy between practice and self-representation in modern academia, an intellectual dodge made possible by a very particular kind of oblivion: that human society is built with things.

Notes

CHAPTER 1

1. This clearly includes a good portion of my own work (e.g., Olsen 1987, 1990).
2. The phrase originates from Karl Marx, but has taken on its own "effective history" since then.
3. Thus the "Tardian moments" ascribed Durkheim by Latour are actually far more (and probably more Durkheimian) than acknowledged (Latour 2005).

CHAPTER 2

1. Miller actually writes "the 19th century," which is obviously a slip of the pen.
2. The statement originates from Edmund Husserl but is more widely adopted as a slogan for phenomenology (see Heidegger 1962:50, 58; Merleau-Ponty 1968:4).
3. The literature is far too vast to be referenced fairly. See Meskell (1996), Hamilakis (2002), and Joyce (2005) for overviews, and Meskell and Joyce (2003) for a particularly well-developed discussion.

CHAPTER 3

1. The concept of *différance* is a hybrid of the concepts of *différence* and *differé*, thus combining the notion of "differing" with "deferral." By doing this, Derrida adds a dimension of postponement (and dispersal) to the concept of difference.

2. The translation of Derrida's phrase *"il n'y a pas de hors-texte"* is somewhat debated. More correct semantic versions may be that there is "no outside-text" or even "nothing outside context."

3. Figure captions borrowed from Thomas (2004).

CHAPTER 4

1. This should not be read as though Husserl's later ("genetic") philosophy influenced Heidegger's founding work, *Sein und Zeit*. The latter work can be seen as a reaction against his teacher's early phenomenology, against which Husserl himself also turned.

2. For some critics, Bergson's notion of image is so close to the thing itself that he has no need to distinguish between the thing and its image (Sartre 1962:39–40).

3. While ontic assertions may be seen as necessary for any discussion of the world and the being of things, the thing's ontological "being-in-itself" cannot be clarified from the present-at-hand only (or primarily; cf. Heidegger 1962:106–7).

4. One important lesson from Heidegger's discussion of things' modes of being is that theoretical thinking about them, or reflexivity about the world, in some sense presupposes a suspension of the referential entanglement, our practical ready-to-hand concern (cf. Dreyfus 1991:79–84). This clearly resonates with Bergson's notion of disentanglement as a necessary condition for "picturing" the world.

5. There are also, of course, obvious links to other bodies of work such as Bourdieu's notion of habitus and the conditions under which the "doxic" mode may be questioned and thus brought to mind (1977).

6. In an interesting discussion of this concept, Harman argues that it involved a "diagonal" dualism on two levels: On one level sky and mortals are related as part of the visible (the present-at-hand, "broken tool"), while earth and gods are part of the concealed (the ready-to-hand, "tool"). On another level, Heidegger's distinction between the "specific something" and the "something in general" relates sky and gods (as something specific), as opposed to earth and mortals (as something at all; Harman 2002:203).

7. In most (English language) literature, this term is used untranslated as Heidegger's term for the violating character of modern technology. Directly translated, it means "rack," "skeleton," "frame" (originally: a position, to place), something that (in a negative sense) "frames up" our modern being (Heidegger 1993:325; cf. Inwood 2000:210–11; Young 2002).

8. Actually, this taxonomy continues to also reproduce itself in the "new" material culture studies, where it appears under new names—one of them being implied in the focus on "inalienable" objects (cf. Appadurai 1986b; Thomas 1991).

9. As one will notice, these concepts are given another, much more negative meaning as compared with *Being and Time*.

10. The term belongs to a poem by Rainer Maria Rilke describing how modernity and monetarism have deprived things of their meaning, turning them into

commodities. Thus, things long back: "The ore is homesick. And it yearns to leave the coin and leave the wheel that teaches it to lead a life inane."

CHAPTER 5

1. In an exchange with Theodor Adorno, Benjamin writes favorably about Simmel ("Isn't it time he got some respect") and *The Philosophy of Money* ("Nevertheless, if one disregards its basic idea, very interesting things are to be found in the book" [Benjamin 2003:209]).

2. Miller uses this term very liberally, and Bruno Latour seems to be a key representative of this category of abstracted thinkers despite his numerous works on scientific practice.

CHAPTER 6

1. This premise is of course widely held in archaeology as well. The archaeological concern with past objects as a source material, a way of recollecting the past, is related to our conception of them as present-at-hand traces, sources, or signs.

2. Mulhall actually describes the past dinner plate in its present context as ready-to-hand ("ready-to-hand as a piece of domestic crockery or an antiquity" [1996:18]), a term very difficult to assign to something consciously singled out as historical and treated in a special way according to this abstraction.

CHAPTER 7

1. Merleau-Ponty's notion of flesh is somewhat ambiguous. It is not matter in any direct sense and "to designate it we should need the old term 'element,' in the sense it was used to speak of water, air, earth and fire, that is, in the sense of a *general thing*, midway between the spatio-temporal individual and the idea" (1968:139). He also speaks of it as "the concrete emblem of a general manner of being" (147). In some ways it can be seen as related to Bergson's concept of the image and the "virtual" (cf. Pearson 2002:2 ff.; see chapters 4 and 6).

2. Gell argues against the distinction between art objects and things in general.

3. "In actuality, many externs become artefacts as they are modified through interactions with people or artefacts" (Schiffer 1999:13). This should probably imply that clouds, for example, may today be conceived of as artifacts.

4. For a while, the name seemed to lack confidence. Latour himself declared in 1999 that "there are four things that do not work with actor-network theory: the word 'actor,' the word 'network,' the word 'theory' and the hyphen!" (1999a:15). These "four nails in the coffin" did not bury ANT as a program or its name, and in 2005 Latour published a heavy introduction to the nailed project (Latour 2005).

5. This concept, borrowed from semiotics, has been suggested as an alternative to that of actors (which has a strong human association), in order to establish a

more democratic, more inclusive approach to "who acts" (cf. Latour 1999b:180–82, 303). As noted by Lee and Stenner, "the being of an actant is contingent upon its capacity to act, and its capacity to act is dependent upon its relations to other actants" (1999:93).

CHAPTER 8

1. Needless to say, the distinction between the habitually useful and the discarded past is a very coarse typology that more expresses two extremes of a continuity, rather than any dichotomy.

References

Alcock, S. 2002. *Archaeologies of the Greek past: Landscapes, monuments, and memories*. Cambridge: Cambridge University Press.

Anderson, B. 1983. *Imagined communities: Reflections on the origins and spread of nationalism*. London: Verso.

Andersson, D. 2001. *Tingenes taushet, tingenes tale*. Oslo: Solum Forlag.

Andreassen, E., H. Bjerck, and B. Olsen. 2010. *Persistent memories: Pyramiden— A Soviet mining town in the High Arctic*. Trondheim, Norway: Tapir.

Appadurai, A. 1986a. Introduction: Commodities and the politics of value. In A. Appadurai (ed.), *The social life of things: Commodities in cultural perspectives*. Cambridge: Cambridge University Press.

Appadurai, A. (ed.). 1986b. *The social life of things: Commodities in cultural perspectives*. Cambridge: Cambridge University Press.

Arendt, H. 1958. *The human condition*. Chicago: University of Chicago Press.

Arntzen, M. 2007. Bilder på stein. En studie av helleristninger på flyttblokker I Nord-Troms og Vest-Finnmark. Master's thesis, University of Tromsø.

Ashmore, W. 2004. Social archaeologies of landscapes. In L. Meskell and R. Preucel (eds.), *A companion to social archaeology*. Oxford: Blackwell.

Ashmore, W., and A. Knapp. 1999. Archaeological landscapes: Constructed, conceptualised, ideational. In W. Ashmore and A. Knapp (eds.), *Archaeologies of landscape: Contemporary perspectives*. Oxford: Blackwell.

Assman, J. 1992. *Das kulturelle Gedächtniss*. Munich: C. H. Beck.

Attfield, J. 2000. *Wild things: The material culture of everyday life*. Oxford: Berg.

Augé, M. 1995. *Non-places: Introduction to the anthropology of supermodernity*. London: Verso.

Baker, F., and J. Thomas (eds.). 1990. *Writing the past in the present*. Lampeter, UK: St David's University College.

Bakker, K., and G. Bridge. 2006. Material worlds? Resource geographies and the "matter of nature." *Progress in Human Geography* 30(1): 1–23.

Barret, J. 1994. *Fragments from antiquity*. Oxford: Blackwell.

Barret, J. 2000. A thesis on agency. In M.-A. Dobres and J. Robb (eds.), *Agency in archaeology*. London: Routledge.

Barth, F. 1961. Diffusjon—Et tema i studiet av kulturelle prosesser. In A. Klausen (ed.), *Kultur og diffusjon*. Oslo: Universitetsforlaget.

Barthes, R. 1975. *S/Z*, trans. R. Miller. London: Cape.

Barthes, R. 1976. *The pleasure of the text*. London: Cape.

Barthes, R. 1977. *Image-music-text*. London: Fontana.

Barthes, R. 1985. *The fashion system*. London: Cape.

Barthes, R. 1986. *The rustle of language*, ed. F. Wahl. Oxford: Blackwell.

Baudrillard, J. 1998. *The consumer society: Myths and structure*. London: Sage.

Beaudry, M. 1978. Worth its weight in iron: Categories of material culture in early Virginia probate inventories. *Archaeological Society of Virginia, Quarterly Bulletin* 33(1): 19–26.

Beek, G. van. 1989. The object as subject: New routes to material culture studies. Review of *Material culture and mass consumption*, by Daniel Miller. *Critique of Anthropology* 9(3): 91–99.

Beek, G. van. 1991. Words and things: A comment on Bouquet's "Images of arte-facts." *Critique of Anthropology* 11(4): 357–60.

Bender, B. 1993. Introduction. In B. Bender (ed.), *Landscape: Politics and perspectives*. Oxford: Berg.

Bender, B. 1999. Subverting the Western gaze: Mapping alternative worlds. In P. J. Ucko and R. Layton (eds.), *The archaeology and anthropology of landscape: Shaping your landscape*. London: Routledge.

Bender, B. 2002. Landscape and politics. In V. Buchli (ed.), *The material culture reader*. Oxford: Berg.

Bender, B., S. Hamilton, and C. Tilley. 2007. *Stone worlds: Narrativity and reflexivity in landscape archaeology*. Walnut Creek, Calif.: Left Coast Press.

Benjamin, W. 1996. *Selected writings, volume 1: 1913–1926*. Cambridge, Mass.: Belknap Press.

Benjamin, W. 1999a. *Selected writings, volume 2: 1927–1934*. Cambridge, Mass.: Belknap Press.

Benjamin, W. 1999b. *The arcades project*. Cambridge, Mass.: Belknap Press.

Benjamin, W. 2002. *Selected writings, volume 3: 1935–1938*. Cambridge, Mass.: Belknap Press.

Benjamin, W. 2003. *Selected writings, volume 4: 1938–1940*. Cambridge, Mass.: Belknap Press.

Benso, S. 2000. *The face of things: A different side of ethics*. Albany: State University of New York Press.

Berger, A. 1992. *Reading matter: Multidisciplinary perspectives on material culture*. New Brunswick: Transaction.

Bergson, H. 1998. *Creative evolution*. Mineola, N.Y.: Dover.

Bergson, H. 2004. *Matter and memory*. Mineola, N.Y.: Dover.

Bickel, B. 2000. Grammar and social practice: On the role of "culture" in linguistic relativity. In S. Niemeier and R. Dirven (eds.), *Evidence for linguistic relativity*. Amsterdam: John Benjamins.

Binford, L. 1962. Archaeology as anthropology. *American Antiquity* 28:217–25.

Binford, L. 1972. *An archaeological perspective.* New York: Seminar Press.

Binford, L. 1983. *Working at archaeology.* New York: Academic Press.

Bintliff, J. 2007. History and Continental approaches. In R. Bentley, H. Maschner, and C. Chippendale (eds.), *Handbook of archaeological theories.* Walnut Creek, Calif.: AltaMira Press.

Bjerck, H. 1995. Malte menneskebilder i «Helvete». Betraktninger om en nyoppdaget hulemaling på Trenyken. Røst. Nordland. *Univ. Oldsaksamlings Årbok* 1993/1994, 121–51.

Bjorvand, H., and F. Lindeman. 2000. *Våre arveord. Etymologisk ordbok.* Oslo: Novus Forlag.

Boast, R. 1997. A small company of actors: A critique of style. *Journal of Material Culture* 2(2): 173–98.

Boivin, N. 2004. Mind over matter? Collapsing the mind-matter dichotomy in material culture studies. In E. DeMarrais, C. Gosden, and C. Renfrew (eds.), *Rethinking materiality: The engagement of mind with the material world.* Cambridge: McDonald Institute for Archaeological Research.

Boivin, N., A. Brumm, H. Lewis, D. Robinson, and R. Korisettar. 2007. Sensual, material, and technological understanding: Exploring prehistoric soundscapes in South India. *Journal of the Royal Anthropological Institute* (n.s.) 13:267–94.

Bouquet, M. 1991. Images of artefacts. *Critique of Anthropology* 11(4): 333–56.

Bourdieu, P. 1973. The Berber house. In I. Douglas (ed.), *Rules and meanings: The anthropology of everyday knowledge.* London: Routledge.

Bourdieu, P. 1977. *Outline of a theory of practice.* Cambridge: Cambridge University Press.

Boyer, M. 1994. *The city of collective memory.* Cambridge, Mass.: MIT Press.

Bradley, R. 1993. *Altering the earth: The origins of monuments in Britain and Continental Europe.* Monograph series 8. Edinburgh: Society of Antiquaries of Scotland.

Bradley, R. 1998. *The significance of monuments.* London: Routledge.

Bradley, R. 2000. *An archaeology of natural places.* London: Routledge.

Bradley, R. 2002. *The past in prehistoric societies.* London: Routledge.

Bradley, R. 2003. The translation of time. In R. Van Dyke and S. Alcock (eds.), *Archaeologies of memories.* Oxford: Blackwell.

Brooker, A. 1999. *A concise glossary of cultural theory.* London: Arnold.

Brown, B. 2003. *A sense of things: The object matter of American literature.* Chicago: University of Chicago Press.

Buchli, V. 1995. Interpreting material culture: The trouble with the text. In I. Hodder, M. Shanks, A. Alessandri, V. Buchli, J. Carman, J. Last, and G. Lucas (eds.), *Interpreting archaeology: Finding meaning in the past.* London: Routledge.

Buchli, V. (ed.). 2002. *The material culture reader.* Oxford: Berg.

Buchli, V. 2004. Material culture: Current problems. In L. Meskell and R. Preucel (eds.), *A companion to social archaeology.* Oxford: Blackwell.

Buck-Morss, S. 1977. *The origin of negative dialectics: Theodor W. Adorno, Walter Benjamin and the Frankfurt Institute.* New York: The Free Press.

Buck-Morss, S. 1999. *The dialectics of seeing: Walter Benjamin and the arcades project.* Cambridge, Mass.: MIT Press.

Burström, M. 2007. *Samtidsarkeologi. Introduktion till et forskningsfält.* Stockholm: Studentlitteratur.

Butler, J. 1993. *Bodies that matter: On the discursive limits of sex.* London: Routledge.

Bygstad, B., and K. H. Rolland. 2004. ANT og Information Systems: En episte-mologisk forelskelse. *Sosiologi i dag* 34(2): 69–86.

Callon, M. 1986. Some elements of a sociology of translation: Domestication of the scallops and the fishermen of St Brieux Bay. In J. Law (ed.), *Power, action and belief: A new sociology of knowledge?* London: Routledge.

Callon, M. 1999. Actor-network theory: The market test. In J. Law and J. Hassard (eds.), *Actor network theory and after.* Oxford: Blackwell.

Callon, M., and J. Law. 1997. After the individual in society: Lessons on collec-tivity from science, technology and society. *Canadian Journal of Sociology* 22(2): 165–82.

Campbell, F., and J. Hansson. 2000. *Archaeological sensibilities.* Gotarc series C, Arkeologiska Skrifter 38. Gothenburg: Department of Archaeology, University of Gothenburg.

Casey, E. 1984. Habitual body and memory in Merleau-Ponty. *Man and World* 17:279–97.

Casey, E. 1987. *Remembering: A phenomenological study.* Bloomington: Indiana Uni-versity Press.

Casey, E. 1998. *The fate of place.* Berkeley: University of California Press.

Childe, V. 1933. Is prehistory practical? *Antiquity* 7:410–18.

Christensen, C. 1993. Tingenes tidsalder. Kitsch, camp og fetishisme. In C. Chris-tensen and C. Thau (eds.), *Omgang med tingene. Ti essays om tingenes tilstand.* Åarhus: Århus Universitetsforlag.

Clifford, J. 1986. Introduction: Partial truths. In J. Clifford and G. Marcus (eds.), *Writing culture: The poetics and politics of ethnography.* Berkeley: University of California Press.

Clifford, J. 1988. *The predicament of culture: Twentieth-century ethnography, literature, and art.* Cambridge, Mass.: Harvard University Press.

Clifford, J. 1997. *Routes: Travel and translation in the late twentieth century.* Cam-bridge, Mass.: Harvard University Press.

Clifford, J., and G. Marcus. 1986. *Writing culture: The poetics and politics of ethnogra-phy.* Berkeley: University of California Press.

Clottes, J. 2007. New discoveries at Niaux Cave in the French Pyrenees. In P.C. Reddy (ed.), *Exploring the mind of ancient man: Festschrift to Robert G. Bednarik.* New Delhi: Research India Press.

Coles, A., and M. Dion (eds.). 1999. *Mark Dion archaeology.* London: Black Dog.

Connerton, P. 1989. *How societies remember.* Cambridge: Cambridge University Press.

Connor, S. 1997. *Postmodernist culture.* Oxford: Blackwell.

Cooney, G. 1999. Social landscapes in Irish prehistory. In P. Ucko and R. Layton (eds.), *The archaeology and anthropology of landscape: Shaping your landscape.* Lon-don: Routledge.

Crane, S. (ed.). 2000. *Museums and memory.* Stanford, Calif.: Stanford University Press.

Cummings, V., and A. Whittle. 2003. *Places of special virtue: Megaliths in the Neo-lithic landscape of Wales.* Oxford: Oxbow Books.

Dant, T. 1999. *Material culture in the social world: Values, activities, lifestyles.* Maid-enhead, UK: Open University Press.

Dant, T. 2005. *Materiality and society*. Maidenhead, UK: Open University Press.

Deetz, J. 1967. *Invitation to archaeology*. New York: Natural History Press.

Deetz, J. 1977. *In small things forgotten: The archaeology of early American life*. New York: Anchor Books.

Deetz, J., and P. Scott Deetz. 2001. *The times of their lives: Life, love, and death in Plymouth Colony*. New York: W. H. Freeman.

Deleuze, G. 1991. *Bergsonism*. Cambridge, Mass.: MIT Press.

Derrida, J. 1973. *Speech and phenomena*. Evanston, Ill.: Northwestern University Press.

Derrida, J. 1977. *Of grammatology*. Baltimore: Johns Hopkins University Press.

Derrida, J. 1978. *Writing and difference*. London: Routledge.

Derrida, J. 1979. Living on: Border lines. In H. Bloom, P. de Man, J. Derrida, G. Hartman, and J. Miller, *Deconstruction and criticism*. New York: Continuum.

Derrida, J. 1987. *Positions*. London: Athlone Press.

DeSilvey, C. 2006. Observed decay: Telling stories with mutable things. *Journal of Material Culture* 11(3): 318–38.

DeVore, I. 1968. Comments. In S. Binford and L. Binford (eds.), *New perspectives in archaeology*. Chicago: Aldine.

Dirven, R., H.-G. Wolf, and F. Polzenhagen. 2007. Cognitive linguistics and cultural studies. In D. Geeraerts and H. Cuyckens (eds.), *The Oxford handbook of cognitive linguistics*. New York: Oxford University Press.

Dolwick, J. 2008. In search of the social: Steamboats, square wheels, reindeer and other things. *Journal of Maritime Archaeology* 3(1): 15–41.

Domańska, E. 2006. The return to things. *Archaeologia Polona* 44:171–85.

Domańska, E., and B. Olsen, 2008. Wszyscy jesteś.my konstruktywistami. In J. Kowalewski and W. Piasek (eds.), *Rzeczy i ludzie. Humanistyka wobec materialności*. Colloquia Humaniorum. Olsztyn: UWM.

Douglas, M., and B. Isherwood. 1979. *The world of goods: Towards an anthropology of consumption*. New York: Basic Books.

Dreyfus, H. 1991. *Being-in-the-world: A commentary on Heidegger's "Being and time," division 1*. Cambridge, Mass.: MIT Press.

Droit, R.-P. 2005. *How are things? A philosophical experiment*. London: Faber and Faber.

Durkheim, E. 1951. *The suicide: A study in sociology*. New York: Free Press.

Edensor, T. 2005. *Industrial ruins: Space, aesthetics and materiality*. Oxford: Berg.

Edmonds, M. 1999. *Ancestral geographies in the Neolithic*. London: Routledge.

Eriksen, T., and T. Sørheim. 2006. *Kulturforskjeller i praksis: Perspektiver på det flerkulturelle Norge*. Oslo: Gyldendal Akademisk.

Evans, J. 2003. *Environmental archaeology and the social order*. London: Routledge.

Fabian, J. 1983. *Time and the other: How anthropology makes its object*. New York: Columbia University Press.

Fabian, J. 1990. Presence and representation: The other and anthropological writing. *Critical Inquiry* 16:753–72.

Fahlander, F., and T. Østigård. (eds.). 2004. *Material culture and other things: Post-disciplinary studies in the twenty-first century*. Gotarc series C, no. 61. Gothenburg: Department of Archaeology, University of Gothenburg.

Falk, H., and A. Torp. 1994/1906. *Etymologisk ordbog over det norske og det danske sprog*. Oslo: Bjørn Ringstrøms antikvariat.

Feldt, S., and K. Basso. (eds.). 1996. *Senses of place.* Santa Fe, N.Mex.: School of American Research Press.

Fenton, W. 1974. The advancement of material culture studies in modern anthropological research. In M. Richardson (ed.), *The human mirror: Material and spatial images of man.* Baton Rouge: Louisiana State University Press.

Fischer, M. 1986. Ethnicity and the postmodern arts of memory. In J. Clifford and G. Marcus (eds.), *Writing culture: The poetics and politics of ethnography.* Berkeley: University of California Press.

Fjellström, P. 1981/1755. *Kort berättelse om Lapparnas björna-fänge samt deras der wid brukade widskeppelser.* Umeå, Sweden: Två Förläggare Bokförlag.

Foster, H. 1996. *The return of the real: Art and theory at the end of the century.* Cambridge, Mass.: MIT Press.

Foucault, M. 1970. *The archaeology of knowledge.* London: Tavistock.

Foucault, M. 1973. *The birth of the clinic: An archaeology of medical perception.* London: Tavistock.

Foucault, M. 1979. *Discipline and punish: The birth of the prison.* Harmondsworth, UK: Penguin Books.

Foucault, M. 1989. *The order of things: An archaeology of the human sciences.* London: Routledge.

Fowler, C. 2001. Personhood and social relations in the British Neolithic with a study from the Isle of Man. *Journal of Material Culture* 6(2): 137–63.

Friedell, E. 1937. *Kulturhistorie 3. Kulturstrømninger fra den sorte død til verdenskrigen.* Copenhagen: Berlingske Forlag.

Frieman, C., and M. Gillings. 2007. Seeing is perceiving? *World Archaeology* 39(1): 4–16.

Fuglestvedt, I. 2005. *Pionerbosetningens fenomenologi. Sørvest-Norge og Nord-Europa, 10200/10000-9500 BP.* AMS-nett 6. Stavanger, Norway: Museum of Archaeology, Stavanger.

Gadamer, H.-G. 1975. *Truth and method.* London: Sheed and Ward.

Gamble, C. 2001. *Archaeology: The basics.* London: Routledge.

Gansum, T., and H. Hansen. 2002. *Fra jern til stål. Mytologiske og rituelle aspekter i teknologiske prosesser.* Borre, Norway: Midtgard historiske senter.

Gaver, W. 1996. Affordances for interaction: The social is material for design. *Ecological Psychology* 8(2): 111–29.

Geertz, C. 1988. *Works and lives: The anthropologist as author.* Cambridge: Polity Press.

Gell, A. 1998. *Art and agency: An anthropological theory.* Oxford: Clarendon Press.

Gibbon, G. 1989. *Explanation in archaeology.* Oxford: Blackwell.

Gibson, J. 1986. *The ecological approach to visual perception.* Hillsdale, N.J.: Erlbaum.

Giddens, A. 1981. *A contemporary critique of historical materialism.* London: Macmillan.

Giles, M. 2001. Taking hands: Archaeology, poetry and photography. *Staple* 51:28–31.

Gjerde, J. 2006. The location of rock pictures is an interpretive element. In R. Barndon, S. Innselset, K. Kristoffersen, and T. Lødøen (eds.), *Samfunn, symboler og identitet—Festskrift til Gro Mandt på 70-årsdagen.* Bergen: Universitetet i Bergen.

Gjerde, J. In press. "Cracking" Landscapes: New documentation—New knowledge? In J. Goldhahn, I. Fuglestvedt, and A. Jones (eds.), *Changing pictures: Rock art traditions and visions in northernmost Europe.* Oxford: Oxbow.

Gjessing, G. 1951. Arkeologi og etnografi. *Viking* 15:115–36.

Glassie, H. 1975. *Folk housing in Middle Virginia: A structural analysis of historical artifacts*. Knoxville: University of Tennessee Press.

Glassie, H. 1999. *Material culture*. Bloomington: Indiana University Press.

Godelier, M. 1977. *Perspectives in Marxist anthropology*. Cambridge: Cambridge University Press.

González-Ruibal, A. 2006. The dream of reason: An archaeology of the failures of modernity in Ethiopia. *Journal of Social Archaeology* 6:175–201.

González-Ruibal, A. 2008. Time to destroy: An archaeology of supermodernity. *Current Anthropology* 49(2): 247–79.

Gosden, C. 1994. *Social being and time*. Blackwell: Oxford.

Gosden, C. 1999. *Anthropology and archaeology: A changing relationship*. London: Routledge.

Grosz, E. 2002. *Architecture from the outside: Essays on virtual and real space*. Cambridge, Mass.: MIT Press.

Gurevich, A. 1992. Wealth and gift-bestowal among the ancient Scandinavians. In J. Howlett (ed.), *Historical anthropology of the Middle Ages*. Cambridge: Polity Press.

Hacking, I. 2001. *The social construction of what?* Cambridge, Mass.: Harvard University Press.

Hahn, H. 2004. *Materielle Kultur. Eine Einführung*. Berlin: Dietrich Reimer Verlag.

Håland, R. 1977. Archaeological classification and ethnic groups: A case study from Sudanese Nubia. *Norwegian Archaeological Review* 10(1): 1–17.

Hall, M. 1996. *Archaeology Africa*. Cape Town: David Philip.

Hamilakis, Y. 2001. Art and the representation of the past: Commentary. *Journal of the Royal Anthropological Institute* 7(1): 153–54.

Hamilakis, Y. 2002. The past as oral history: Towards an archaeology of the senses. In Y. Hamilakis, M. Pluciennik, and S. Tarlow (eds.), *Thinking through the body: Archaeologies of corporeality*. New York: Kluwer/Plenum.

Hamilakis, Y., M. Pluciennik, and S. Tarlow. (eds.). 2002. *Thinking through the body: Archaeologies of corporeality*. New York: Kluwer/Plenum.

Hamilton, S., R. Whitehouse, K. Brown, P. Combes, E. Herring, and M. Seager Thomas. 2006. Phenomenology in practice: Towards a methodology for a "subjective" approach. *European Journal of Archaeology* 9(1): 31–71.

Hansen, L., and B. Olsen. 2004. *Samenes historie fram til 1750*. Oslo: Cappelen.

Haraway, D. 1991. *Simians, cyborgs and women: The reinvention of nature*. New York: Routledge.

Harman, G. 2002. *Tool-being: Heidegger and the metaphysics of objects*. Chicago: Open Court.

Hastrup, K. 1992. Writing ethnography: State of the art. In J. Okely and H. Callaway (eds.), *Anthropology and autobiography*. London: Routledge.

Hastrup, K., and P. Hervik. (eds.). 1994. *Social experience and anthropological knowledge*. London: Routledge.

Hatt, E. Demant. 1913. *Med lapperne i høyfjeldet*. Stockholm: Nordiska Bokhandelen.

Hauptman Wahlgren, K. 2002. *Bilder av betydelse. Hällristningar och bronsåldersland-skap i nordöstra Östergötland*. Stockholm Studies in Archaeology 23. Gothenburg: Bricoleur.

Hawkes, C. 1954. Archaeological theory and method: Some suggestions from the Old World. *American Anthropologists* 56:155–68.

Heidegger, M. 1962. *Being and time.* New York: Harper and Row.

Heidegger, M. 1966. *Discourse on thinking.* New York: Harper and Row.

Heidegger, M. 1971. *Poetry, language, thought.* New York: Harper and Row.

Heidegger, M. 1982. *Basic problems of phenomenology.* Bloomington: Indiana University Press.

Heidegger, M. 1993. The question concerning technology. In D. Farell Krell (ed.), *Martin Heidegger: Basic writings.* San Francisco: Harper Collins.

Held, D. 1980. *Introduction to critical theory: Horkheimer to Habermas.* London: Hutchinson.

Helskog, K. 2004. Landscapes in rock-art: Rock-carving and ritual in the old European North. In C. Chippindale and G. Nash (eds.), *The figured landscape of rock-art: Looking at pictures in place.* Cambridge: Cambridge University Press.

Helskog, K., and E. Høgtun. 2004. Recording landscapes in rock carvings and the art of drawing. In G. Milstreu and H. Prøhl (eds.), *Prehistoric pictures as archaeological source.* Tanumshede, Sweden: Tanums Hällristningsmuseum.

Hesjedal, A. 1992. Helleristninger som tegn og tekst. Magister thesis, University of Tromsø.

Hesjedal, A. 1994. The hunters' rock art in northern Norway: Problems in chronology and interpretation. *Norwegian Archaeological Review* 27(1): 1–14.

Hicks, D. 2005. "Places for thinking" from Annapolis to Bristol: Situations and symmetries in "world historical archaeologies." *World Archaeology* 37(3): 373–91.

Hodder, I. 1982a. Theoretical archaeology: A reactionary view. In I. Hodder (ed.), *Structural and symbolic archaeology.* Cambridge: Cambridge University Press.

Hodder, I. 1982b. *Symbols in action.* Cambridge: Cambridge University Press.

Hodder, I. 1985. Post-processual archaeology. *Advances in Archaeological Method and Theory* 8:1–26.

Hodder, I. 1986. *Reading the past: Current approaches to interpretation in archaeology.* Cambridge: Cambridge University Press.

Hodder, I. 1989. This is not an article about material culture as text. *Journal of Anthropological Archaeology* 8:250–69.

Hodder, I. 1999. *The archaeological process: An introduction.* Oxford: Blackwell.

Hodder, I. 2004. The "social" in archaeological theory: An historical and contemporary perspective. In L. Meskell and R. Preucel (eds.), *A companion to social archaeology.* Oxford: Blackwell.

Hodder, I., and S. Hutson. 2003. *Reading the past: Current approaches to interpretation in archaeology.* Cambridge: Cambridge University Press.

Hodder, I., and R. Preucel. (eds.). 1996. *Contemporary archaeology in theory: A reader.* Oxford: Blackwell.

Hodder, I., M. Shanks, A. Alessandri, V. Buchli, J. Carman, J. Last, and G. Lucas. (eds.). 1995. *Interpreting archaeology: Finding meaning in the past.* London: Routledge.

Hodgson, D. 2008. The visual dynamics of Upper Palaeolithic cave art. *Cambridge Archaeological Journal* 18(3): 341–53.

Holm, P. 2000. Ressursforvaltning som heterogent nettverk. In H. Gammelsaeter (ed.), *Innovasjonspolitikk, kunnskapsflyt og regional utvikling.* Trondheim, Norway: Tapir.

Holtorf, C. 1998. The life-history of megaliths in Mecklenburg-Vorpommern (Germany). *World Archaeology* 30(1): 23–38.

Holtorf, C. 2002. Notes on the life history of a pot sherd. *Journal of Material Culture* 7:49–71.

Holtorf, C. 2008. Comment on A. González-Ruibal, "Time to destroy: An archaeology of supermodernity." *Current Anthropology* 49:265–66.

Husserl, E. 1970. *The crisis of European sciences and transcendental philosophy.* Evanston, Ill.: Northwestern University Press.

Husserl, E. 1976. *Logical investigations.* London: Routledge.

Husserl, E. 1982. *Ideas pertaining to a pure phenomenology and to a phenomenological philosophy*, first book. Dordrecht, Netherlands: Kluwer Academic.

Huyssen, A. 2003. *Present pasts: Urban palimpsests and the politics of memory.* Stanford, Calif.: Stanford University Press.

Ingold, T. 2000. *Perception of the environment: Essays in livelihood, dwelling and skill.* London: Routledge.

Ingold, T. 2007a. Materials against materiality. *Archaeological Dialogues* 14(1): 1–16.

Ingold, T. 2007b. Writing texts, reading materials: A response to my critics. *Archaeological Dialogues* 14(1): 31–38.

Ingold, T. 2008. Bindings against boundaries: Entanglements of life in an open world. *Environment and Planning A* 40:1796–1810.

Inwood, M. 2000. *A Heidegger dictionary.* Oxford: Blackwell.

Iser, W. 1974. *The implied reader.* Baltimore: Johns Hopkins University Press.

Iser, W. 1978. *The act of reading: A theory of aesthetic response.* Baltimore: Johns Hopkins University Press.

Jameson, F. 1984. Postmodernism, or the cultural logic of late capitalism. *New Left Review* 146:53–92.

Jameson, I. and R. Shaw. 1999. *A dictionary of archaeology.* Oxford: Blackwell.

Jay, M. 1998. Scopic regimes of modernity. In N. Mirzoeff (ed.), *The visual culture reader.* London: Routledge.

Joerges, B. 1988. Technology in everyday life: Conceptual queries. *Journal for the Theory of Social Behaviour* 18(2): 219–37.

Johansen, T. 1992. *Kulissenes regi. En sosiomateriell analyse av forutsetningene for makt og mestring.* Oslo: Universitetsforlaget.

Johnsen, H., and B. Olsen. 1992. Hermeneutics and archaeology: On the philosophy of contextual archaeology. *American Antiquity* 57(3): 419–36.

Johnsen, J.P. 2004. Latour, nature og havforskere—hvordan produsere nature? *Sosiologi i dag* 34(2): 47–67.

Johnson, M. 1999. *Archaeological theory: An introduction.* Oxford: Blackwell.

Johnson, M. 2006. Archaeological and theoretical culture. *Archaeological Dialogues* 13(2): 167–72.

Jones, A. 2003. Technologies of remembrance: Memory, materiality and identity in Early Bronze Age Scotland. In H. Williams (ed.), *Archaeologies of remembrance: Death and memory in past societies.* New York: Kluwer/Plenum.

Jones, A. 2007. *Memory and material culture.* Cambridge: Cambridge University Press.

Joyce, R. 1994. Dorothy Hughes Popenoe: Eve in an archaeological garden. In C. Claasen (ed.), *Women in archaeology.* Philadelphia: University of Pennsylvania Press.

Joyce, R. (with R. Preucel and J. Lopiparo). 2002. *The languages of archaeology: Dialogue, narrative and writing*. Oxford: Blackwell.

Joyce, R. 2003. Concrete memories: Fragments of the past in the Classic Maya present (500–1000 AD). In R. Van Dyke and S. Alcock (eds.), *Archaeologies of memory*. Oxford: Blackwell.

Joyce, R. 2005. Archaeology of the body. *Annual Reviews in Anthropology* 34:139–58.

Julien, M.-P., and C. Rosselin. 2005. *La culture matérielle*. Paris: La Découverte.

Kagge, E. 1993. *Alene til Sydpolen*. Oslo: Cappelen.

Kalstad, J. 1997. Noaidier og trommer: Samiske religiøse tradisjoner fra vår nære fortid. *Ottar* nr. 217.

Kant, I. 2001/1783. *Prolegomena to any further metaphysics*. Indianapolis: Hackett.

Karlsson, H. 1998. *Re-thinking archaeology*. Gotarc series B, Archaeological Theses 8. Gothenburg: Department of Archaeology, University of Gothenburg.

Keyser, J., and G. Poetschat. 2004. The canvas as the art: Landscape analysis of the rock-art panel. In C. Chippindale and G. Nash (eds.), *The figured landscapes of rock-art: Looking at pictures in place*. Cambridge: Cambridge University Press.

Klausen, A. 1981. *Antropologiens historie*. Oslo: Gyldendal.

Knappett, C. 2005. *Thinking through material culture: An interdisciplinary perspective*. Philadelphia: University of Pennsylvania Press.

Knappett, C., and L. Malafouris. 2008. *Material agency: Towards a non-anthropocentric approach*. New York: Springer.

Kopytoff, I. 1986. The cultural biography of things: Commoditization as process. In A. Appadurai (ed.), *The social life of things*. Cambridge: Cambridge University Press.

Körner, S. 1955. *Kant*. Harmondsworth, UK: Penguin Books.

Kristeva, J. 1982. *The power of horror: An essay in abjection*. Oxford: Blackwell.

Kristeva, J. 1986. *The Kristeva reader*, ed. Toril Moi. Oxford: Blackwell.

Kuper, A. 1978. *Anthropologists and anthropology: The British school 1922–72*. Harmondsworth, UK: Penguin Books.

Latour, B. 1986. The power of association. In J. Law (ed.), *Power, action and belief*. London: Routledge.

Latour, B. 1987. *Science in action: How to follow scientists and engineers through society*. Cambridge, Mass.: Harvard University Press.

Latour, B. 1992. Where are the missing masses? The sociology of a few mundane artifacts. In W. E. Bijker and J. Law (eds.), *Shaping technology/holding society*. Cambridge, Mass.: MIT Press.

Latour, B. 1993. *We have never been modern*. London: Harvard University Press.

Latour, B. 1999a. On recalling ANT. In J. Law and J. Hassard (eds.), *Actor network theory and after*. Oxford: Blackwell.

Latour, B. 1999b. *Pandora's hope: Essays on the reality of science studies*. London: Harvard University Press.

Latour, B. 2002. Bodies, cyborgs and the politics of incarnation. In S. Sweeney and I. Hodder (eds.), *The body*. Cambridge: Cambridge University Press.

Latour, B. 2003. Is re-modernization occurring? *Theory, Culture and Society* 20(2): 35–48.

Latour, B. 2005. *Reassembling the social: An introduction to actor-network-theory.* Oxford: Oxford University Press.

Law, J. 1999. After ANT: Complexity, naming and topology. In J. Law and J. Hassard (eds.), *Actor network theory and after.* Oxford: Blackwell.

Law, J., and J. Hassard. (eds.). 1999. *Actor network theory and after.* Oxford: Blackwell.

Law, J., and A. Mol. (eds.). 2002. *Complexities: Social studies of knowledge practices.* Durham, N.C.: Duke University Press.

Layton, R., P. Stone, and J. Thomas. (eds.). 2001. *The destruction and conservation of cultural property.* London: Routledge.

Leach, E. 1973. Concluding address. In C. Renfrew (ed.), *The explanation of culture change: Models in prehistory.* Pittsburgh: University of Pittsburgh Press.

Lee, N., and P. Stenner. 1999. Who pays? Can we pay them back? In J. Law and J. Hassard (eds.), *Actor network theory and after.* Oxford: Blackwell.

Lefebvre, H. 1987. The everyday and everydayness. *Yale French Studies* 73(Fall): 7–11.

Lemonnier, P. 1992. *Elements for an anthropology of technology.* Anthropological Papers 88, Museum of Anthropology, University of Michigan. Ann Arbor: University of Michigan.

Lemonnier, P. 1993. *Technical choices: Transformations in material cultures since the Neolithic.* London: Routledge.

Leone, M. 1977. The new Mormon temple in Washington, D.C. In L. Ferguson (ed.), *Historical archaeology and the importance of material things.* Special Series 2. Lansing, Mich.: Society for Historical Archaeology.

Leone, M. 2007. Beginning for a postmodern archaeology. *Cambridge Archaeological Journal* 17(2): 203–7.

Leroi-Gourhan, A. 1964. *Le geste et la parole I, Technique et langage.* Paris: Albin Michel.

Leroi-Gourhan, A. 1965. *Le geste et la parole II, La mémoire et les rythmes.* Paris: Albin Michel.

Löfgren, O. 1997. Scenes from a troubled marriage: Swedish ethnology and material culture studies. *Journal of Material Culture* 2(1): 95–113.

Lucas, G. 2001. *Critical approaches to fieldwork: Historical and contemporary archaeological practice.* London: Routledge.

Lucas, G. 2004. Modern disturbances: On the ambiguities of archaeology. *Modernism/modernity* 11:109–20.

Lucas, G. 2005. *The archaeology of time.* London: Routledge.

Lucas, G. 2008. Time and the archaeological event. *Cambridge Archaeological Journal* 18(1): 59–65.

Lyotard, J.-F. 1984. *The postmodern condition: A report on knowledge.* Manchester: Manchester University Press.

Macann, C. 1993. *Four phenomenological philosophers: Husserl, Heidegger, Sartre, Merleau-Ponty.* London: Routledge.

Malafouris, L. 2008. Beads for a plastic mind: The "blind man's stick" (BMS) hypothesis and the active nature of material culture. *Cambridge Archaeological Journal* 18(3): 401–14.

Marcus, G., and M. Fischer. 1986. *Anthropology as cultural critique*. Chicago: University of Chicago Press.

Marx, K. 1968. *The Eighteenth Brumaire of Louis Bonaparte*. New York: International Publishers.

Marx, K. 1975. *Early writings*. Harmondsworth, UK: Penguin Books.

Matthews, E. 2002. *The philosophy of Merleau-Ponty*. Montreal: McGill–Queen's University Press.

Mauss, M. 1979. The notion of body techniques. In M. Mauss, *Sociology and psychology*. London: Routledge and Kegan Paul.

McGuckin, E. 1997. Tibetan carpets: From folk art to global community. *Journal of Material Culture* 2(3): 291–310.

Merleau-Ponty, M. 1962. *The phenomenology of perception*. London: Routledge and Kegan Paul.

Merleau-Ponty, M. 1968. *The visible and the invisible*. Evanston, Ill.: Northwestern University Press.

Meskell, L. 1996. The somatisation of archaeology: Institutions, discourses, corporeality. *Norwegian Archaeological Review* 29(1): 1–16.

Meskell, L. 2004. *Object worlds in ancient Egypt: Material biographies past and present*. Oxford: Berg.

Meskell, L. 2005. Introduction: Object orientations. In L. Meskell (ed.), *Archaeologies of materiality*. Oxford: Blackwell.

Meskell, L., and R. Joyce. 2003. *Embodied lives: Figuring ancient Egypt and the Classic Maya*. London: Routledge.

Miller, D. (ed.). 1983. Things ain't what they used to be. Special issue on material culture, *Royal Anthropological Institute News* 59.

Miller, D. 1985. *Artefacts as categories: A study of ceramic variability in central India*. Cambridge: Cambridge University Press.

Miller, D. 1987. *Material culture and mass consumption*. Oxford: Blackwell.

Miller, D. 1994. Artefacts and the meaning of things. In T. Ingold (ed.), *Companion encyclopedia of anthropology*. London: Routledge.

Miller, D. 1998a. Why some things matter. In D. Miller (ed.), *Material cultures: Why some things matter*. London: University College London Press.

Miller, D. 1998b. *A theory of shopping*. Cambridge: Polity Press.

Miller, D. 2001. *The dialectics of shopping (The 1998 Morgan Lectures)*. Chicago: University of Chicago Press.

Miller, D. 2002. Consumption. In V. Buchli (ed.), *The material culture reader*. Oxford: Berg.

Miller, D. 2005a. Materiality: An introduction. In D. Miller (ed.), *Materiality*. Durham, N.C.: Duke University Press.

Miller, D. 2005b. Afterword. In L. Meskell (ed.), *Archaeologies of materiality*. Oxford: Blackwell.

Miller, D. 2007. Stone Age or Plastic Age? *Archaeological Dialogues* 14:23–27.

Moore, H. 1986. *Space, text and gender: An archaeological study of the Marakwet of Kenya*. Cambridge: Cambridge University Press.

Moser, I., and J. Law. 1999. Good passages, bad passages. In J. Law and J. Hassard (eds.), *Actor network theory and after*. Oxford: Blackwell.

Mulhall, S. 1996. *Heidegger and "Being and time."* London: Routledge.

Mullarkey, J. 2000. *Bergson and philosophy*. Notre Dame, Ind.: University of Notre Dame Press.

Müller, S. 1884. Mindre Bidrag til den forhistoriske Archæologis Methode II. Den archæologiske Sammenligning som Grundlag for Slutning og Hypothese. *Aarbøger for nordisk Oldkyndighed og Historie* 1884:183–203.

Mullins, P. 2004. Ideology, power, and capitalism: The historical archaeology of consumption. In L. Meskell and R. Preucel (eds.), *The Blackwell companion to social archaeology*. Oxford: Blackwell.

Myrstad, R. 1996. *Bjørnegraver i Nord-Norge: Spor etter den samiske bjørnekulten.* Stensilserie B, historie/arkeologi, no. 46. Tromsø, Norway: University of Tromsø.

Naum, M. 2008. *Homelands lost and gained: Slavic migration and settlement on Bornholm in the early Middle Ages.* Lund Studies in Historical Archaeology 9. Lund, Sweden: Lund University.

Nilsson, B. 2003. *Tingens och tankarnas landskap.* Acta Archaeologica Lundensia in 8°, 44. Stockholm: Almqvist and Wiksell International.

Nora, P. 1984. Entre mémoire et histoire: La problématique des lieux. In P. Nora (ed.), *Les lieux de mémoire, volume 1: La République*. Paris: Gallimard.

Nora, P. 1989. Between memory and history: Les lieux de mémoire. *Representations* 26:7–24.

Norman, D. 1988. *The design of everyday things*. New York: Doubleday.

Norris, C. 1982. *The deconstructive turn: Essays in the rhetoric of philosophy*. London: Methuen.

Olivier, L. 2001. Duration, memory and the nature of the archaeological record. In H. Karlsson (ed.), *It's about time: The concept of time in archaeology*. Gothenburg: Bricoleur Press.

Olivier, L. 2008. *Le sombre abime du temps: Mémoire et archeologie*. Paris: Seuil.

Olsen, B. 1987. *Arkeologi, tekst, samfunn: Fragmenter til en post-prosessuell arkeologi*. Stensilserie B, historie/arkeologi 24. Tromsø, Norway: University of Tromsø.

Olsen, B. 1990. Roland Barthes: From sign to text. In C. Tilley (ed.), *Reading material culture*. Oxford: Blackwell.

Olsen, B. 1991. Metropolises and satellites in archaeology: On power and asymmetry in global archaeological discourse. In R. Preucel (ed.), Processual and post-processual archaeologies: Multiple ways of knowing the past. Occasional Paper 10. Carbondale, Ill.: Center for Archaeological Investigations.

Olsen, B. 1997. *Fra ting til tekst: Teoretiske perspektiv i arkeologisk forskning*. Oslo: Universitetsforlaget.

Olsen, B. 2001. The end of history? Archaeology and the politics of identity in a globalized world. In R. Layton, P. Stone, and J. Thomas (eds.), *The destruction and conservation of cultural property*. London: Routledge.

Olsen, B. 2003. Material culture after text: Remembering things. *Norwegian Archaeological Review* 36(2): 87–104.

Olsen, B. 2004. Momenter til et forsvar av tingene. *Nordisk Museologi* 2004(2): 25–36.

Olsen, B. 2006. Archaeology, hermeneutics of suspicion and phenomenological trivialisation. *Archaeological Dialogues* 13(2): 144–50.

Olsen, B. 2007. Keeping things at arm's length: A genealogy of asymmetry. *World Archaeology* 39(4): 579–88.

Olsen, B., and A. Svestad. 1994. Creating prehistory: Archaeology museums and the discourse of modernism. *Nordisk Museologi* 1994/1:3–20.

Oskal, N. 1995. Det rette, det gode og reinlykken. PhD thesis, University of Tromsø.

Parker Pearson, M. 1995. Tombs and territories: Material culture and multiple interpretation. In I. Hodder, M. Shanks, A. Alessandri, V. Buchli, J. Carman, J. Last, and G. Lucas (eds.), *Interpreting archaeology: Finding meaning in the past.* London: Routledge.

Parkin, D. 1999. Mementoes as transitional objects in human displacement. *Journal of Material Culture* 4(3): 303–20.

Patrik, L. 1985. Is there an archaeological record? *Advances in Archaeological Method and Theory* 8:27–62.

Pearce, S. 1997. *Collecting in contemporary practice.* London: AltaMira Sage.

Pearson, K. 2002. *Philosophy and the adventure of the virtual: Bergson and the time of life.* London: Routledge.

Pearson, M., and M. Shanks. 2001. *Theatre/archaeology.* London: Routledge.

Pels, P. 1998. The spirit of matter: On fetish, rarity, fact and fancy. In P. Spyer (ed.), *Border fetishisms: Material objects in unstable spaces.* London: Routledge.

Pétursdóttir, Þ. 2007. "Deyr fé, deyja frændr": Re-animating mortuary remains from Viking Age Iceland. Master's thesis, University of Tromsø.

Pickering, A. 1994. After representation: Science studies in the performative idiom. *PSA: Proceedings of the Biennial Meeting of the Philosophy of Science Association* 1994(2): 413–19.

Piggot, S. 1965. *Ancient Europe.* Edinburgh: Edinburgh University Press.

Pinney, C. 2005. Things happen; or, From which moment does that object come? In D. Miller (ed.), *Materiality.* Durham, N.C.: Duke University Press.

Popper, K. 1972. *Objective knowledge.* Oxford: Clarendon Press.

Prattis, J. 1985. Dialectics and experience in fieldwork: The poetic dimension. In J. Prattis (ed.), *Reflections: The anthropological muse.* Washington, D.C.: American Anthropological Association.

Preda, A. 1999. The turn to things: Arguments for a sociological theory of things. *Sociological quarterly* 40(2): 347–66.

Preucel, R. (ed.). 1991. Processual and post-processual archaeologies: Multiple ways of knowing the past. Occasional Paper 10. Carbondale, Ill.: Center for Archaeological Investigations.

Preucel, R. 2006. *Archaeological semiotics.* Oxford: Blackwell.

Preucel, R., and A. Bauer. 2001. Archaeological pragmatics. *Norwegian Archaeological Review* 34(2): 85–96.

Price, N. 2002. *The Viking way: Religion and war in late Iron Age Scandinavia.* Uppsala, Sweden: Uppsala University Department of Archaeology and Ancient History.

Proust, M. 1999. *Time regained (In search of lost time, vol. 6).* New York: Modern Library.

Proust, M. 2003. *Swann's way (In search of lost time, vol. 1).* New York: Modern Library.

Rathje, W. 1984. The garbage decade. *American Behavioral Scientist* 28(1): 9–29.

Rathje, W. 1991. Once and future landfills. *National Geographic* 179(5): 116–34.

Rathje, W. 1996. The archaeology of us. *Encyclopaedia Britannica's yearbook of science and the future* 1997:158–77.

Rathje, W., and M. McCarthy. 1977. Regularity and variability in contemporary garbage. In S. South (ed.), *Research strategies in historical archaeology*. New York: Academic Press.

Renfrew, C. 1989. Comments. *Norwegian Archaeological Review* 22(1): 33–41.

Renfrew, C. 2001. Symbols before concept: Material engagement and the early development of society. In I. Hodder (ed.), *Archaeological theory today*. Cambridge: Polity Press.

Renfrew, C. 2003. *Figuring it out: What are we? Where do we come from? The parallel visions of artists and archaeologists*. London: Thames and Hudson.

Renfrew, C. 2004. Towards a theory of material engagement. In E. Marrais, C. Gosden, and C. Renfrew (eds.), *Rethinking materiality: The engagement of mind with the material world*. Cambridge: McDonald Institute for Archaeological Research.

Renfrew, C., C. Gosden, and E. DeMarrais (eds.). 2004. *Substance, memory, display: Archaeology and art*. Cambridge: McDonald Institute for Archaeological Research.

Richards, C. 2008. The substance of Polynesian voyages. *World Archaeology* 40(2): 206–23.

Ricoeur, P. 1970. *Freud and philosophy: An essay on interpretation*. New Haven: Yale University Press.

Ricouer, P. 1981. *Hermeneutics and the human sciences*. Cambridge: Cambridge University Press.

Rowlands, M. 1993. The role of memory in the transmission of culture. In *World Archaeology* 25:141–51.

Rowlands, M. 2002. The power of origins: Questions of cultural rights. In V. Buchli (ed.), *The material culture reader*. Oxford: Berg.

Rowlands, M. 2005. A materialist approach to materiality. In D. Miller (ed.), *Materiality*. Durham, N.C.: Duke University Press.

Sackett, J. 1982. Approaches to style in lithic archaeology. *Journal of Anthropological Archaeology* 1:59–112.

Sackett, J. 1985. Style and ethnicity in the Kalahari: A reply to Wiessner. *American Antiquity* 50:154–60.

Sartre, J.-P. 1962. *Imagination: A psychological critique*. Ann Arbor: University of Michigan Press.

Scarre, C. 2002. Situating monuments: The dialogue between built form and landform in Atlantic Europe. In C. Scarre (ed.), *Monuments and landscape in Atlantic Europe*. London: Routledge.

Scarry, E. 1985. *The body in pain: The making and unmaking of the world*. Oxford: Oxford University Press.

Schiffer, M. 1991. *The portable radio in American life*. Tucson: University of Arizona Press.

Schiffer, M. (with A. Miller). 1999. *The material life of human beings: Artifacts, behavior, and communication*. London: Routledge.

Schiffer, M. (with K. Hollenback and C. Bell). 2003. *Draw the lightning down: Benjamin Franklin and electrical technology in the Age of Enlightenment*. Berkeley: University of California Press.

Sennett, R. 2008. *The craftsman*. New Haven: Yale University Press.

Serres, M. 1987. *Statues*. Paris: Bourin.

Serres, M. 1995a. *Genesis.* Ann Arbor: University of Michigan Press.

Serres, M. (with B. Latour). 1995b. *Conversation on science, culture and time.* Ann Arbor: University of Michigan Press.

Shanks, M. 1992. *Experiencing the past: On the character of archaeology.* London: Routledge.

Shanks, M. 1995. *Classical archaeology: Experiences of the discipline.* London: Routledge.

Shanks, M. 2004. Three rooms: Archaeology and performance. *Journal of Social Archaeology* 4(2): 147–80.

Shanks, M. 1998. The life of an artifact in an interpretive archaeology. *Fennoscandia Archaeologica* 15:15–30.

Shanks, M. 1999. *Art and the early Greek state: Experiences of the discipline.* London: Routledge.

Shanks, M. 2007. Symmetrical Archaeology. *World Archaeology* 39(4): 589–96.

Shanks, M. 2010. *The archaeological imagination.* Walnut Creek, Calif.: Left Coast Press.

Shanks, M., and C. Tilley. 1982. Ideology, symbolic power and ritual communication: A reinterpretation of Neolithic mortuary practices. In I. Hodder (ed.), *Structural and symbolic archaeology.* Cambridge: Cambridge University Press.

Shanks, M., and C. Tilley. 1987. *Reconstructing archaeology: Theory and practice.* Cambridge: Cambridge University Press.

Sharp, L. 1952. Steel axes for Stone-Age Australians. *Human Organization* 11(2): 17–22.

Shaw, R., and C. Stewart. 1994. Introduction: Problematizing syncretism. In C. Stewart and R. Shaw (eds.), *Syncretism/anti-syncretism: The politics of religious synthesis.* London: Routledge.

Simmel, G. 1978/1906. *The philosophy of money.* London: Routledge.

Smith, A. 2003. *The political landscape: Constellations of authority in early complex polities.* Berkeley: University of California Press.

Soja, E. 2000. *Postmetropolis: Critical studies of cities and regions.* Oxford: Blackwell.

Solli, B. 1996. Narratives of Veøy: On the poetics and scientifics of archaeology. In P. Graves-Brown, S. Jones, and C. Gamble (eds.), *Cultural identity and archaeology.* London: Routledge.

Sørensen, K. 2004. Tingenes samfunn. Kunnskap og materialitet som sosiologiske korrektiver. *Sosiologi i dag* 34(2): 5–26.

Stocking, G. 1982. *Race, culture, and evolution: Essays in the history of anthropology.* New York: Free Press.

Strathern, M. 1988. *The gender of the gift: Problems with women and problems with society in Melanesia.* Berkeley: University of California Press.

Strathern, M. 1990. Artefacts of history: Events and the interpretation of images. In Jukka Siikala (ed.), *Culture and history in the Pacific.* Helsinki: Finnish Anthropological Society.

Sturrock, J. (ed.). 1979. *Structuralism and since: From Lévi-Strauss to Derrida.* Oxford: Oxford University Press.

Suthrell, C. 2004. *Unzipping gender: Sex, cross-dressing and culture.* Oxford: Berg.

Svestad, A. 1995. *Oldsakenes orden. Om tilkomsten av arkeologi.* Oslo: Universitetsforlaget.

Sweeney, S., and I. Hodder (eds.). 2002. *The body.* Cambridge: Cambridge University Press.

Tallgren, A. 1937. The method of prehistoric archaeology. *Antiquity* 11:152–61.

Taylor, W. 1948. *A study of archaeology.* Memoirs of the American Anthropological Association 69. Menasha, WI: American Anthropological Association.

Thomas, J. 1993. The politics of vision and the archaeologies of landscape. In B. Bender (ed.), *Landscape: Politics and perspectives.* Oxford: Berg.

Thomas, J. 1996. *Time, culture and identity: An interpretive archaeology.* London: Routledge.

Thomas, J. 1998. Some problems with the notion of external symbolic storage, and the case of Neolithic material culture in Britain. In C. Renfrew and C. Scarre (eds.), *Cognition and material culture: The archaeology of symbolic storage.* Cambridge: McDonald Institute for Archaeological Research.

Thomas, J. 2000. Reconfiguring the social, reconfiguring the material. In M. Schiffer (ed.), *Social theory in archaeology.* Salt Lake City: University of Utah Press.

Thomas, J. 2004. *Archaeology and modernity.* London: Routledge.

Thomas, J. 2006. Phenomenology and material culture. In C. Tilley, W. Keane, S. Kuechler, M. Rowlands, and P. Spyer (eds.), *Handbook of material culture.* London: Sage Press.

Thomas, J. 2007. The trouble with material culture. *Journal of Iberian Archaeology* 9/10:11–24.

Thomas, N. 1991. *Entangled objects: Exchange, colonialism and material culture in the Pacific.* Cambridge, Mass.: Harvard University Press.

Thomas, N. 1998. Foreword. In A. Gell, *Art and agency: An anthropological theory.* Oxford: Clarendon Press.

Tilley, C. 1989. Discourse as power: The genre of the Cambridge inaugural lecture. In D. Miller, M. Rowlands, and C. Tilley (eds.), *Dominance and resistance.* London: Unwin Hyman.

Tilley, C. (ed.) 1990a. *Reading material culture: Structuralism, hermeneutics and poststructuralism.* Oxford: Blackwell.

Tilley, C. 1990b. Michel Foucault: Towards an archaeology of archaeology. In C. Tilley (ed.), *Reading material culture: Structuralism, hermeneutics and poststructuralism.* Oxford: Blackwell.

Tilley, C. 1991. *Material culture and text: The art of ambiguity.* London: Routledge.

Tilley, C. 1994. *A phenomenology of landscape.* London: Berg.

Tilley, C. 1999. *Metaphor and material culture.* Oxford: Blackwell.

Tilley, C. 2004. *The materiality of stone: Explorations in landscape phenomenology.* Oxford: Berg.

Tilley, C., S. Hamilton, and B. Bender. 2000. Art and the re-presentation of the past. *Journal of the Royal Anthropological Institute* (n.s.) 6(1): 36–62.

Trentmann, F. 2009. Materiality in the future of history: Things, practices, and politics. *Journal of British Studies* 48(2): 283–307.

Turi, J. 1987. *En bok om samernas liv.* Umeå, Sweden: Två Förläggare Bokförlag.

Turner, B. 2003. Foreword: The phenomenology of lived experience. In L. Meskell and R. Joyce, *Embodied lives: Figuring ancient Maya and Egyptian experience.* London: Routledge.

Van Dyke, R., and S. Alcock. 2003. Archaeologies of memory: An introduction. In
    R. Dyke and S. Alcock (eds.), *Archaeologies of memory*. Oxford: Blackwell.
Wagner, R. 1991. The fractal person. In M. Godelier and M. Strathern (eds.), *Big
    man and great man: Personifications of power in Melanesia*. Cambridge: Cambridge
    University Press.
Waskul, D., and P. Vannini. (eds.). 2006. *Body/embodiment: Symbolic interaction and
    the sociology of the body*. Burlington, Vt.: Ashgate.
Webmoor, T. 2007. What about "one more turn after the social" in archaeological
    reasoning? Taking things seriously. *World Archaeology* 39(4): 563–78.
Webmoor, T., and C. Witmore. 2008. Things are us! A commentary on human/
    things relations under the banner of a social archaeology. *Norwegian Archaeo-
    logical Review* 41(1): 53–70.
Welsch, W. 1997. *Undoing aesthetics*. London: Sage.
White, H. 1973. *Metahistory: The historical imagination of nineteenth-century Europe*.
    Baltimore: Johns Hopkins University Press.
White, H. 1978. *Tropics of discourse: Essays in cultural criticism*. Baltimore: Johns
    Hopkins University Press.
White, H. 1990. *The content of the form: Narrative discourse and historical representa-
    tion*. Baltimore: Johns Hopkins University Press.
Wiessner, P. 1983. Style and social information in Kalahari projectile points.
    American Antiquity 48:253–76.
Willey, G., and P. Phillips. 1958. *Method and theory in American archaeology*. Chi-
    cago: University of Chicago Press.
Williams, H. (ed.). 2003. *Archaeologies of remembrance: Death and memory in past
    societies*. New York: Kluwer/Plenum.
Williams, S., and G. Bendelow. 1998. *The lived body: Sociological themes, embodied
    issues*. London: Routledge.
Williams, T. 2007. Where worlds collide: The past in the present at Leskernick. In
    B. Bender, S. Hamilton, and C. Tilley, *Stone worlds: Narrativity and reflexivity in
    landscape archaeology*. Walnut Creek, Calif.: Left Coast Press.
Witmore, C. 2004. Four archaeological engagements with place: Mediating bodily
    experience through peripatetic video. *Visual Anthropology Review* 20(2): 57–72.
Witmore, C. 2006. Vision, media, noise and the percolation of time: Symmetrical
    approaches to the mediation of the material world. *Journal of Material Culture*
    11(3): 267–92.
Witmore, C. 2007. Symmetrical archaeology: Excerpts of a manifesto. *World Ar-
    chaeology* 39(4): 546–62.
Yates, F. 1966. *The art of memory*. London: Routledge and Kegan Paul.
Yates, T. 1990. Jacques Derrida: "There is nothing outside of the text." In C. Tilley
    (ed.), *Reading material culture: Structuralism, hermeneutics and poststructuralism*.
    Oxford: Blackwell.
Yates, T. 1993. Frameworks for an archaeology of the body. In C. Tilley (ed.), *In-
    terpretative archaeology*. Providence, R.I.: Berg.
Young, J. 2002. *Heidegger's later philosophy*. Cambridge: Cambridge University
    Press.
Young, R. 1995. *Colonial desire: Hybridity in theory, culture and race*. London: Rout-
    ledge.

Index

About the Author

Bjørnar Olsen is professor in archaeology at the University of Tromsø, Norway. He has written a number of papers and books on northern and Sámi prehistory and history, museology, and on archaeological theory. His latest book (with Elin Andreassen and Hein Bjerck) is *Persistent Memories: Pyramiden–a Soviet Mining Town in the High Arcti* (2010).

ACKNOWLEDGEMENTS

This book has taken a long time to complete. Much of the research for it was conducted during my sabbatical year at Stanford University in 2003 and the writing was completed during my second year at Stanford in 2007/2008. I thank the Stanford Archaeology Center for providing work space and allowing me to use their facilities, and the Norwegian Research Council and the University of Tromsø for funding my research. A special thank to Michael Shanks for hosting me at his Metamedia Lab and proving such a vibrant and generous research environment.

I am very grateful to a number of colleagues and friends who have shared ideas and literature and discussed various issues related to this book. In particular I want to thank Douglass Bailey, Cathrine Baglo, Hein Bjerck, Ewa Domanska, Ian Hodder, Bill Rathje, Alfredo Gonzáles Ruibal, Michael Shanks, Tim Webmoor and Christopher Witmore. I am also grateful to Ian Hodder, Robert Preucel and two other anonymous reviewers for their detailed comments to an earlier draft of this book. Thanks also go to Elin Rose Myrvoll, Alfredo Gonzáles Ruibal, and Karin Tansem for allowing me to use their photographs.